CASE STUDIES IN A SENSE OF PLACE

by Thomas de Monchaux

Stella and David are up on the roof. A House Without Walls, a narrow ladder rattling up its side, is under construction. It is a blustery day and the high white clouds move quickly across the blue sky. As the clouds pass over the surrounding tall pines, light scintillates through the iridescent pine needles. The architects are talking for a long time with the roofer—about drainage: how to get snow and rain from the sky to the ground, around the house in between. The already much-folded construction documents crinkle and flip around in the gusts, flashing white. A flat roof is never, of course, truly flat: it is itself always creased and tilted with near-imperceptible hills and valleys to channel water this way and that. The architects and the roofer are together improvising something called a cricket: a low and hump-backed origami arrangement, an inches-high hillock that sheds water in the right directions. Everything here is a miniature landscape of folding, of infinitesimal but essential gradations achieved by how one drapes the waterproof membranes like a bedsheet with hospital corners—even under, as here, what will eventually be a planted sedum bed, a true miniature landscape to echo and continue the landscape beyond. With the technical problem solved, the talk turns to that landscape, to the trees, the distant ridge lines of the lower Berkshire and higher Adirondack Mountains that frame this part of the Hudson Valley to the east and west a couple hours north of New York City. "Columbia County," the roofer gestures down at his pickup truck parked at the base of the ladder and says, "when you drive across the county line—they don't always have the sign on every road—but you can just feel it."

That sense of place applies—in two ways—to these baker's dozen of houses in the work of Stella and David, completed over about as many years, of which a core quorum are located in Columbia County. First, these houses are grounded in a sense of place—in a complex constellation of you-can-just-feel-it intimations and interpolations about how earth and sky, summer and winter, year and day and night, all work in this place: how there is a late but fast winter dawn as the sun crests the nearby hills to the east; how there is a slow summer evening as it angles across the valley among the far hills to the west; how the summer nights are colder with even small increases in elevation, among so many microclimates of wind and water; how the east-to-west angles of sunlight rake across prevailing north-to-south angles of the geography; how second-growth forests spill across former fields, full of their own hillocks and crickets between the Berkshires and Adirondacks, and Catskills beyond. These generally modestly scaled but experientially ambitious houses are to their landscapes as the celebrated mid-twentieth-century Case Study Houses by Craig Ellwood and others were to their pockets of Los Angeles County, or as the work of Albert Frey and others were to the edge of the Colorado Desert along suburban tracts edging the Coachella Valley: investigations, through physical siting and visual framing, by indoors into outdoors, by small places into big places. (There's a particular kind of New Yorker who comes from out West—Stella, formerly of a city in the Sonoran Desert, is one. She said once: "I would be so happy to do a desert house in CMU [concrete masonry unit] block. It would be cheap and gorgeous." "It would keep me up at night," David said, "thinking of all the mortar joints during our Northeast freeze-thaw cycles. But we can try.")

Upstate New York was a kind of American West—for better and for worse—before the American West. It's easy to be Romantic about Columbia County. It is an origin point of one of the most influentially romantic imaginaries in American history: the Hudson River School of landscape painters, legendarily dating to the artist Thomas Cole's steamship ride up the Hudson River from New York City to West Point, in the autumn of 1825—and a subsequent pictorial vision of the cozily pastoral adjacent to the luminously sublime. And it's necessary to critique that romance: as a template for a falsely soothing view of a colonial American frontier as a peaceable kingdom; later as a place of fraught adjacencies between the year-rounders and the summer people; and still more recently, a platform for an aesthetically nostalgic mercantilism, tracking the economic exile, no matter how picturesquely documented, of crafty hipster influencers from a gentrified Brooklyn all the way—almost like their actual hippie precursors—back to the land. Here in a rural landscape up toward the northern tip of what is, geologically speaking, the Appalachian ridge and valley that runs from Alabama to New York and beyond, is a visible American history of social mobility and immobility, possession and dispossession taken toward extremes. The houses in this book map a little of that landscape too: they are for self-made entrepreneurs of noteworthy privilege, for those carefully consolidating their lifelong resources into a forever home; for folks who are the first in their families to own such land and to make such places; for working people who have yet to build their house of the future, but believe that they will and have organized action around that belief. The houses in this book map a domestic landscape as well: in their teaching, Stella and David often explore multi-unit, multi-generational housing, configured at high urban density; and in their practice they design city apartments big and small—yet to all of this residential research they bring a special and specific idea of home life: of living with expansiveness at any scale; in a dignity that is not a luxury; with a formal rigor that enables an informal atmosphere; and with a feeling of agency that is not conceded or directed within any hierarchy—all organized around what they call (with capital letters, if you please) an Open House.

Transcending any particular locality, there's another way you can *just feel it*, in and around these houses, that is as much about the domestic landscape as any one geographic landscape—or perhaps about the lessons of this specific geographic landscape of the Hudson Valley, this specific sense of place, distilled and applied to domestic scale, even if that domestic building finds itself on Long Island or New Jersey or parts of the West. Like the roads without border signs into Columbia County, Stella and David's houses don't always have signposted front doors—or every door can be a front door if you use it as one. The borders are open. The houses don't tell you how you must get in—or how you must keep out. Yet you know, when you go in and out and about, that you have crossed from a *there* to a *here*. Sometimes inside feels like outside—in a way that is more about moments of deeply sheltered exteriority (the miniature box-canyon open-to-above staircase to the roof garden of A Square House, the oblique dog-trot porch at the heart of A House with a Swerve) than the razor-thin metal thresholds and indoor gravel pits and fig trees of those Los Angeles case studies. But these thirteen houses all, in distinct but related ways, offer that feeling of arrival and departure—and reward a reliance on that feeling, as much as on awakening and dreaming, to construct each day of a life.

This is, in part, because these thirteen houses are descriptive, not prescriptive—for the way that they make legible a landscape of options to their dwellers, but don't dictate how those options be taken. There tend to be as many ways *through* these houses as there are ways into and out of them. The conventional prescriptiveness of the pre-modern house was dictated by chambers: a place for everything and everything in its place: sewing rooms, nurseries, and butler's pantries. The conventional prescriptiveness of the early modern house was the fantasy that a different type of architectural object could, or even should, construct a different type of architectural subject: that a so-called free plan (free-floating partition walls liberated from structural duties by a point-grid of skinny columns) would somehow make a free people: athletic and ecstatic—or perhaps just antic or frantic in a new way. The so-called open plan of 1920 was by 2020 still somehow a new-and-modern-seeming idea in popular culture, popularized by interior decoration television (which tends to be filmed in Vancouver and Toronto) as the brainy-sounding Canadianism: "open concept"; and as an expression of the other decorative watchword of that era, the desirable phenomenon of "flow." This is an echo of the old modern idea that space itself somehow oozes or sloshes around—or can be induced to—rather than of course it being simply our own bodies, our feet and eyes, that move through space over time. It's an appealing word—flow—evocative of the neurological flow-state of a well-occupied mind, or even merely of the sequence of moves in, say, a gratifying exercise routine. But it's reductive and prescriptive. The well-lived life has its stops and starts, too.

These thirteen houses stop and start, in the sense that they are *formal*—in the geometrical sense. They are bounded and composed. As compositions in three dimensions, they are sourced from primary elements—platonic solids, circles, squares, grids, planes thick and thin—that have been intelligibly subjected to subtle but almost savagely severe operations: trimming, overlapping, superimposing, shifting, and stretching by way of a circle into an ellipse or a line into a curve by way of a fillet or chamfer or swerve. Sometimes these primaries, triangle above a rectangle, conspire even to make a house-shaped house. There goes another Monopoly hotel, in the phrase attributed to Louis Kahn. A great deal of tectonic legerdemain—furring and edging—goes into sustaining all the crispiness with which the houses assert that they are forms, as much as they are deeply and finely layered laminations of materials.

But these thirteen houses are also *informal*. Whether by isolated rooms in a closed-plan layout or insistent islands of mechanized amenities and furnishings in an open-plan layout, both pre-modern and modern houses tend toward hierarchy: on-stage and back-stage, space for company and others for family, served and service. Corridors, famously, came into the domestic architecture of the developed West to accommodate domestic servants—who had to be deflected from the processional enfilade of aligned doorways between rooms; for the same reason, corner doors traditionally opened toward the wall, not the room—to delay the view of the subservient and to prepare the served to be seen. In these thirteen houses, you'll find far fewer corridors than you might expect, and far fewer doors. The houses are neither exclusively articulated into successive enclosures, nor conceived of as blank, un-landmarked slates: there is an abundance and a care, in these houses, for landings, thresholds, porches, bridges—to all the in-between places where life, more often than not, actually gets lived. These are littoral zones—interstitial parts of the landscape washed across by different waves of eventfulness and emotion, just as tide pools are periodically animated and quieted by wind and water, between sea and land. Rooms that you might assume have to be big, are not. Rooms that you might assume have to be small, are not. Different qualities of intimacy and expansiveness apply. Upstairs at Stella and David's own house—A House of One Shape—the bedroom and the bathroom are the same size—save for the intrusion of the stair and secret closet. Is it a big bathroom or a small bedroom? Yes. Formally, they are identical rooms mirrored across an oblique, but for the informal difference that one centers on a bed and another on a tub, of equal and complementary presence. All rooms, as Stella and David have postulated, are created equal. Thus created, they offer to their users a freedom of choice.

This all goes to what Stella and David have called the *politics of the plan*. At first, when I heard them say this, I thought they meant the *poetics* of the plan, for the work has a self-evident poetry to it: details that rhyme with each other and with the whole, measured meters of proportion, evocation without imitation of vernacular archetypes and collective memories of places seen in films, in dreams, in all states of distraction. *Poetics* is a word that non-architects, and even architects, resort to for a kind of indeterminate and evocative *mattering*. But Stella and David were thinking about politics—because they were thinking about power and status, about inclusion and exclusion, about centering and marginalizing, about identities and their performances—and about how, especially at home, the configuration of spaces and their adjacencies can break down hierarchies that have been unwillingly or unwittingly inherited—even at the scale of family politics, internalized politics, and domestic politics of the kitchen table. The intimacy of daily routines and the sometimes long durations of our residencies in houses—places of our inner lives and our interior lives—makes houses precisely into places for habituated thoughts and deeds, and their resistance.

Democracy is coming, sang Leonard Cohen, *to the USA. From the homicidal bitchin' that goes down in every kitchen, to determine who will serve and who will eat*. Stella and David are standing in the kitchen in their own home, and talking about it. "A kitchen," Stella says, "how do we make our kitchens look less *kitchen*. How to make our houses less domesticated?" "I like the ambiguity," David answers, "Does a kitchen have to do what it's supposed to do? We don't hide kitchens like houses used to—but it is still so distinct, still a place of so much particularity because of the equipment. But that particularity gets so co-opted into style, into all the trappings." "It doesn't have to be a *received* domesticity," says Stella, "it can be something else, something wilder, something freer." "A big thing we like to do," says David, "is not to design a kitchen around a big refrigerator. Not around this beast of equipment, this one component, or any one component. There's a difference between components and architectural elements. We talk about components—fixtures, pipes, stairs. They are technical but they are also culturally produced, culturally received. We look at the way that they get looked at." "We do like to clear the deck," says Stella, "It makes room for life to happen. The act of sweeping is powerful." In Stella and David's own house the broom—just a regular broom—hangs candid on the wall in that kitchen. Stella gestures to it. "Our piece of land doesn't have a view. It doesn't have a pond. The land itself is like a room," she says, "One of the first things we did, even before we built a house, is sweep the forest floor." Outside, the tended earth encircles a fire pit, which is another kind of kitchen. The room is an open landscape, the land is an open room.

America is a land of houses. Some seventy percent of Americans live in detached single-family houses. (About twenty percent of Americans now live in apartments.) Most of those houses are wood—an inadvertently sustainable fact, one that may be further sustained with the advent of mass timber construction. Most are about 2,600 square feet. That some eighty percent of Americans nonetheless live in cities tells you something about the sprawling municipality of the American exurban and urban—and the self-evident unsustainability of this kind of land use during the climate crisis and Holocene extinction. Hyper-urbanization—the emptying out of the global countryside into megacities—will make the model of the detached single-family house increasingly peculiar. Even in the United States, in our characteristically shambolic way, we are beginning to understand the benefits of intergenerational and multi-family dwellings traditionally more characteristic of the so-called old and developing worlds; beginning to understand the benefits of the lively densification, or mere economic efficiency, offered by the ever-more-approved-by-zoning accessory dwelling unit, the extra house in the backyard. The percentage of dwellings owned by the people who live in them—the so-called homeownership rate—boomed after the Second World War, amplified by public policy that also segregated and redlined Americans by race and class, away from access and equity. This percentage reached a peak around 2004, declining with the subsequent federal mismanagement of the economy and predatory private-equity-distorted lending that lead to the housing crisis and Great Recession of 2008. Partly as a consequence, we are also a nation of the underhoused and unhoused. Yet America remains invested—emotionally, intuitively, romantically, practically, fiercely, dedicatedly—to the house and the idea of the house.

One way of looking at a house is as an interpretation of a dream. And of course it is an American dream—confirmed as an essential component of the achievement of that dream by seventy percent or more of respondents in recent annual polls. Those cynics who in one generation sold you on a Cape Cod and picket fence—or on a Modern-esque McMansion with an open concept—might be the same who sold you, in another, on the inevitable ennui, on the stultifying middle-class subdivision propriety, of same, in order to sell you something else. Americans are always escaping from or to the suburbs. Dreams are of course an impossible mix of memory and prophecy—and for many Americans, houses hold a sense of the past and of the future, as well as a sense of place. The only place we love more is the open road.

A home, as Reyner Banham said, is not a house. But here in America, the country that fascinated that Englishman and became his second homeland, houses have become the maps for that territory. They are maybe the least bad map we have. A discourse of houses is a discourse on how to live, on how to make yourself at home. Down to the smallest detail, to the moment when your hand finds of its own accord the light switch in the dark and you breathe out. This is the most intimate and direct action of architecture. The discourse of this book, of these thirteen houses, is an open-ended discourse because its end is openness—a free-spirited agency in the face of contingency. That is the sensibility that these houses, with their descriptive-not-prescriptive quality, all imbue—one hopes—on their dwellers. There are some bigger and some smaller houses here. There are some richer and some poorer houses here. There are square houses and linear houses. There are houses that make you dream of California and there are houses that make you dream of Vermont. But maybe they are all the same house, all ways of looking at a house. More than one novelist has been attributed with the observation that there are really only two stories: someone leaves home, and a stranger comes to town. Maybe the beauty of the houses of Stella and David is that in these houses, with their open-ended arrivals and departures, these two stories are able to become one: the return to the unfamiliar, the strangeness of homecoming.

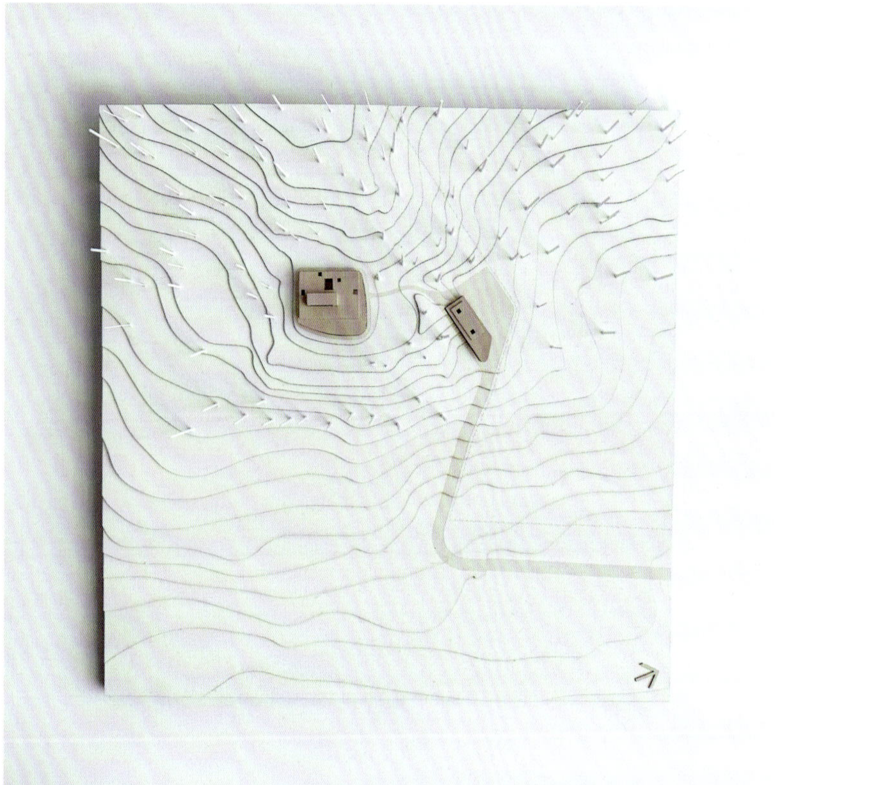

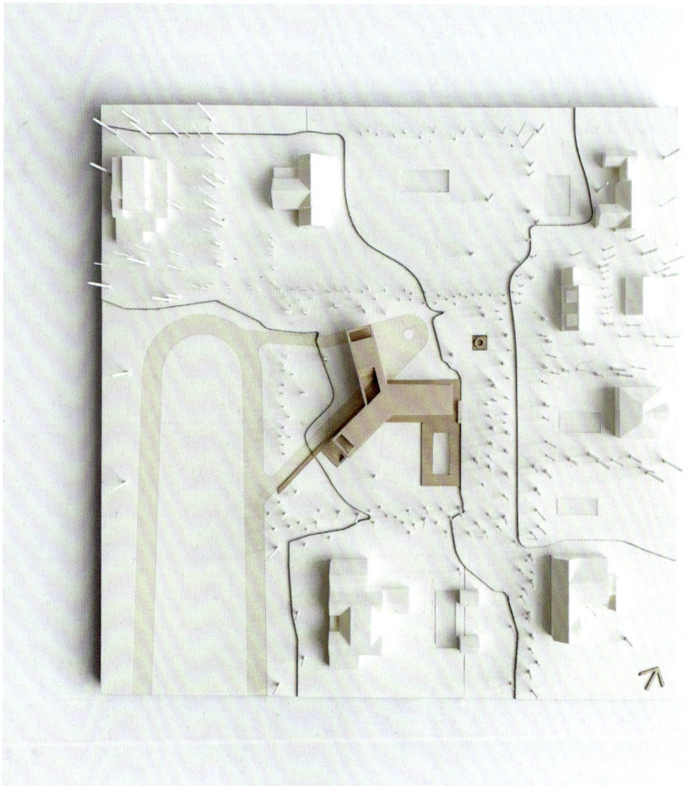

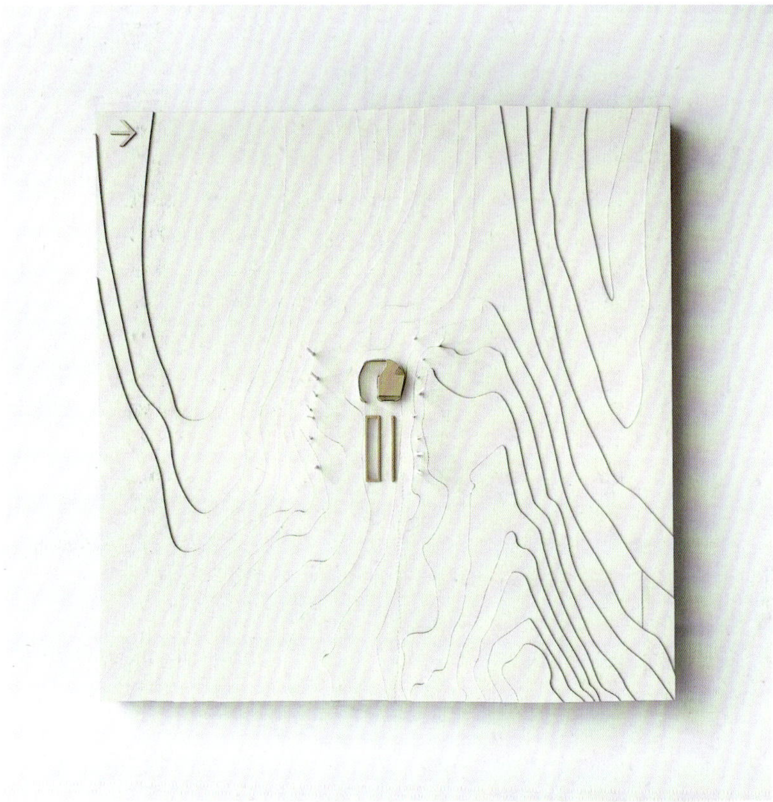

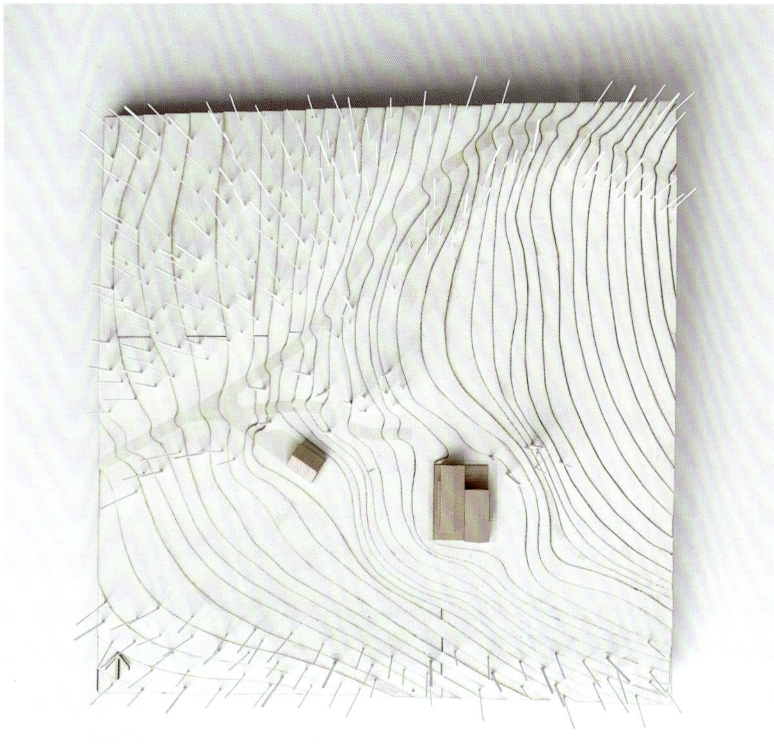

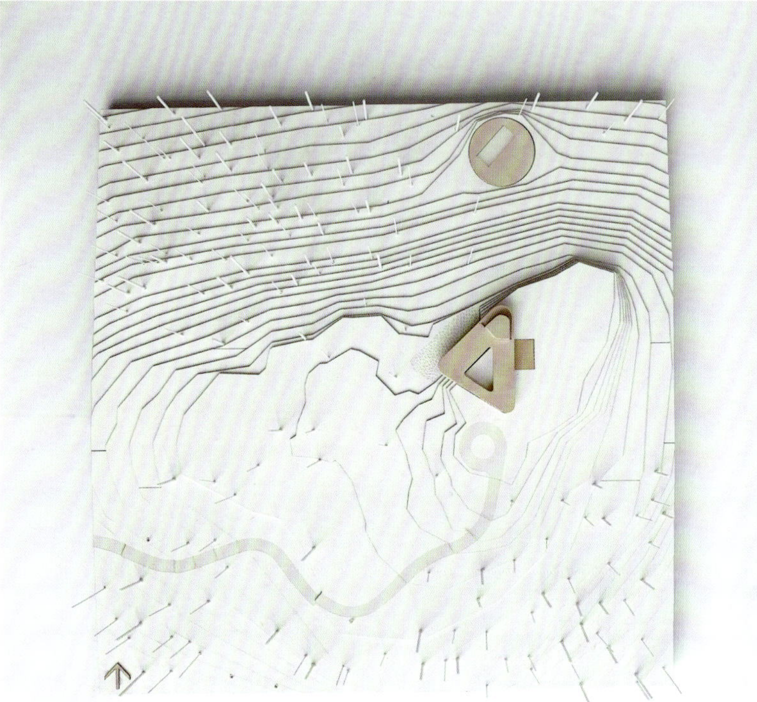

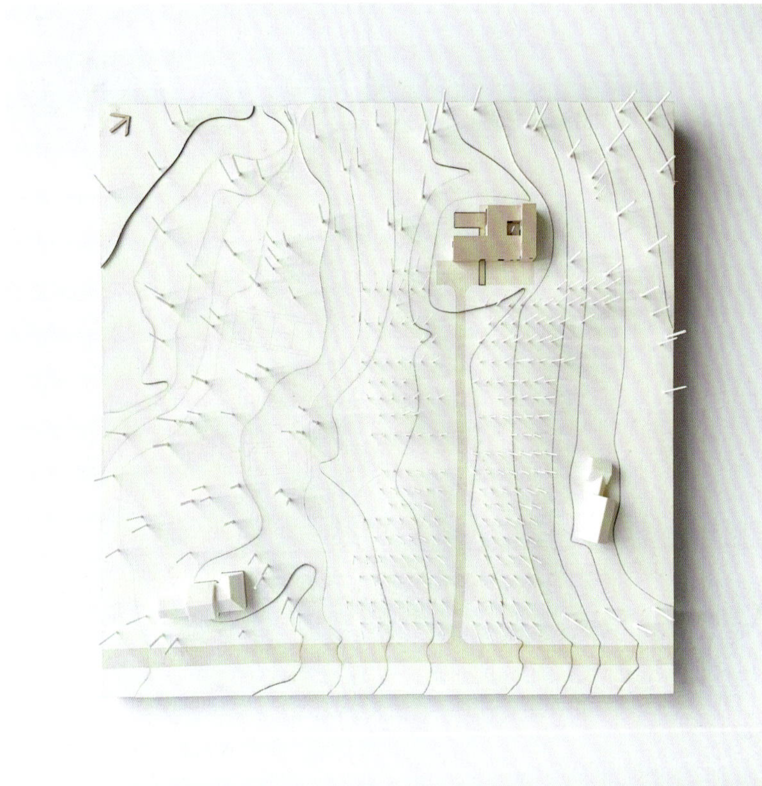

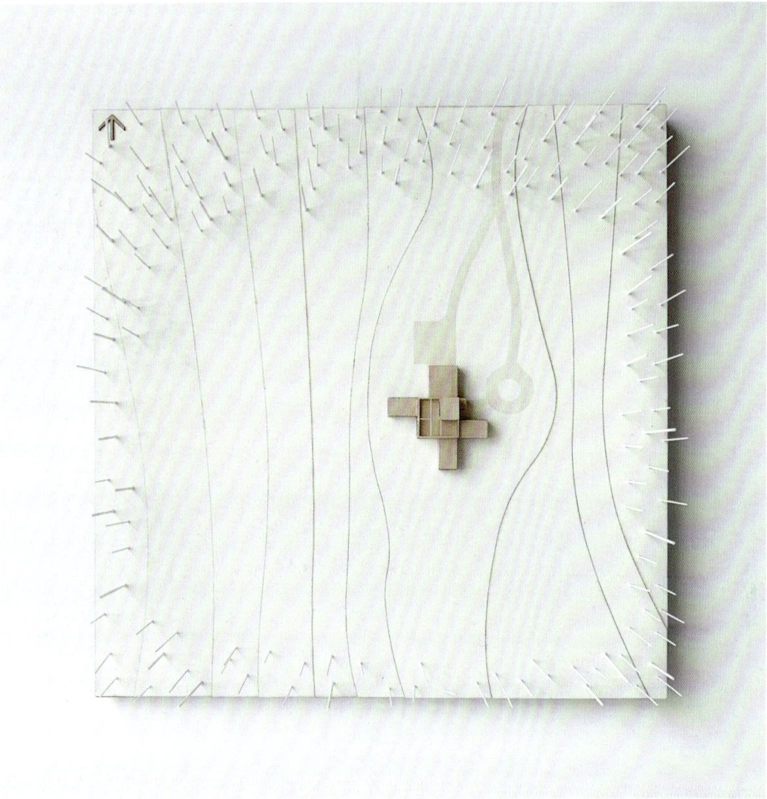

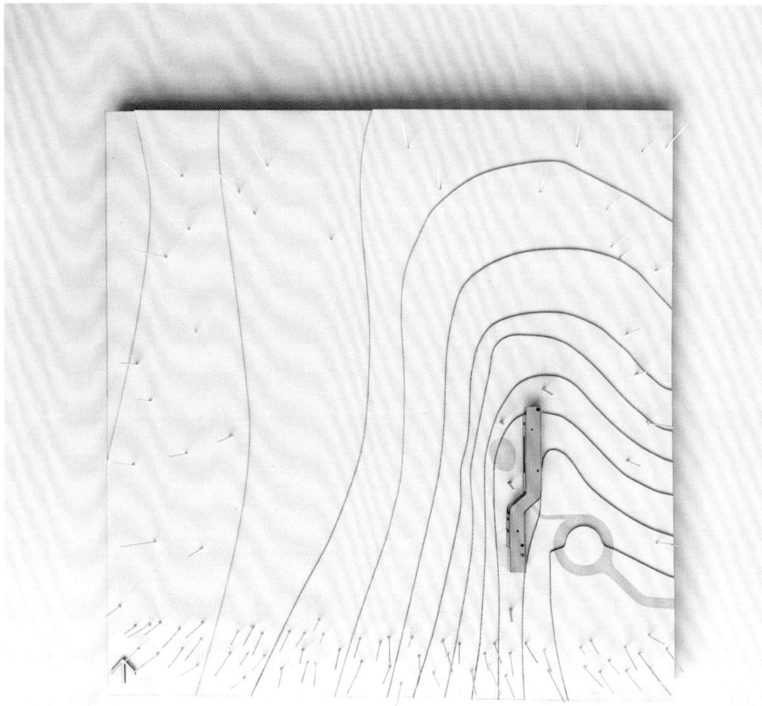

Open House. The phrase has been made familiar by residential real estate brokers who use it to describe a day of display to prospective buyers—generally a moment of performance and artifice. We use it in a different way. For us, the phrase is a prompt to reimagine "the house"—to rethink how it is enclosed; organized; occupied; used (and misused); and to rethink how the house might retain a quality of informality, while taking on calibrated formal explorations within its building type. Open House has become for us a way of thinking; a way of working that challenges and changes assumptions and expectations; a framework for surprise. It's also about being welcoming: an invitation to come on in. It should also be said that when speaking about "the house," an open house is not defined simply by visual or mechanical openness to the outside—the glass house with glass doors—but is more situated as a place without overriding preconceptions of what it is or should be.

This book assembles thirteen of the houses that we have designed in recent years—nine built, four unbuilt—along with thirteen topical texts, including this one, that consider the elements and aspects of domestic space to be found, in different ways, in all thirteen of the houses. These texts on the topical elements of domestic space don't encyclopedically explicate every part and piece. Instead, these selected topics establish an open and incomplete framework for looking at an open house. The topics are viewed through frames of architecture—how did architect so-and-so in such-and-such an era design that house as interpreted through these ideas of the house?—as well as through other forms of cultural production such as film and fine art. The practice of architecture has the purview of making and inventing new forms for the elements of buildings. But it has, by no means, the last word in how these elements are used, understood, misused, interpreted and represented in relation to human habitation. Is a stair in a suburban tract house just a stair? Or—when the American filmmaker John Cassevetes locates the moments of intense domestic psychology between characters on stairs, does such use prompt us to think differently about this seemingly incidental, but often very central architectural element and the space it establishes?

We have been designing and building houses since the early years of our practice. We started out in a New York City loft, where we virtually camped out in an open space for five years. During that time, we continuously renovated and relocated rooms and activities from one end of the space to the other. The space was open and its programmatic designations were fluid. We have also spent years camping in upstate New York, and living outdoors—in tents and trailers on our own piece of land long before, during, and after we built a small house there. We lived with intention and deliberation, which was its own privilege, without walls and without roofs. We tested our assumptions about enclosures and essentials. Consciously and unconsciously, we have been living into the question of what constitutes domestic space: how is it defined; and can it be defined in ways we might not expect. And as architects, intentionally and sometimes narrowly selective of our chosen lineages, within and outside of architecture, we rethink this space as less defined, as more informal, as open.

Many years ago, we were speaking with a colleague who is a landscape designer in Japan. We were sharing with him what was then a new obsession with the woods near a clearing on our land outside of the city of Hudson, New York. He recommended that we bring a broom to the woods and sweep the forest. He said that, "if you swept a square or round piece of forest floor, and kept at it for a year, you would have a space that has all the aesthetic qualities of a traditional Japanese garden: quiet, understated, natural, mossy." The history of modern architecture in the West is, of course, full of distortions and appropriations of the Far East—though for us this became less an abstract fascination than a physical action, less with a faraway place than with what was under our very feet. Our act of sweeping the forest compelled us. A broom—a simple tool for sweeping—can be used to define the space of a garden, an outdoor living space, or just a space, at both its most abstracted and most engaged with a natural environment. This is an establishment by caretaking, not by enclosing. A space thus established defines a region of intention and occupation—much like a campsite and not unlike the iconic blanket that becomes a measure of all things in the celebrated 1977 film *Powers of Ten* by Ray and Charles Eames. Such a space is also reminiscent of a traditional cabin, with its floor of tamped and swept earth. As soon as you start to sweep that forest floor and tend to the space around it, that swept and tended landscape immediately becomes domesticated in some way. A new conversation between the seemingly domesticated and the seemingly wild is established—along a shifting boundary that is not an enclosure. An Open House evokes these simple moves while at the same time, keeping the definition of space open to interpretation.

We have also been fascinated by explorations in art, architecture, design, and criticism that challenge assumptions about domestic life and domestic space. We enter through the critic and novelist Umberto Eco's 1962 book of critical theory, *The Open Work*, in which the production of the art work is the production of the framework that deliberately leaves a lot to chance, contingency, and discovery. In her essay from 1978 called "Sculpture in the Expanded Field", Rosalind Krauss writes about the transformation of sculpture in the 1960s and 1970s from a singular modernist idea to one that is more expansive and inclusive with elements of both architecture and landscape—denying categorization of type or discipline. Krauss writes "Sculpture is rather only one term on the periphery of a field in which there are other, differently structured possibilities. And one has thereby gained the "permission" to think these other forms." Following Krauss, we can think of architecture and space making in the expanded field. We are liberated from the confines of "type" and can encourage—through space making—alternative narratives and experiences of place and space.

The artist-architect Allan Wexler's madcap furnishings and ritual constructions, (such as 1988's *Bed / Sitting Room for an Artist in Residence*, and 1990's *Coffee Seeks Its Own Level*) upend so many preconceptions about domestic space. Architect Albert Frey's jagged boulder—that invades his signature 1964 Frey House II in Palm Springs, California, yet domesticates itself by accommodating the intrusion of an electrical outlet into the rock itself—that may be read as a critique of the urbane modernism that the house elsewhere so boldly professes. Frey's house is open in its own way, yet the open project of modernism comes with costs both psychological and energetic; there is a boldness in living with fragility. And Frey's explorations at the industrial scale, in his 1933 Canvas Weekend House that suggest the mass-manufacture of domestic space, also call into question received ideas of what a house is. Alvar Aalto in his 1952 Muuratsalo Experimental House, Frank Lloyd Wright in his Usonian Houses (some sixty odd houses designed by Wright beginning in 1934), and Richard Neutra at the 1935 Von Sternberg House all seem to crack open, in different ways, the very forms of the house as those forms were preconceived in those men's traditional contexts. Aalto sends those forms skittering across a landscape. Wright unfolds the space of the house in complicated resistance to the grid-bound American lot. Neutra recasts the form of the house in deference to the movement of the car. Paul Rudolph—Wright's near-equal as a prodigious and singular formalist—found in coastal Florida a climate in which to explicate the relationship between cave-like enclosure and sky-like exposure. Both of these are conditions that modern spatial design can achieve. Rudolph's 1952 Walker Guest House is basically a tent: a low-tech mechanistic, the house spiders out past the bounds of the "interior," deploying pulleys and panels to shade, cool and climatize within that extreme Florida climate. Lina Bo Bardi's 1952 Casa de Vidro (Glass House), sited among a densely forested Brazilian landscape, lifts off the ground—much farther than Mies Van der Rohe's canonical 1951 Farnsworth House, that could not get high enough to escape the waters of the flood plain in which it was built—to capture breezes; to both approach and evade the substantial greenery that surrounds it; and, as modernists must, to capture aerie-like views. Bo Bardi's skinny steel stair at the Casa de Vidro, something like Wright's stair at Fallingwater from 1939 that descends down to the stream as if to pull cooling breezes up into the house—the lightest of nods to access and thermal delight. These are usual subjects in a line-up of mid-twentieth-century houses. Yet we are always trying to open them up, to understand them less as objects—slides in the lecture—than as clues to ways of dwelling.

The non-heirachical, non-prescriptive and informal project of Open House, as we call it, is both to domesticate space—to make a place to live—while at the same time to un-domesticate and re-wild the American house. We question strictures and norms about domesticity, while remaining highly conscious of the parts, pieces, and cultural representations of the house, and of the design lineages within which the open house is constructed.

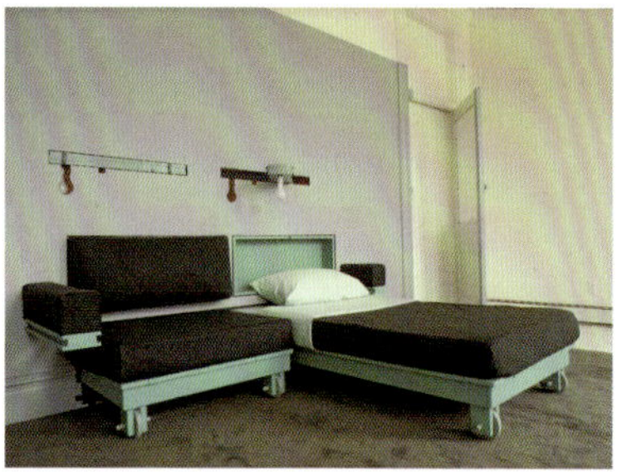

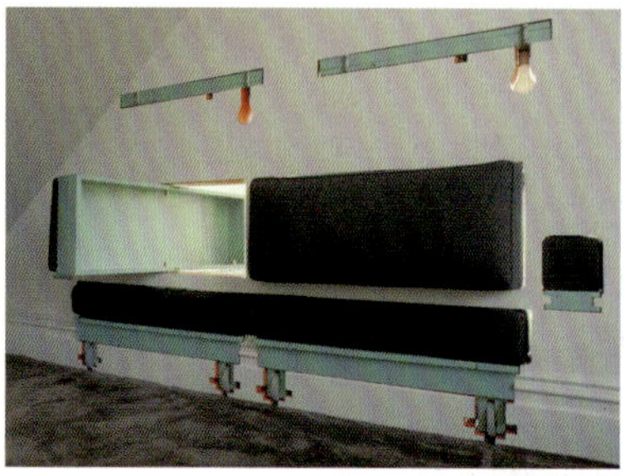

It's a perfect summer afternoon. A couple, after having eaten their lunch, rests on a striped blanket that's about six feet square and holds almost everything needed for a lunch in the grass. *Powers of Ten*, the 1977 educational film produced for IBM by the Eames Office, famously zooms in and out from that image to a microscopic and cosmic scale. But it also defines the space and tools of the meal in the grass as something that contains all you need to rest, eat, read and almost fully dwell in a modern American urban park. In the iconic still image from the film, the basket has broken the frame of the seemingly circumscribed space of one square meter, thereby beginning to establish a relationship between what is inside the frame of the blanket and what lies outside—a visual reminder of a critical component of Campsite as architecture.

It's significant that this couple—proto-yuppies, maybe—*choose* a moment of life outdoors. In consciousness of the scarcity and precarity of housing, the instructions of the campsite—of life outside of rooms and routines—depends on the privilege to make that choice. But it also empowers and requires us to think about how much we actually need to make a home, to ask whether one can live more with less—and perhaps, in so doing, to enable resources of domesticity to be distributed even more broadly—to ask whether luxury equals a costly material or the ability to hear an owl call at sunset.

Campsite thinking recalls both early forms of human settlement and low-tech and nomadic occupation of land. If Campsite begins pre-house then what are its forms, tools, patterns? In architectural discourse, we tend to think: a Bedouin tent, an iron-age encampment, a grouping of teepees, a Long House—looking back in time, with questionable nostalgia, from the hard-shell convenience and hydrocarbon-energy-laden circumstances of our contemporary enclosures. But culturally produced forms of critique, of desire or perhaps of mere nostalgia for ways of living outside of the house can all be instructive about the contemporary relationship between the house and the desire to break free from the house. The iconic American Airstream—somewhere between modern design and modernist stylization—and entire industries of less shiny Winnebagos and tow-behind pods all evoke endless summers and the open road: even, problematically, the way that the great American road trip reruns legends of the colonial frontier, the so-called Wild West with its great cities from Pueblo to Cahokia. The architectural artist

Andrea Zittel occupies the American West desert as the locus of Campsite, with an artful practice of living beyond the grid and an evocation of the Back to the Land encampments and intentional communities of the 1960s and 1970s. Alphabetically-acronymed outdoor equipment supply companies like EMS and REI will sell you all that you need for getting to the land, fully geared up. Go to a park and sit under an open-roof structure. Or go to Louis Kahn's Trenton, New Jersey, Bathhouses of 1955 and listen to the Marco Polo game in the adjacent swimming pool and the wind through the trees. The Bathhouses enclose space and remain open, in a sheltered but not enclosed assemblage of earth and sky—their roofs touching down lightly, ever so lightly, on masonry walls. The Bathhouses are aware of forms—pyramids, cubes—but they deliberately don't cohere, enclose into those forms, and so enable a certain liveliness within and without. The crux in Campsite, and work that inhabits this space, is informality.

Campsite is an intentionally stripped-down version of domestic space: a living light on the land. It is reductive. It eradicates boundaries between indoors and outdoors, in that it is essentially outdoors but establishes a domestic space and establishes a mindfully minimal presence of shelter. Campsite is also flexible, adaptable, changeable—because it is comprised of a contingent arrangement of essential elements. There is no set way that a campsite is organized: it is often laid out in relation to its immediate surroundings and circumstances. And if it's not quite right, you can move it. Moreover, in Campsite domestic elements are physically separated from one another. The tent does not have a bathroom or a sink, so you leave the tent to go fetch water. The fire is its own element. So each time that you have to get water, cook, sleep or attend to bodily functions, you are going from the outside to some other kind of place of some other kind of shelter—or just a hint of designated space that is defined by only a platform or a piece of stone.

Campsite is informal, though not formless. But it defies architectural formality in its domestic openness. It establishes a space in which you are an inhabitant, but in which you have escaped the strictures and structures of a received idea of a house. Its luxury, however spartan its details, is in that liberation. But Campsite has its own order, its own rule: each component that constitutes the site is closely curated for its technical efficiency; everything counts; everything weighs in its carrying. This is a structured open-endedness.

Once we think of the house itself as its own kind of Campsite, one that can be occupied in various ways—this changes the way that we can experience living, and changes the way that we can organize a house. It does away with one kind of formality. It does away with one kind of programmatic specificity. It does away with certain hierarchies. It does away with certain singularities. And it un-privileges one space over the other. It looks toward a more open set of relationships that link a diverse set of spaces to one another. This is the idea of Campsite within the idea of Open House. It's a memory of the myriad ways that human dwellers, home-makers of every description, have established spaces of collective domesticity across time and space.

A-Z WS 04

Is there a difference, really, between a door and a window? In a passage from William Faulkner's 1935 novel *As I Lay Dying*, the character Darl walks around an old house, while the character Jewel simultaneously passes through it, using its windows as doors:

> *Square, [the house stood] in shimmering dilapidation in the sunlight, a single broad window in two opposite walls giving onto the approaches of the path. When we reach it I turn and follow the path which circles the house. Jewel, fifteen feet behind me, looking straight ahead, steps in a single stride through the window. Still staring straight ahead, his pale eyes like wood set into his wooden face, he crosses the floor in four strides [...] and steps in a single stride through the opposite window and into the path again just as I come around the corner. In single file and five feet apart and Jewel now in front, we go on up the path toward the foot of the bluff.*

In Blake Edwards' 1961 film *Breakfast at Tiffany's*, based on Truman Capote's 1958 story of the same name, a central role is played by the space of domesticity that is Holly Golightly's New York City apartment. She has a neighbor whom she befriends. She and the neighbor visit each other not by the interior building corridor, but via the connecting exterior fire escape. They use their windows as doors—going in and out of each other's apartments. This means of passage is essentially the back door, the back porch, the informal entry. As in John Cassavetes' stairs and landings, in his films from the late 1950s through the 1980s, the fire escape becomes a central player in Edwards' film. In a way, this escape is the most secret space, yet it is also outside in the public air of the city—a domestic twist on private and public space. In a more self-referential pivot around such ambiguities, at Marcel Duchamp's 1927 installation into *11 Rue Larrey*, Paris, a swing door is hinged to two frames connected to two rooms. When the door is closed to one frame it is open to the other. And when it is closed to the second frame it creates openness to the first. Both rooms can never be closed at the same time, but they can both be open.

An Open House dispenses with the formality of how openings are defined—that is: what a window is and what is a door is—preferring an ambiguity of what might be open or closed, and how their openness and closedness are produced in the architecture. In Open House there is rarely a designated front or back door. Rather there are multiple doors and rooms, including bathrooms, that have access to the outside through a door. In this way, where you might expect a window, there is more often a door. And even windows that look and act like windows, are, in fact, often doors—named as such by their manufacturers or usable as such, just as Jewel uses them in Faulkner.

A swinging door is very different from a sliding door. Sliding doors are more like zipping and unzipping your tent to go outside. A swinging door privileges one space over another and implies an intended direction of movement. In an Open House, the choices between swinging doors and sliding doors are carefully considered. Often sliding and or pocket doors are preferred in that they not only disappear in the pocket of an exterior or interior wall, they do not assume any particular direction of movement from one room to another or from outside to inside. They don't tell you where to go.

Between the late 1950s and the late 1980s, John Cassavetes made a dozen films. Much of the action of these films take place in homes. The films are about relationships. They are shot in a *cinema verité* style, in which the actors, often the same ones from one film to the next, are improvising. There is a rawness and an informality to the filmmaking. Cassavetes gave his actors a loose script or story line and they would play out the scene. Our idea of Open House—it loves a loose script.

As you watch one Cassavetes film to the next, there is a buildup of a sort of intimacy with the characters and the actors. And because a lot of the scenes are shot inside houses, there is also an intimacy with architecture. You, the viewer, are brought into the private space; into the private lives of the characters and the interior architecture of their spaces. Stairs are often a central place where activities occur. The space of the stair in a Cassavetes film is not only transitory space, but is a room, a place unto itself. Characters spend time on the stairs; couples sit on the stairs working out their marital issues (*Faces*, 1968); a club owner transitions between the stage and the backstage by going up and down the stairs (*Killing of a Chinese Bookie*, 1976); people jump up and down on the stairs working out the issues of their relationships, both between the characters in a play and the actors playing them (*Opening Night*, 1977). All of these scenes place the stair as a central location, a central architectural character.

The act of stepping alters human locomotion. But stepping can also be an action figuratively undertaken by the floor plate or ground plane of an entire house itself, altering the experience of the house. Landscapes step. Houses can step too. In the spatial rubrics of Corbusian free plan and Loosian *raumplan*—those canonically familiar, and traditionally opposed concepts of interior space—stepping is utilized to architectural effect. Le Corbusier's 1931 Villa Savoye mechanizes movement through the house through the formal twisting of the stair figure at the core of the house—arriving at indoor and outdoor living spaces and then translating further up to the roof. Loos' 1930 Villa Mueller steps perhaps less lively but more methodically between spaces, creating a different kind of spatial distinction. Curzio Malaparte's singular Villa Malcontenta, designed in 1937 makes a stair the roof of the house—and like Cassavetes, the director Jean-Luc Godard, in his 1964 film *Contempt*, uneasily spatializes a fraught romantic relationship on this very stair. As we noted in the topic of Open House, both Lina Bo Bardi and Frank Lloyd Wright realize the power of the stair to touch down into nature—or to seem to—and to conceive the space of the stairwell as a shaft for thermal convection.

In Open House, steps and stairs are not incidental. A landing or a stair is as much a dwelling place in the house as any other room—it has equal importance. Where is a step or stair placed? Is it open or closed? What rooms or spaces does it connect? Is it its own room or is it part of larger open circulation space? In this kind of house, steps and stairs are primary, they connect levels, create varied ceiling heights in section as well as connect above and below. Stairs are not hidden. Stairs have natural light. They are a place to be: to stay, to sit, to pause, to slow down between up and down. Stairs deepen and elevate our movement in a house away from the horizontal, away from the flat—speeding and slowing and varying the pace of our domestic life by varying its places.

The seemingly ordinary architectural element of the corridor has an extraordinary impact in the way that we organize space. Embedded in the corridor can be social implications, hierarchies, accessibilities, and more. In his 1978 essay, *Figures, Doors and Passages*, Robin Evans illustrates the historical impact of the corridor, comparing Andrea Palladio's 1556 Villa Antoni in the Veneto, to Roger Pratt's Colehill Manor, in Berkshire, England, built exactly a century later. The absence of corridors in Palladio's Italian villa created an enfilade of adjacent rooms, in which circulation and lived space are collapsed as the occupant passes from one room to another: in the language of a 19th-century critique quoted by Evans, all rooms were "thoroughfare rooms." In 17th-Century England, the introduction of the corridor tightly conducted the passage of the body through space and separated male from female, servant from served: the politics of the corridor in action.

The director Wong Kar Wai's 2000 film *In the Mood for Love* is a story of two neighbors renting rooms in an urban apartment. The city is Hong Kong. The corridor plays the essential role. The two neighbors often meet and pass each other in the corridor—a narrow passage where they politely engage each other as they enter or leave their private rooms. This active passageway is a central architectural player. It extends the urban corridor of the street beyond, where both neighbors frequent the local noodle shop for take-out—an expansion of the domestic kitchen. The urban corridor, in this case, conducts the growing connection between the members of the couple, and their two adjacent apartments and the corridor/street itself is the catalyst that sparks their relationship and the circuit that carries its current.

Traditionally canonical houses of the modern movement have innovated the corridor in paradoxical ways—by both denying and doubling the space of circulation. Mies van der Rohe's 1951 Farnsworth House is an early example of the doubling of circulation in the architecture of the house, around volumes and spaces. This doubling was not done with formal corridors as confined spaces between walls—but conceived of as channels for motion between mismatched surfaces: at Farnsworth, one solid-wood veneer on one side and glass on the other—a kitchen in a hallway or a hallway in a kitchen. The same is so, in so many other modern and modernist houses. In these houses, we don't see boxed-in corridors like those of earlier centuries, but we see secondary linear spaces nonetheless, encircling the spaces of stasis: snaking around living rooms, dining rooms, and so forth. Around such an encircled center, the corridor is both denied and doubled.

The artist Bruce Nauman characterized the corridor as a space of anxiety, performance and surveillance and unsettling self consciousness—as in his 1970 *Green Light Corridor*, his 1969 *Performance Corridor*, and his 1970 *Live-Taped Corridor*. Forcing uncomfortably tight spaces, Nauman shed light (often beautiful, all-encompassing light) on this narrow place, making his subjects all the more aware of the capacities of these spaces to evoke emotion. Director Stanley Kubrick's high-art pop-culture 1980 horror film *The Shining* plays the corridor, in the semi-domestic setting of an off-season hotel and lensed in ways that complicate its seeming depth and shallowness of field, for full emotional and psychological affect.

In Open House, corridors are not peripheral. When and how they are deployed is significant and intentional: central. If a space does not need a corridor then there is no need to design spaces around an unactivated conduit. This creates not only an efficiency of space (significant when designing small houses), but more importantly, it creates an informality of rooms (and of people) and their relationship to each other. There is literally less separation, and therefore more interaction and overlap. In some cases, this requires rooms to have more than one door—also not an insignificant occurrence, as Evans notes of Palladio and Pratt. Where corridors do occur, in Open House, we celebrate and program them. In other words, some of life happens in the corridor (as for John Cassavetes, for whom life occurs on the staircase). The corridor is a place to be, not just a place to pass through. Often we expand the dimension of a corridor to allow for activities, making it less a corridor than another room in the house—albeit a linear room—where all spaces, in their distinct yet continuous ways, are valued and inviting.

In director Alfonso Cuarón's 2018 film *Roma*, a family's city house features prominently in that family's complex story of love and social class. The film takes place in Mexico City in the 1970s. There are many aspects of the house that are noteworthy, but the courtyard plays a central role. The entry to the house is from the driveway court. This space is narrow—barely fitting the car, such that when the car is parked in this court, it becomes difficult to enter the house without squeezing between car and walls. This space also functions as an open courtyard to the side of the house. But it is also the yard where the dog shits. So there is an interesting mix between the formality of entry to the house and the informality of the yard where the dog does what dogs do. This driveway/courtyard also serves as the exterior room that connects the housekeeper's living quarters to the family's living space, and contains the exterior stair that winds up to the second floor bedroom and then further up to the roof, where housekeepers do laundry. This exterior stair—an open steel stair, like a fire escape—is central to the courtyard space. Inside the house, the stair again is a supporting actor. Many scenes in the film occur on the stairs, with the film's protagonist going up and down, as she brings things to the homeowner. This inside stair is both more open and more formal. Many scenes in the film show the protagonist ascending and descending these two stairs—one in the courtyard and one in the house—and the film ends with her going up the exterior courtyard stair to the roof, and disappearing out of the camera's view.

In an open house, a courtyard has the capacity to blur boundaries between inside and outside. This in-between space establishes a nuanced complexity in place of the usual indoor/outdoor duality that sets the house as a confined object in opposition to the great outdoors. If the courtyard is outside, but inside the body of the houses, is it outside? The answer, as in the complex societal and spatial topology in Cuarón's film, may be complicated by social and familial dynamics and politics. And in Open House, the courtyard, whether fully contained or cracked open to the world beyond the house, presents a challenge to domestic space. Alvar Aalto's 1952 Muuratsalo Experimental House, in its bucolic forested and watery setting, is one such cracked courtyard. The space is so open that it barely holds together as a courtyard, and its relationship to indoors and its borderline non-cohesive surface treatments throw into question the very enclosures and limits of the house itself. In more defined, encircled spaces, from traditionally circular Fujianese Tulou houses and urban compounds like Beijing's residential Hutongs; through the different vernacular courtyard houses in the Islamic world from the Levant to the Maghreb; to such a particular modern example as Jørn Utson's 1956 Kingo Houses, all these kinds of domestic landscapes wrap the house program around an open space as a spatial island of calm and protected/tempered thermal opportunity. Toyo Ito's White U House in Tokyo, built in 1976 and demolished in 1997, and White O House in Marbella, Chile in 2009 play the courtyard two ways: White U is a classic space of calm and contemplation while White O uses the topography of the land to crack the courtyard open not in plan but in section, as the encircled space situates down the hill below the house, opening outward and downward, conveying the understory garage spaces up to the living spaces of the house.

AZD-27

Curtains, really, are tents—prototypical forms of architecture. Vestiges of past lighter modes of enclosure, curtains shield and modulate light; deny exposure to a framed image; reveal or conceal activity from view; and through that visual concealment alone make you feel secure—falsely or not—from what lies beyond their folds. Curtains, as tents do, make you believe you are protected from perceived or real danger; warm up the cold castle; and interweave the hard and soft extremes of architecture. Curtains are the territory of the dynamic—soft, mobile, transformable—that other architectural materials cannot achieve. Conversely, non-curtain architecture appears to own the static and the resistance to gravity against which curtains cannot stand.

Curtains provide soft luxury against hard efficiency. Yet, as in the collaborative work of textile-expert Lilly Reich, and her sometime professional and romantic partner Mies Van Der Rohe, the seemingly efficient glass wall also relies on the shade of the seemingly only ornamental but actually essential curtain. Many historical and vernacular architectures were either actually just curtains—that is, tents—or relied on curtains for actual warmth, perceived warmth, and status-signifying display. But modernism needed curtains to soften hard edges as well. Heating and cooling were not the issue for architectural modernism as a style, even for totally glass buildings, thanks to the once-in-the-history-of-the planet blip of hydrocarbon energy extraction—cheap heat from oil. Modernism brought back the tent. Another thin layer, the glass and steel membrane that constituted the so-called curtain wall of modern buildings, requires the curtain itself to connote protection for the psychologies of the modern subject.

Akira Kurosawa plays the curtain for psychological dramatic effect, in his 1963 film *High and Low*, by having the protagonists of the film, the family under a perceived but poorly-understood threat, hide behind their curtains when anxious or scheming, and then throw them open to attempt to see the danger, peering from their modern perch down to the still mostly pre-modern building fabric of the city below. Establishing an oppositional set-up of a seemingly clean and clear modernism at odds with the seemingly messy and even threatening traditional city, Kurosawa plays up the heightened anxiety when the curtains are cast aside.

It seems that we look to curtains for a sense of completeness and clothed-ness, at whatever level or cost, to our naked buildings and inhospitable spaces. Shigeru Ban's 1995 Tokyo Curtain Wall House is probably the most noteworthy architectural one-liner around this topic: bundling the ethereal curtain, in this case a two story tall drape of fabric, around the set back hard edges of a modern sliding-glass-walled urban house, invoking a double-meaning pun of the curtain wall. Designer Petra Blaise, in her work over decades with Rem Koolhas of OMA, ran a material range from heavy to light in all kinds of fabrics, and as proscenium curtains for stage sets of a putatively hard-edged modern life, and as animate and mutable elements for a changeable post-modern life.

The openness that we try to build into the houses that we design also requires the possibility of closures—so we bundle the environmental enclosure with the spatial and material layering the architecture of the tent, both fundamentally basic and associatively luxurious. After all, open is open only when there is closure adjacent, or the capacity for open to be closed.

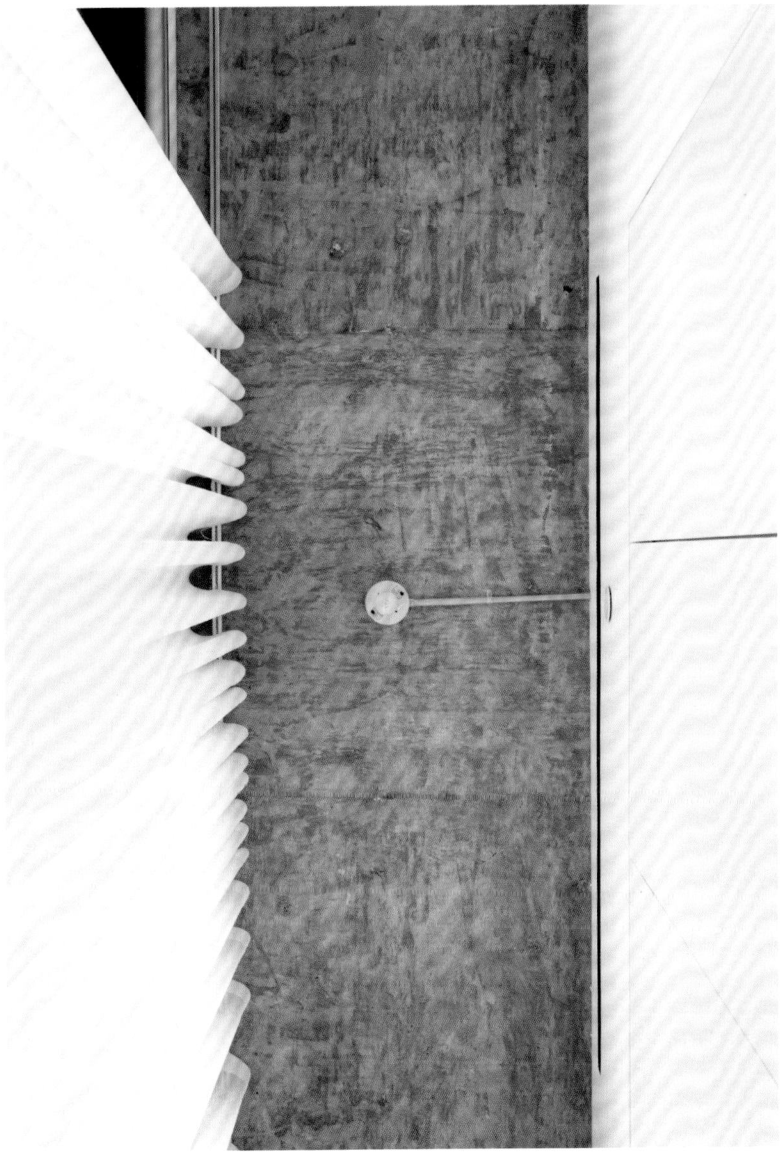

Happy Together, the 1997 film by director Wong Kar-Wai, is the story of a couple and their troubled relationship. The film is shot in Hong Kong and Argentina, cities on opposite sides of the world from one another—a displacement that the director highlights by shooting Hong Kong upside down. In one scene, the couple are seen dancing in a room that has a minimum apparatus for cooking and cleaning. The plumbing fixtures (at their most basic and austere) are not boxed in by cabinetry or otherwise concealed, but cantilevered candidly from the wall in a room that doubles as a kitchen and a living room.

Fountain is the once notorious 1917 sculpture by the artist Marcel Duchamp, created as part of his *readymade* series. It is constituted by a standard wall-mounted urinal that is rotated 90 degrees through its long axis, mounted supine on a pedestal, and signed with one of the artist's many pseudonyms as an artwork—thereby objectifying, the story goes, what would be unlikely to have been considered art at the time. In the 1980s, the artist Robert Gober, riffing off of Duchamp's urinal, created a series of pieces that were fabrications of manipulated porcelain utility sinks. Unlike Duchamp's, these pieces are not in fact sinks, but plaster fabrications made to look like sinks. And unlike Duchamp's urinal, Gober's sinks hang on the wall: they are manipulated, doubled, mirrored—and so objectified for their full surreal consideration, extracted from their usual bathroom or kitchen locations. In the streamlined plumbing world of machined minimal luxury fixtures, Gober's reconstructed sinks look bulbous and strange. In the wake of 1960s and 1970s design, the original sinks found in New York City tenements where the bathtub may have been in the kitchen—likely the fixture source of Gober's pieces—already had the same strangeness and the ability to evoke nostalgia for loft-living of days gone by.

Plumbing is an opportunity to rethink the conventions surrounding bathing and cooking, and all that stuff that is sold as standardized and normalized for our bodies to become nourished and cleansed. As at a campsite, in a house there is no reason not to liberate the sink from its conventionally designated location in bathroom and kitchens. These elements, when considered for their functional and object-like inherent intricacy, can be elevated when seen the kinds of contexts we describe in our topics Open House and Campsite. In fact, plumbing's exposure heightens our sense of their aesthetics and frees up the function from so much that has become over-built, over-commodified and over-sold. In 1931, Le Corbusier placed a freestanding sink just inside the front door at the canonical Villa Savoye in the Parisian suburb of Poissy—an insistent reminder in those tubercular times to wash your hands. At the inception of this book, Le Corbusier's sink made us think that in our times, this move can be made less didactically, but also that the Covid pandemic has reminded so many that plumbing and exposure are to be taken seriously, and that plumbing can provide a threshold as well as some sanctuary at the terminus of some circulation sequence.

At the same time in Paris in the late 1920s to early 1930s, the furniture designer and occasional architect Pierre Chareau designed, at his 1932 Maison de Verre, a bathroom in which the toilet pivots around its own waste line. The bathroom is also ambiguously privatized by a mesh screen. Both the pivot and the screen create a keen awareness of privacy and infrastructure around this all important domestic fixture. Rudolph Schindler's 1922 King's Road House in West Hollywood, California (built nine years before the Villa Savoye) exposes and doubles the use of its plumbing by having the bathroom faucet serve both the sink and the tub: a Duchampian plumbing sleight of hand or the architect cleverly saving money on his own house? Lilly Reich's 1927 Frankfurt Kitchen project neatly equips the kitchen its rightful space, cleaning up and sorting out storage, plumbing and cooking appliances. Alison and Peter Smithson's 1956's House of the Future, a speculative model house displayed in the Daily Mail Ideal Home Exhibition in London, opened up the house to shared courtyards, natural light and early swingin' plans of irregular flowing shapes—and the plumbing got tucked away in cubicles behind accordion doors. In post-war Western cultures of convenience, plumbing is hidden from view so that a flowing lifestyle can be unencumbered by the stuff that does the work for you or that you have to work in order to live. Of course, another English architect, the reliably provocative Michael Webb of Archigram, designed his 1964 Cushicle to provide all the infrastructure that the post-war urban nomad needed to subsist, reducing the house to a selectively inflatable spacesuit-like apparatus that the nomad would wear and deploy. In the Cushicle, counter to the Smithson's House of the Future, all plumbing and appliances are exposed to view and use—the bowels are like veins in its skin. Sou Fujimoto's 2011 NA House in Tokyo exposes plumbing in an overall ethos of abundant domestic exposure—liberating plumbing, privacy and function from walls and norms in a seriously open Open House.

Enter our contemporary world of luxury fixtures and bespoke bathing, ever upping the ante on costly but acquirable soulfulness, in which all that piping and construction needed to create a privileged calm is boxed in, hidden away. Open House, as we conceive it, seeks a different relationship between plumbing and space and so an alternative aesthetic. Where the plumbing is not hidden, the relationship between the body and the device that is the house plus its plumbing becomes clarified, not suppressed from consciousness. So what does all this mean for plumbing? Can the sink, the tub, the shower, the stove stand alone, have their own identities and be free of rooms, of counters, of one another, and of vanities of all kinds?

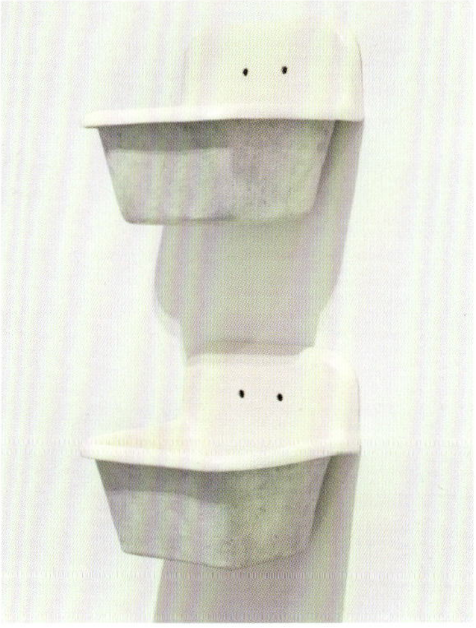

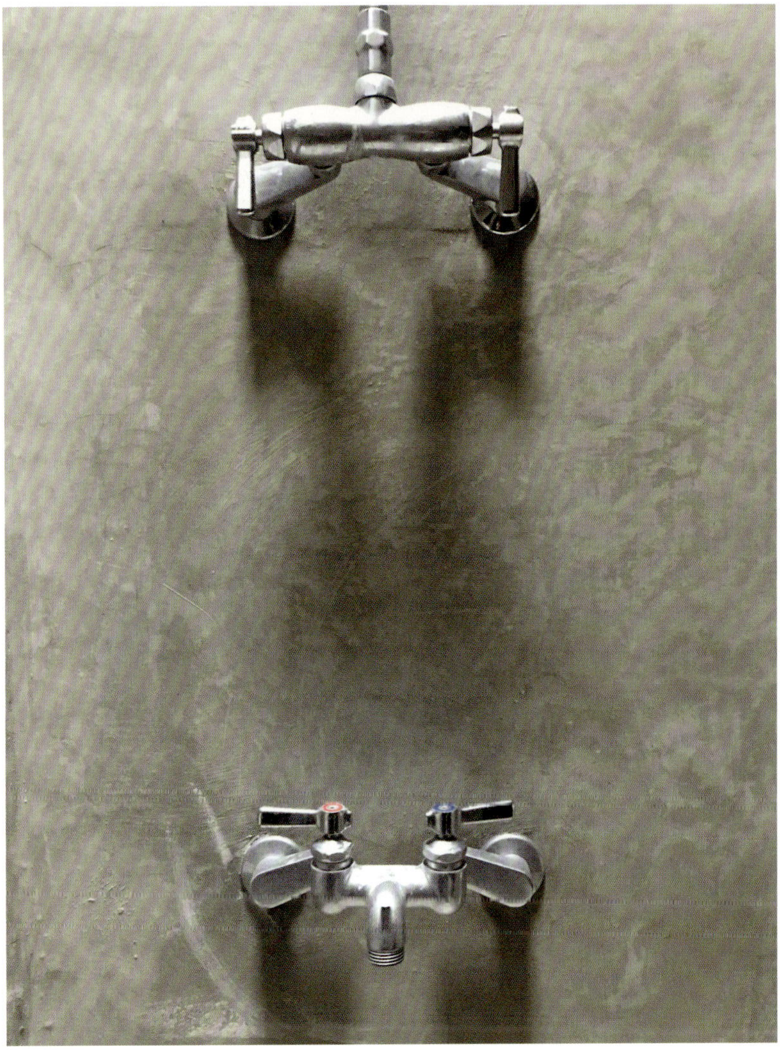

House Plants, in Open House, are often *on* the house not *in* the house. These House Plants are not meant to imitate the "natural" surroundings of the house. Typically, as plants get closer to houses, they become more curated, less informal and less seemingly "natural"—like many things relating to the typical environment of the house. Open House celebrates the informality of a meadow, ground cover, trees. But conversely, as Open House celebrates informality, it formalizes House Plants. Roberto Burle Marx's landscapes are instructive: his gardens deploy the layered paradox of the artificial "organic" found in certain strains of modernist architecture, textile, furniture, and industrial design from the mid 20th century. Burle Marx applied the geometrically "organic" pattern to the design of gardens, themselves made of actual organic material. Patterns and colors of plantings curve and radius around one another like those in a Jean Arp painting, in the forms of Picasso's figures, or in a Le Corbusier mural.

Gardens and houses have intimate histories. The kitchen garden can exist at many scales. In the city, a garden can be the size of a window box. In the Hudson Valley, a garden can become quite elaborate: elevated raised beds, hardscaped pathways, fencing and irrigation, all approaching levels of architecture. These are gardens for the practical purpose and/or pleasure of growing some portion of one's food or flowers. But the garden that tames nature into formalized environments have been planted by queens, kings and weekend warriors alike. The garden maze turns nature into a full-scale human game. As rendered sinister in Stanley Kubrick's 1980 *The Shining*, the maze can be murderous. Alain Resnais' 1961 *Last Year at Marienbad*, (written by Alain Robbe-Grillet), casts the garden, arguably more than the Baroque hotel, as the central significant environment within which relationships play out across space and time. As in the suburban spaces as presented by John Cassavetes, Resnais sets the stage for relationships between people in a space, in this case surrealist space-time and in a triangular relationship of modern/baroque proportions. Back in the Hudson Valley, and back at the scale of Open House, Russell Wright's own home, Manitoga, built between 1941 and 1961 into the stone walls of a former quarry, blurs the interior-exterior boundary with landscape materials and mossily greens the roof to reinforce a lush, hobbity-habitat stage of house and House Plants.

We formulate an intentionally-designed environment made up of the colors, shapes and textures of plants: one that extends the space of an open house to the space around the house—not trying to lift "Nature" onto an upper plane on which it can act natural, but to add a design counterpoint to the environment of interior and exterior. As designed components, House Plants carry form and texture but do so while insulating the interior (unrewarded at this point by energy code) and marking the passage of seasons. The recollection and anticipation of what the plants did last year and what they may do this year in relation to the hard and fixed surfaces of the building sets an open house on a seasonal trajectory that is both of the environment and separate from it. House Plants are natural, unnatural, aesthetic, performative—and deeply intentional.

Architects have a lot to say about plans and the architectural plan. Writing in 1891, Daniel Burnham, the celebrated Chicago architect, advised to "make no little plans; they have no magic to stir men's blood..." In 1923 in *Towards a New Architecture*, Le Corbusier declared, "The Plan is the generator. Without a plan, you have lack of order, and willfulness. The Plan holds in itself the essence of sensation. The great problems of tomorrow, dictated by collective necessities, put the question of "plan" in a new form. Modern life demands, and is waiting for, a new kind of plan, both for the house and for the city." Le Corbusier's comment about the house and the city evokes Leon Battista Alberti's famous observation from the 15th century that, "The city is like a great house, and the house in its turn a small city," and so evokes the plan, order and sensation of the house. The architect Stan Allen, who also works in the Hudson Valley, writes about "The Agency of the Plan" in his 2017 publication *Four Projects*. Building on Le Corbusier, Allen says that "the plan is a 'generator' in the sense that it produces a whole series of architectural consequences beyond the literal reproduction of its own internal formal relationships. The plan is a catalytic device." He also speaks to the work of architectural historian Robin Evans, who writes in 1997 in *Translations from Drawing to Building and Other Eassys* that, "If anything is described by an architectural plan, it is the nature of human relationships, since the elements whose trace it records—walls, doors, windows, and stairs—are employed first to divide and then selectively to re-unite inhabited spaces."

So much about spatial ideology, temporal ethos, social construct and how humans see themselves living in space is contained in the plan. Across cultures, time and the willfulness of design, the plan tracks spatial consequences, the metabolics of the house/machine/human interaction and the progression (but not necessarily progress) of styles of living. As noted about the element of the corridor in our text on that topic, Palladio's 1592 Villa Rotunda collapses domestic space and its inhabitants in the enfilade arrangement of spaces, while in many Palladian-seeming country houses in England in the 17th and 18th Centuries, the plan employs corridors that segregate classes and genders. Frank Lloyd Wright's Usonian plans, though American, are ingeniously compact and boat-like, with intricate logics that extend to the organization of their small suburban lots. Mies van der Rohe designs houses to appear, in their plans, to flow freely around or bracketed by dense and compact cores—as at Farnsworth

House or Resnor House, built in 1939 in Jackson Hole. But in his Brick Country House of 1923, the forms of the plan pivot pinwheelingly, bracketing spaces more like the figures in Piet Mondrian's painting *Piers and Ocean* of 1905—centrifugal as much as centripetal. Put plans of Brick Country House next to Rudolph Schindler's 1922 King's Road House and Frank Lloyd Wright's Usonian Houses and see a conversation among architects about how to live in a house in the early 20th Century. Le Corbusier's domestic explosion of his, "new kind of plan," is seemingly modern—as we've come today to apply the word—in its mechanized succinctness. But even though Le Corbusier famously established the "free plan" as one of his polemical "Five Points of a New Architecture", published in 1923 in *Towards a New Architecture*, the interior walls were free to move around, at the direction of the architect, since the building had its own structural system free from interior constraint—within their tight compositional edges and volumetric envelopes, his houses, seen through their plans, are decidedly not as open and free-flowing as Mies van der Rohe's later open plans. The painter needs the frame.

Near the very end of Alfonso Cuarón's 2018 film *Roma*, the privileged family that is the film's subject returns from a holiday and enters their comfortable urban home. While they were away, the housekeeper has rearranged the designation of the upstairs bedrooms. Everyone gets a different room from what they had before their holiday. It is time for a change—a new beginning. What is significant about this scene for us is that the spaces of the home are not prescribed or designated for one type of use or person. They are interchangeable, and open to interpretation; to use, misuse, and reuse. Open House starts with calibrations of the organization of domestic space. Always conscious of what space lies beyond, whether interior or exterior, the plan of Open House formalizes informality—seeking to catalyze the domestic conversation amongst spaces and Robin Evans' human relationships. These are the domestic, (as well as the architectural, as defined by Stan Allen) consequences of the plan. Open House plans are fluid in possibility yet precisely calibrated. Since the houses are usually not large, parameters are as critical as perimeters. There is not excess room to spread out—but also, there doesn't have to be. When designing the plans of houses of the scales presented in this book, every inch counts.

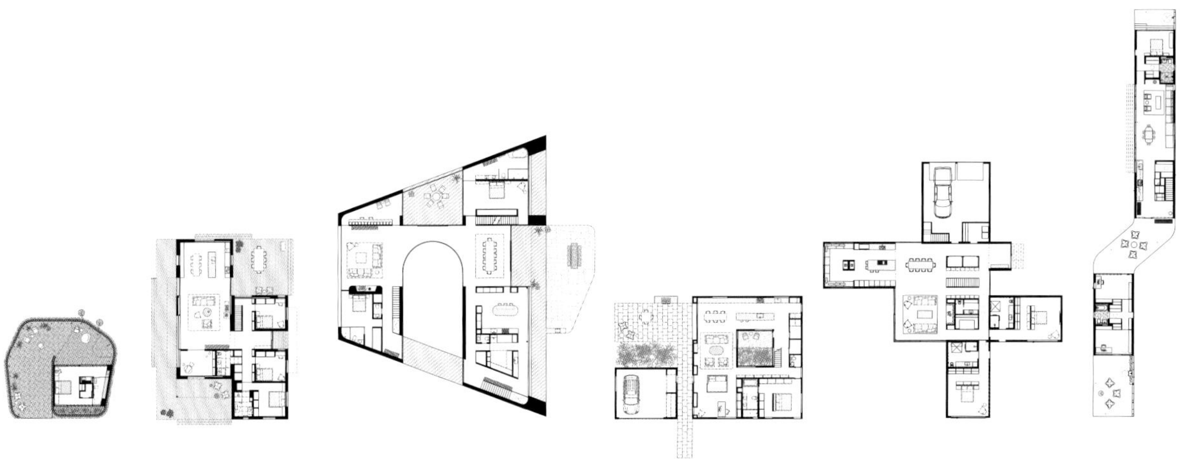

Structural systems seek continuity and efficiency, but in the end rarely attain total rational uniformity. Within any single project, changes in course, budget and other unforeseen inputs can make for contingent and hybrid structural systems. The flitch beam exemplifies hybridity in structure. A traditional construction component, dating to before the advent of structural steel, the flitch beam combined a harder more expensive wood with a softer, more prevalent, and easier-to-machine wood in order to make a stronger beam. Currently, a flitch refers to a steel plate grafted into framing or engineered lumber with through-bolting in order to increase the spanning capacity of a member. The plate height is most often constrained by the adjacent lumber, but the width can increase incrementally, within limits, to effectively backfill wherever depth can't be achieved.

We can exercise this hybridity, contingency, nimbleness, and whatever tool is best for the job. But structure cannot be taken lightly. Structural systems in our open houses can start out simply as: Western or wood platform frame, hybrid-wood platform frame + steel moment frame, hybrid-wood platform frame + steel column, steel frame + wood-frame infill, wood-frame + concrete panel, mass wall site cast concrete + wood-frame roof.

The interplay between structure and the space that it both occupies and defines particularizes the specific relationships in a house that make the open, open and make space, space. An open house as we conceive of it does not expose structure for structure's sake—as, say its own kind of ornament or gesture of prowess—but establishes a mutual influence between structure and space—such that underlying patterns of structures and fundamental relationships between spaces coexist: as a both-and mash-up, as an either-or edit, or something in-between. In this way, structure declares its presence as structure but also as a prime player in how space is conceived and directed. Structure in our houses is a study in contingency. But it is not passive, nor is it intended to be overbearing.

The necessities of domestic space and the positioning of openness sets up a range of shared duties between the structure-ruling gods of gravity and shear—the dead drop of the straight fall down, and the rectangle-to-parallelogram-racking of lateral forces going sideways. It is fully possible that in a single structure, duties to gravity can be shared by columns or volumes comprised of inglorious walls. But shear is always in the walls, unless it is in moment frames needed to support openings that have migrated too far from solid walls. Structure may be dictated by budget but it often gets arm-wrestled into a range of contortions, or simply slipped from rational rules of construction in order to wrest an architectural tectonic from construction—for example, the rules that instructs that the rim joist must sit on the outside edge of the stud below; that sheathing overlaps the foundation; that exterior wall studs are always 2×6; that windows install flush to the outside of sheathing; that rough openings have the same relationship to framing throughout the building; or that simply all structure aligns.

We honor these rules by comprehendingly breaking them. And this is the heart of the matter: tectonically speaking, these rules are necessary starting points that are tweaked in deference to an architectural idea, the clarity of the assembly, the resolution of the detail. Seemingly the one inflexible frame of an architecture, especially of a house, structure is the medium of compromise—it is what gives. And Structure and Tectonics are never the same thing, for this reason. Especially at the scale of a house, systems of load-bearing and elements of construction are mutually complicit, but distinct. Like Paul Rudolph's 1952 Walker Guest House, a little tectonic jewel of a frame, his 1966 Bass Residence, 1968 Green Residence and 1959 Milam Residence, examples of houses that prioritize the legibility of the systems that establish the tectonics of these buildings, over pure efficiency. In these projects, as in so much of his work, Rudolph starts with *module* but evolves into *system*. Structures are implicated but (and here Walker may be an exception) never subsume tectonics, as they do at Mies van der Rohe's 1951 Farnsworth House. Farnsworth, as in so much of Mies's work, collapses the structural and the tectonic in an explicit structural/visual celebration of the I-Beam. In Open House, we explore and exploit contingency, but engage a conversation between gravity and shear, box and column, wall and frame—knowing that Structure and Tectonic are both formal constructions and figurative constructs.

That rift in the matrix when a building or a city street is in the midst of demolition offers a mystifying glimpse into the inner working of the grand machine, in which what is inside the once apparently solid walls is laid messily bare. Urban buildings from as long ago as the late 19th or early 20th century, that present their façades as pure heavy stone, are revealed to be in fact iron or steel structures, with what seems to our curtain-wall-conditioned eyes to be a very thick veneer—but still a veneer—with rubble and the actual structure behind. Modern life presents a paradoxical surface: a veneer, at best, of calibrated layers. The precarious work of Gordon Matta-Clark—from his large-scale 1975 incisions into metal sheds on Manhattan's Pier 52, through his *Conical Intersect* project of that same year, excavating deep into the masonry of condemned Paris apartment buildings, to the smaller and rather quaintly domestically scaled *Building Cuts* documented at the Whitney Museum's 2007 retrospective in a show *You are the Measure*—actualizes the conceptual cut into buildings that is stipulated in architectural drawings. These works reveal cross-sections and destabilize any conceptions of architectural safety and domestic security. *Building Cuts* begins to reveal the paradoxical architectural spectrum that spans from thickness to thinness. And that can only be fully revealed through a practice of destructive probing—of which Matta-Clark's work is a critical example. Or better, (and less expensively) through the representational convention of the architectural wall section.

Wall sections of a building reveal—like the diagnostic tool of magnetic resonance imaging (MRI) through a body—performance-laden slices through the construction systems. These sections are elemental: air, fire, earth, and water all require special consideration. At the position in a wall section where the wall meets the sky, the detailing must especially address water; where the wall meets the ground, it must especially address heat and cold. These questions of where the water or thermal barrier is placed relative to the structural or thermal mass of the building is, on the one hand, a technical issue; but on the other hand it speaks to the craft: to the understanding of a house as a field of dryness or cloud of warmth or coolth, achieved not just through mechanical equipment but through fine calibrations of material and sequential arrangement. The wall section reveals a consideration of atmospheric conditioning—heating, cooling, dehumidifying—that is independent of the mere operations of mechanical systems. The wall section prompts a consideration of the openness of an Open House, down to the finest calibrations of impermeability and porosity.

The wall section cuts through a series of the systems, layers, products and building qualities most often in order to describe to a builder how these layers adhere and aggregate to comprise various performance profiles of the building. The wall section also has the capacity to describe sculptural qualities of the exterior perimeter of the building. But given the performance pressures on the layers in the wall in our contemporary crises and conditions of ecology and technology, descriptions of plasticity may be relegated to other more focused—and limited—representations, while systems and performance are now front and center. Previously, the wall section emphasized formal behavior describing, say, entablatures, volutes, the gentle curve of entasis. But the wall section did this in the form of profiles of the outermost layer—the line where the drawing ends, leaving the internal layers and edges to the builders. (Consult, for instance, the contours of Alberti's sections in the *Ten Books of Architecture* from 1452 to find nothing but blank hatchwork inside the walls.) Nowadays, the wall section calibrates the very fine layers of construction meant to hold up, to keep warm, to keep dry—and also establish a building's outer form—among which the most reductive of layered systems is the curtain wall. The wall section is also a diagram of efficiency, carrying costs and sequences of production. Across time, the wall section describes the wall, prescribing how the building meets the sky and the ground and how the necessities of both the shedding of water and the ingenuities of drainage shape the appearance of the enclosures—and hence of all the architectures of the building, from tip to toe and everything in between.

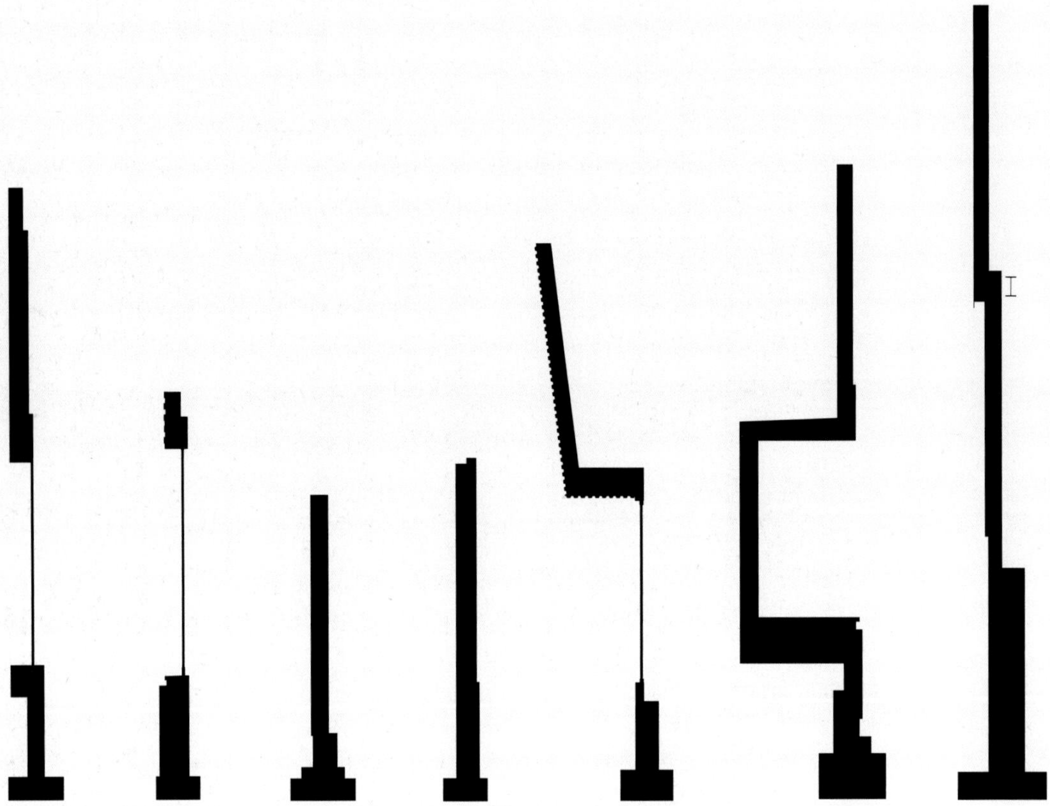

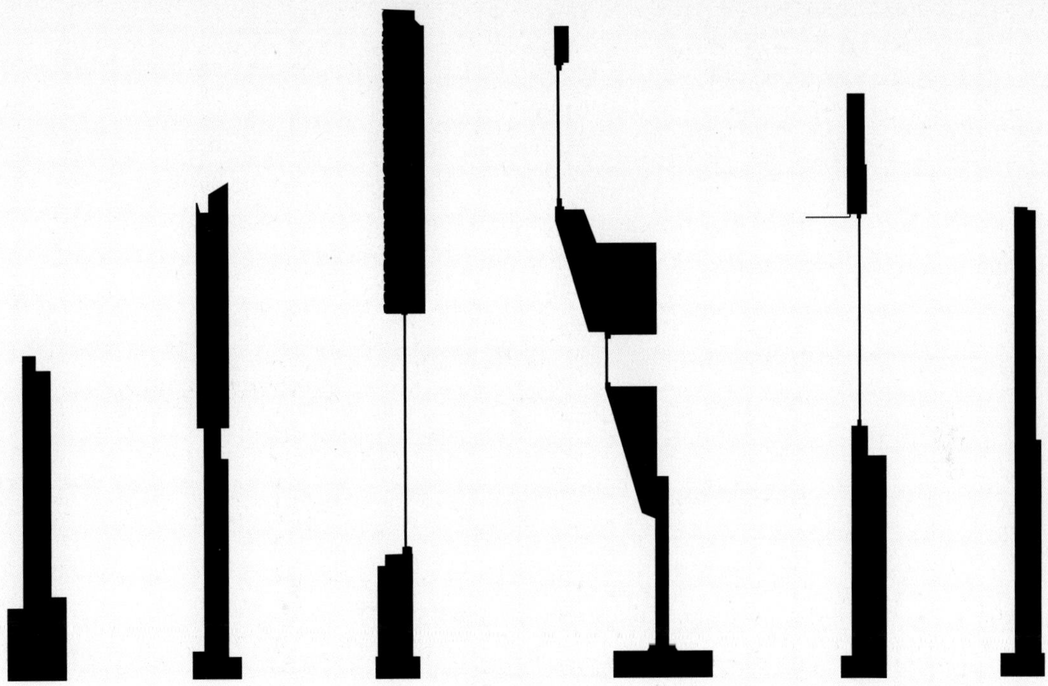

Between 1969 and 1971, the southern Californian photographer Lewis Baltz produced 25 photos, that he called *The Tract Houses*. These photos capture ubiquitous suburban development houses that utilize stock elements of standard construction in American homebuilding. The photos are taken just after the houses' completion, but before anyone has moved in. Exterior and interiors are unfinished and unfurnished; the landscaping is still incomplete. The cookie-cutter houses have been designed without a particular site or owner in mind. They adhere to late-mid-20th-Century culturally-accepted norms and received ideas for how a house should be designed, organized, and inhabited. Doors and windows are standardized off-the-shelf elements and are placed without any consideration of site-specific conditions of light, views, winds, moods, and more. And in many of his photos, Baltz highlights the unconsidered afterthought and haphazard placement of the overlooked but all-too-visible fragments of infrastructure (gas meter, dryer vent, hose bib, and so forth) onto the facade of the house. It is only in this seemingly random aftermath of infrastructural attachments that actual site-specificity finally asserts itself.

Baltz's tract houses are placeless houses. These are not homes—or, that is, they are made homes only by the actions and intentions of their dwellers, not the other way around. In Open House, home is about place. It is defined not only by the house, but also by the surrounding landscape and the relationship between the architecture and its site. A three-winged house defines three distinct yards or a courtyard house incorporates the outdoors into the interior living room. Different kinds of openings—and windows, provide access to adjacent outdoor and indoor landscapes, and provide views and daylight. A campsite can, by great necessity or great luxury, serve as a home if it has been tended to and inhabited. You choose where you pitch your tent, whether under a tree or near a stream, whether facing south or facing a view, whether on top of a hill or down in the valley.

In conservation biology, *rewilding* is the practice of reintroducing keystone or apex species to their former habitats, of returning the offspring of captive animals or cultivated plants to a natural state—or at least to a deliberately less controlled environment. If the project of what we call Open House aims to define domestic space and define the experience of home, it also, paradoxically, aims to un-domesticate the house.

This is a house of one shape.

Located in Hudson, New York, this house is composed of several rooms of one shape. Each room in the house is a three-dimensional right trapezoid—what we call a *zoid*—that is repeated, mirrored, and flipped. When applied to space, this geometry produces a smaller opening at one end and a larger opening at the other. When mirrored, flipped, and nested together, the rooms each look towards a particular view of the landscape and a particular orientation towards the sun.

Each zoid is a discrete room, used either as a covered porch, a kitchen, a dining room, a living space, a bedroom or a bathroom. And each of these rooms has direct access to the outdoors through a sliding or swinging door. There are no windows—only doors. There is no predetermined designation of spaces: all rooms are created equal and interchangeable. Only the plumbing fixtures are fixed. And there is no material distinction between walls, floors, or ceilings; all rooms are finished in Baltic birch plywood.

An enclosed stair brings you up to a second floor "pop-up" space that overlooks a planted roof—a landscape of house plants. The pop-up space is a parallelogram—not a zoid—it breaks the rule. This space has two open ends, one facing north and the other facing south. By structurally resolving the two long glass spans on the first floor, the solid walls on the second floor become beams for the first-floor spans. The stair bisects the parallelogram figure, creating two equally-sized triangle rooms that are open and accessible to the roofscape garden.

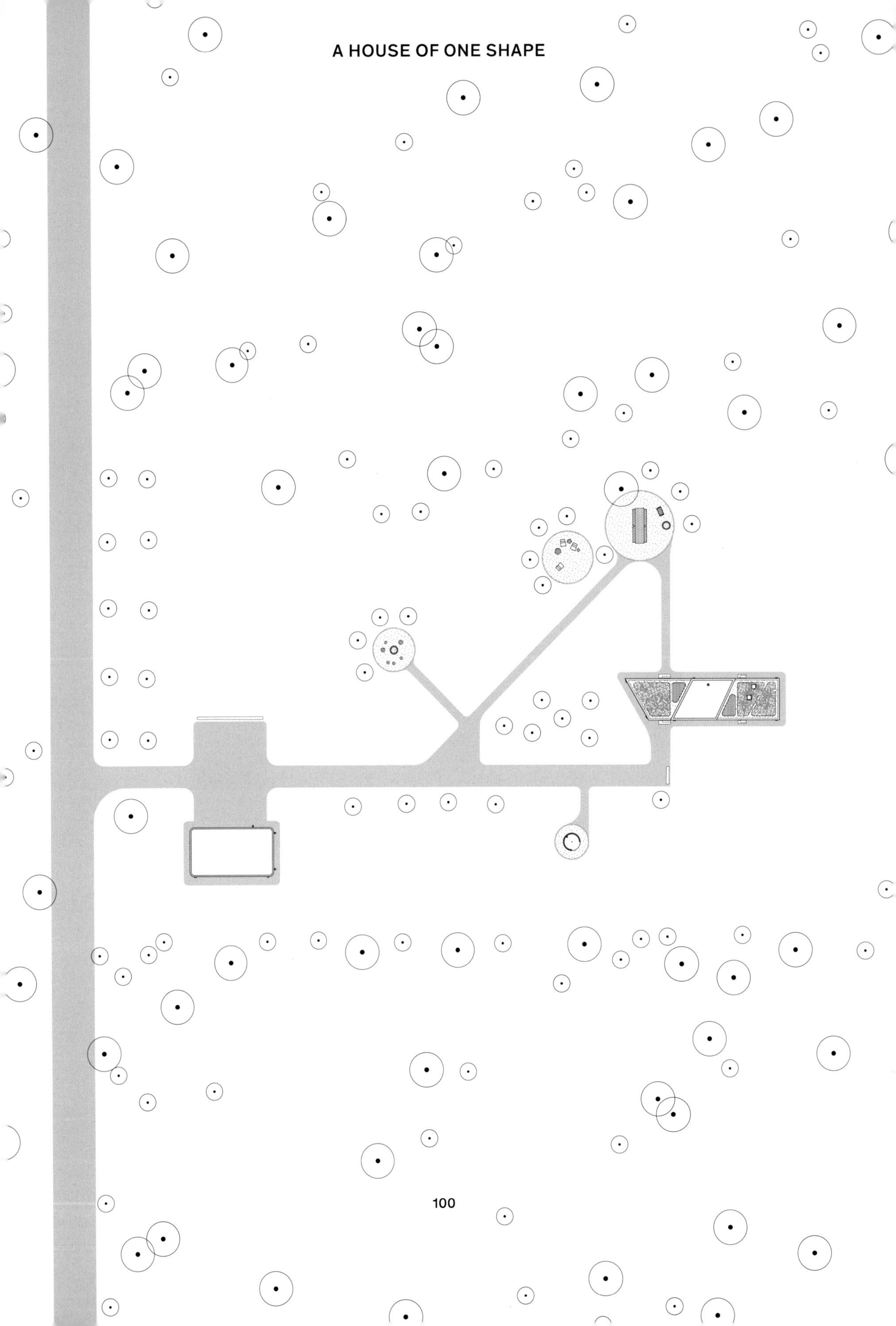

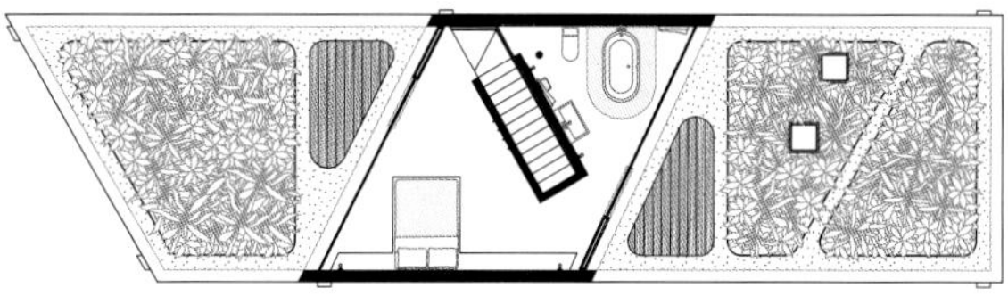

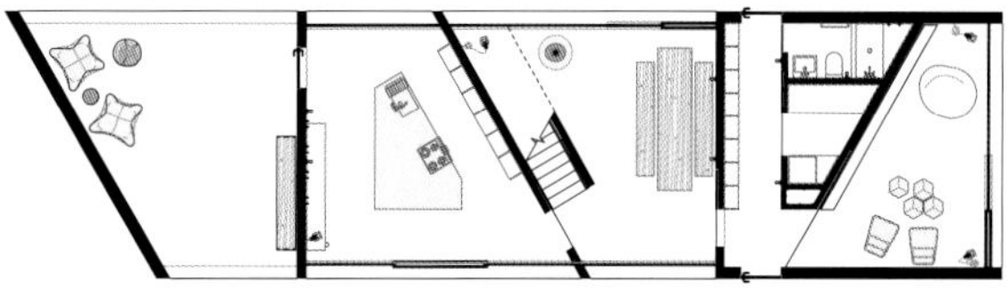

A HOUSE OF ONE SHAPE

Every house has its own particular narratives that are tightly connected to the metrics of its architecture: yielding dimensions, taking measures, telling stories about the building. The metric stories of this house are twofold: a singular geometric shape and a campsite on the land that predated the house. The shape is a right trapezoid that constitutes the plan of almost all the spaces of the house.

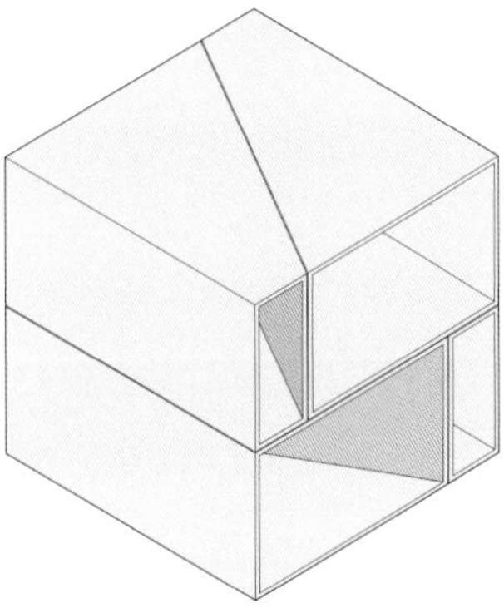

The right trapezoid is four-sided, with one right angle and two complimentary angles (30 and 60 degrees, for example, or any two angles that add up to 90 degrees); it has one fixed leg, one hypotenuse and two opposing faces that become both long and short as a function of the complimentary angles.

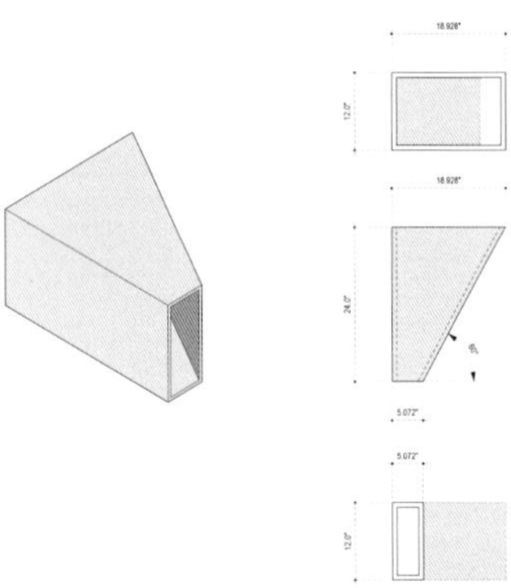

This house is part of four distinct studies of this geometry that have built upon one another to create several different projects: (chronologically) an art installation, public seating in the Miami Design District, this house, and a pavilion at a nearby art and architecture park called Art Omi.

This shape was first studied for the 2016 Unpacking the Cube exhibition at the Chamber Gallery on West 23rd St. in New York City. The deceptively simple shape proved to be virtually infinitely reconfigurable, inviting combinations and forms that were constrained only by how many pieces could be made. Using Ultra High Performance Concrete (UHPC), 24 units of this same shape were made. UHPC is a specialized mixture made even more specialized by the sequencing of ingredients added to the mix that can achieve a compressive strength of 11,000 pounds per square inch, a far cry from concrete used for house foundations that typically achieve 3,500 psi. As a result of this strength, the material was able be poured thin to create the pieces for the art installation. The walls of the trapezoidal shapes are 3/4" thick, as are the benches in the Miami Design District.

These shapes were called "nts" (as in "not to scale"), also the name of the LEVENBETTS contribution to Unpacking the Cube, because these shapes, although fixed at dimensions that when aggregated × 4 would equal a 24" × 24" × 24" cube. These were also dimensions that later were to become significant for the space of this House—when they were multiplied by a factor of 10. In contrast to the nts study, in which the same shape aggregates and proliferates ad infinitum, this house is a study in geometries that aggregate and disaggregate into sub-geometries only so far as needed to assemble a 1,600-square-foot house.

Each "zoid" of the house has two opposing solid walls, at an angle to one another, and two fully open parallel glass walls. The open walls are 9' long and 18' long, respectively. Each room, or "zoid space," is 18' wide (outside dimension), which sets the width of the house. Three successive spaces (one of which is an outdoor space) alternate their large and small dimensions as they stack against one another in plan. This "zoiding" of spaces focuses your perspective outward in opposite directions as you move along the long axis of the house: narrowing, broadening, and narrowing in turn.

The fourth space in this succession of spaces also uses the right trapezoid, conceived not as a void but as a solid utility zone, and turns the view 90 degrees from the other zoid spaces in order to capture a vista and a cooler internal microclimate toward the north, and to establish two shear walls that counteract the lateral loads that the open glass walls, unsupported by steel moment frames, cannot resist.

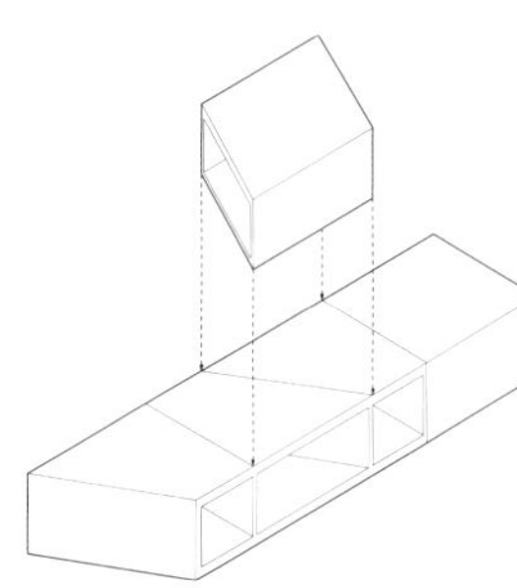

On the second floor, the geometry plays out as a parallelogram-shaped space that shifts the orientation of the open walls of the spaces below by 90 degrees, and posts down onto outer structural points of the right trapezoids. Engineered wood beams span across to the structural points and enable the walls of the second-floor space to be open. The other two walls of the second floor are solid in opposition to the open walls of the spaces below and act as deep upset beams over the glass expanses. The shift of the solid to void walls from ground to second floor resets the passage of light and solar aspect of the house to align with the diurnal patterns of life in the house. Furthermore, the space of the parallelogram is intersected by the internal staircase, yielding two smaller triangular spaces, one in the bedroom and the other in the bathroom.

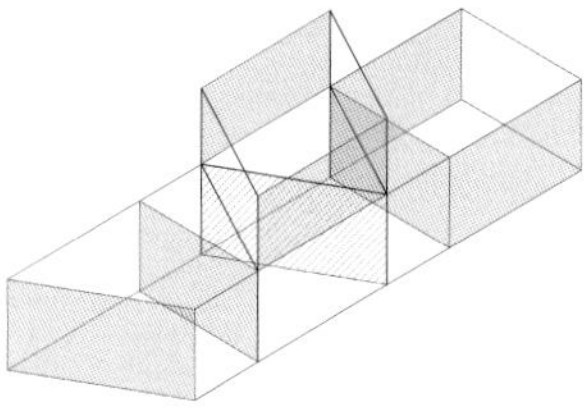

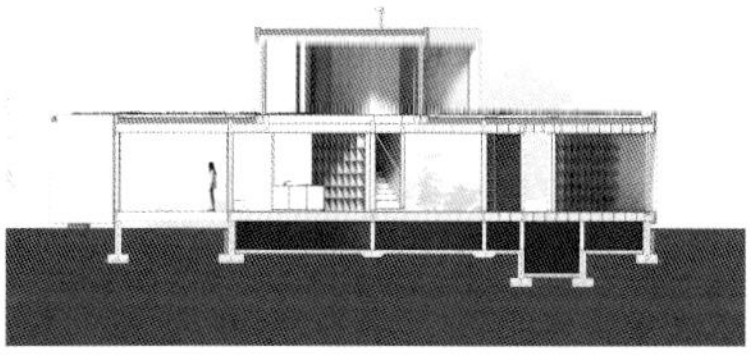

Preceding all this geometry was the campsite—another type of calibration that had relatively little to do with the study of shapes. The house embodied the activities of camping and then reestablished outdoor spaces on the sites of the former campsite. The campsite was first a 16' × 8' tent platform and a two-person tent; a hand-operated well pump; a 16-gallon lockbox (the garage); two chairs (the living room); a 36" diameter × 12" tall concrete ring fire pit (the kitchen); the woods themselves (for enjoyment and relief), and a clearing (for the space of inhabitation). The campsite provided for all that was needed for human inhabitation during northeast North American summertime and established a way of living on the land that would intersect with the open zoid spaces of the house. Like the campsite, the domestic elements of the house are both informally composed and highly specific. A bathroom sink is bolted to the wall without a vanity or other support.

The kitchen is an island, offset from the walls of the room in which it sits: a solid trapezoid within a spatial trapezoid, with all appliances incorporated into its prismatic volume. The wood-burning stove floats in front of nearby glass, sitting on a 30"-diameter fiber cement dot.

The landscape surrounding the house reestablishes the spatial definition of the campsite elements by placing three galvanized-edged gravel circles (bigger dots) outboard of the house. These dots both encircle and are encircled by black locust and ash shade trees, and define the space of the barbeque and table (36' in diameter), a sitting area (24' in diameter), and a radially laid out garden (also 24' in diameter). The house, although a conceptual consequence of a geometric study, takes on the characteristics of the campsite in its spaces, and translates its originating metrics into the geometries of itself and its site.

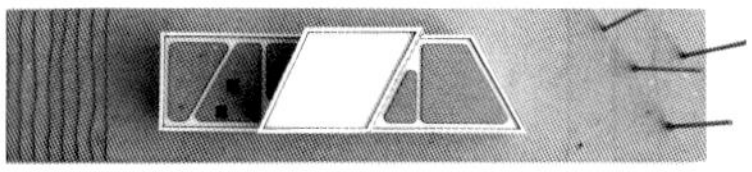

This is a square house.

Located in Stone Ridge, New York, the house is a 43' × 43' in plan. It has ten doors and no windows. There is no front door or back door. There is no formal entry. Rather, the house is organized as a series of rooms that face the landscape and can all be accessed directly from the outside. The square plan reinforces a non-hierarchical informal organization to the house, while still allowing each face of the building to offer a different experience of the landscape and orientation to the sun.

Organized like a raumplan, (the matrix of levels associated with the domestic designs of interwar Austrian architect Adolf Loos) each room is a discreet space or volume with a different dimension in plan and in section. The roof is flat but the floors step with the existing sloped landscape, creating a variation in height as you move through the house. At the center of the house is a sunken living space that drops you below the height of the ground outside, sinking you deeper in to the earth.

The house sits in the ground—not just on the ground. Made of board-formed cast concrete, it is heavy. The deep perimeter walls act as both massive thresholds and as permeable surfaces through which domestic space and nature commingle. Accessed from the outside, a stair brings you up to the roof, to a campsite deck and roof garden where you can set up a tent, bathe in the outdoor shower, and eat vegetables from the garden.

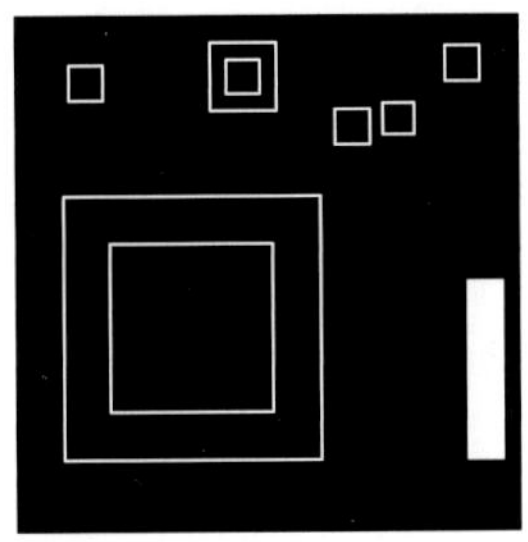

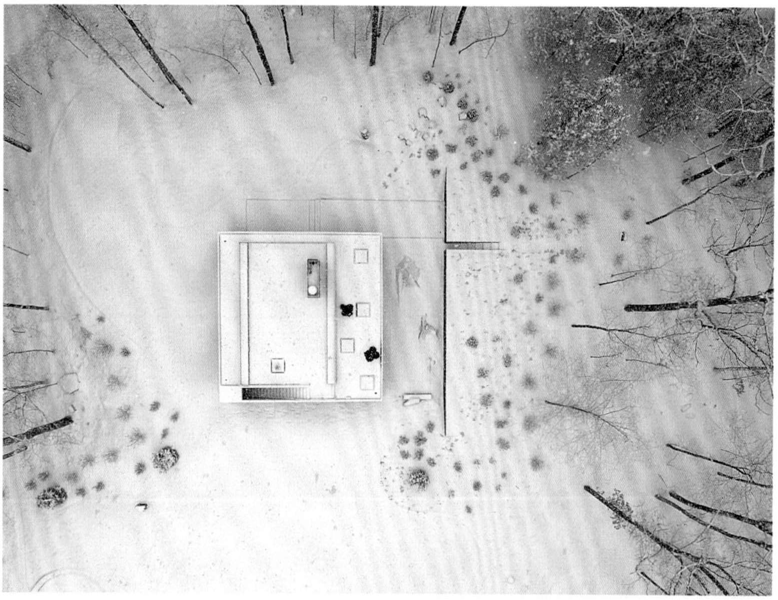

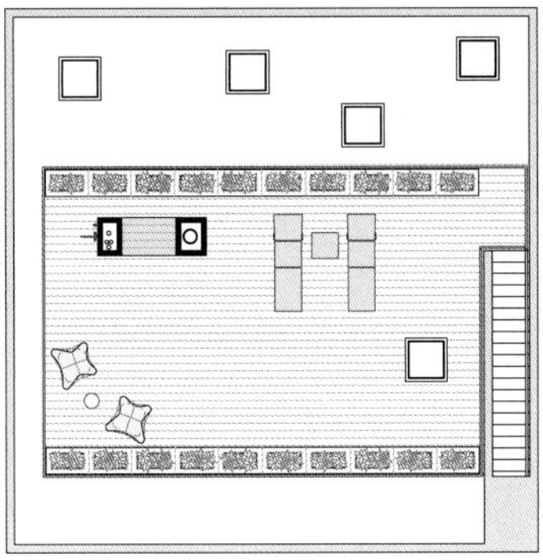

A SQUARE HOUSE

The formal metrics of this house begin with the shape—the square and extends to a series of squares. The house is 43' × 43' and embeds a 16' × 16' sunken pit within a square living room—a hedonistic place in which to sink softly into the earth around the fire.

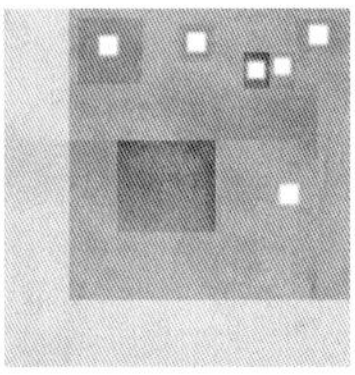

The pit, at the lowest "level" in the house and an exemplar of swingin' 1960s and 1970s American architectural hedonism, found in the Paul Rudolph's house, Eero Saarinen's Mueller House and (who could forget) the sunken trapezoidal shapes of John Lautner's house in Beverly Crest—made famous by its formal concrete ingenuity, by the structural daring of the house itself, and by its perpetual use in film and fashion shoots.

This house's pit, focused on both the fireplace and the view of woods and moss garden to the south, constitutes a deep space at the epicenter of the house. Silky and soft shag carpet blurs its base, while a three-sided ring of irregular shaped cushions (a nod to Lautner) rounds out the comfort metric of this hard and soft space.

Another square, a sunken 8' × 8' hot tub, is set into the concrete floor, anchoring this one of several bathing elements of this house. The other elements in this bathing space are a traditional wood soaking tub, made of Hinoki, a Japanese Cedar; a steam shower; a rinsing bench; and a tree—all daylit from above by square skylights.

The overall spatial composition of squares is comprised of six stepped platforms, eight doors of two primary dimensional types, four skylights, and eight distinct water programs—comprised of a series of tubs, sinks, and showers. The interconnection of square spaces and stepped spaces is very different from the linear metric of a long thin plan. In this house, a constellation of spatial relationships prioritizes flow over static organization, but calm stasis within each space over linear movement from one space to the next.

The house is heavy. Made of mass wall construction, the site-cast concrete of the building weighs 432,150 pounds. Constituting the second-thickest walls in this collection of houses, the wall sections speak to the tectonic, plastic and thermal opportunities of the stereotomic construction: surface interplay of formwork and ties, insulation, pocketing of sliding doors or fixed glass, integrated cabinetry, and wall surfaces. Those surfaces expose the ties that keep the boards of the formwork in place when the pressure of the pour pushes outward. The filled tie ends, 1,920 conical concrete thimble shaped plugs, form an 8" × 16" pattern of concrete dots across the walls of the house.

Board-formed walls turn the four outside corners of the building and play off against the 19 jamb and nine head transitions at apertures where the back-and-forth variance of board-formed edges (stepping between 1/8" and 1/4") are revealed against the smooth formed walls where glass fills in the voids in the walls. Rough-sawn pine boards, 4" wide in the shifting misalignment, establish the horizontally striated pattern across the exterior walls of the building, a carefully calibrated corduroy cast against the pine. The formwork is tuned to the heights of apertures and required a double layering of the 4" boards and an entire additional exterior layer of plywood and 2 × 6 gunwales to resist the pressure of the pour.

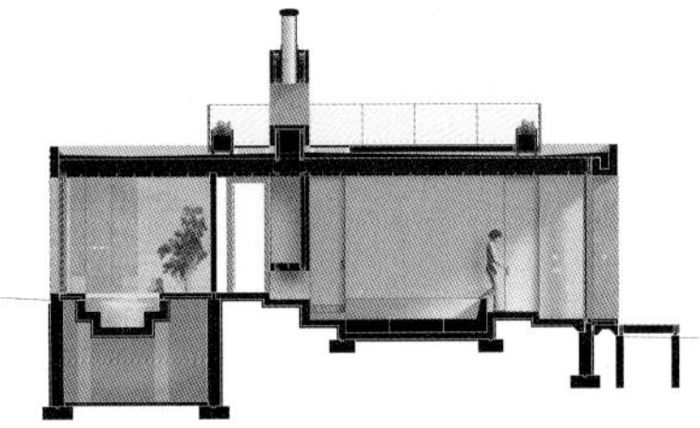

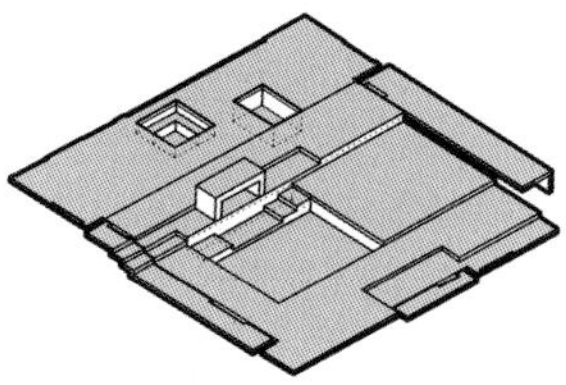

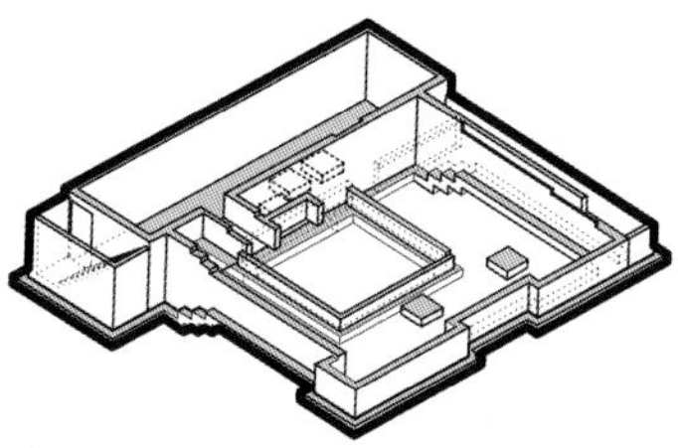

The 16 steps in the formwork, that mirror the stair steps above that lead to the roof, are consequences of the 4" pine boards. At 8" each and aligning with the jagged stepped profile in concrete—which is also serves as an angled beam that spans the angled glass panel at the guest room/studio of the building—the formwork continues the horizontal banding of the facade.

Prioritizing the incessant pattern, the stepping of these doppelgänger steps highlights the precision of the formwork and reinforces the tectonic legibility of the building's textured surfaces. As a poured liquid, concrete establishes textures, takes the shape of desired patterns, or of a needed foundation—all of which are at work in this house. The foundation consisted of seven independent pours, each sequenced to allow access to connection points to one another and to facilitate the removal of formwork post-pour. Unlike the additive process of wood frame construction, the concrete walls and foundations were formed in the negative of the walls themselves and were subtracted after the concrete hardened.

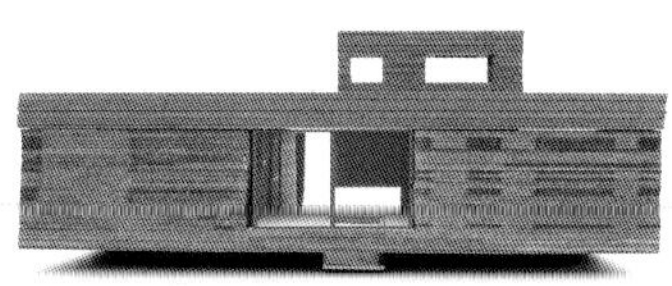

As a result of its heavy response to the topography, the house settles deeply into its site. You can feel it pushing into the earth in increments: in the steps and recesses that follow the topography of the hill and that push deeper to hold water in the Japanese spa tub and envelop conversations in the padded pit. Models that were made to study the surfaces of the building walls simulated the pattern of horizontal striation, and the stereotomic nature of the building. In those models, layers of stacked chipboard served to create the visual and textural surface while also representing the mass wall construction of the building itself.

This is a house without walls.

Located in Hillsdale, New York, the house takes its cues from our topic, Campsite. It is an open pavilion. It is comprised of a series of boxes—volumes comprising domestic elements: bathroom, kitchen, fireplace, closet, storage, and utilities—that all sit under a simple flat roof supported by a constellation of 2.5-inch steel columns. Each volume is placed in a loose perpendicular pattern (like the marks in Mondrian's 1915 painting *Pier and Ocean*), creating informal enclosures yet providing for privacy and openness to the outdoors. Like a campsite, one can meander from one domestic element to another through a series of partially enclosed spaces. The roof supports a planted sedum garden with a "pop-up" room that invites you to camp outside under the stars.

The house has only doors, no windows. It is organized as a series of rooms that open directly to the outside, creating a fluid relationship between interior and exterior. The roof has seven apertures—some inside and some outside that bring light and air from above to the interior and exterior living spaces below. The rounded-square roof plan reinforces a soft, non-hierarchical organization of the house, while the play of light and shadow, through the spaces and field of slender columns, tracks the sun throughout the day.

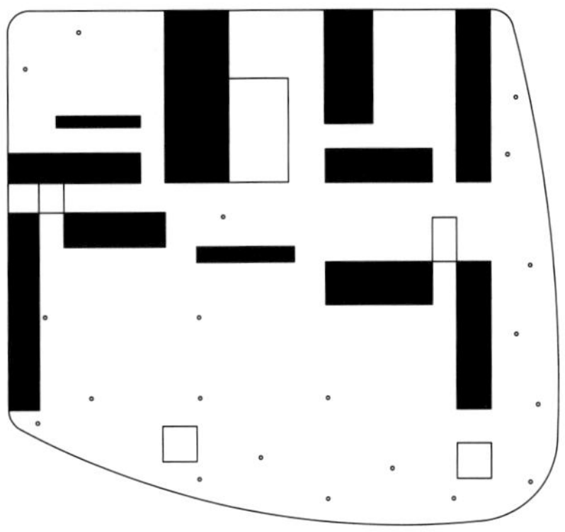

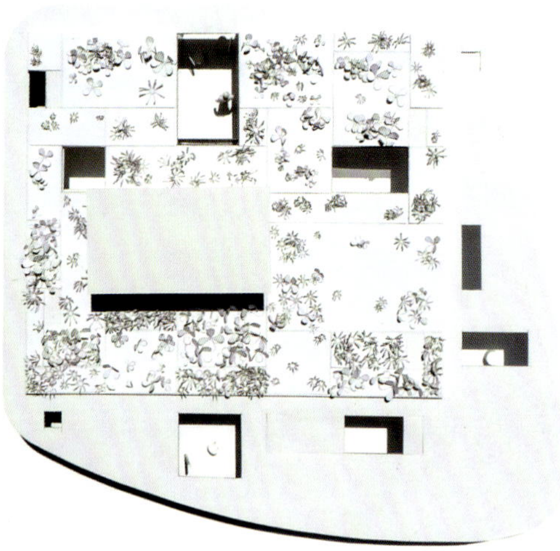

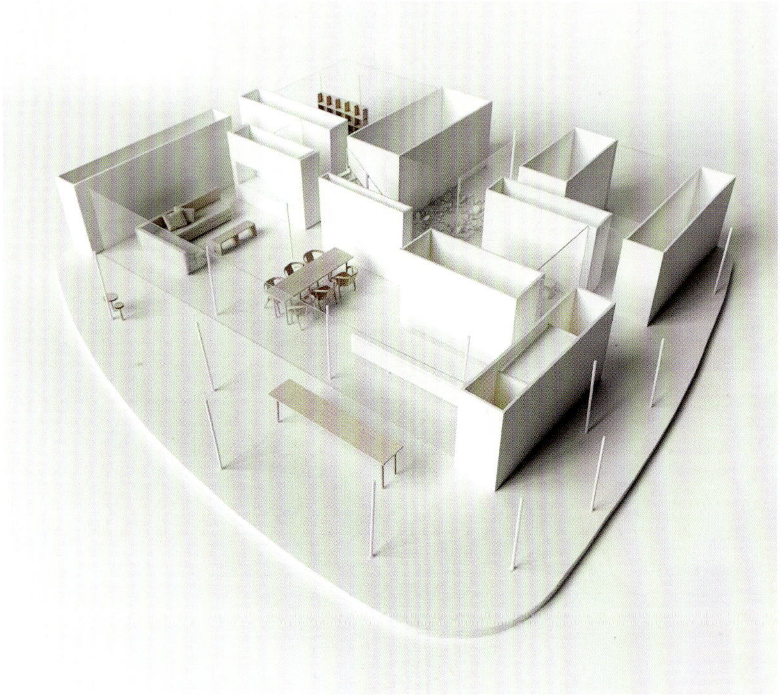

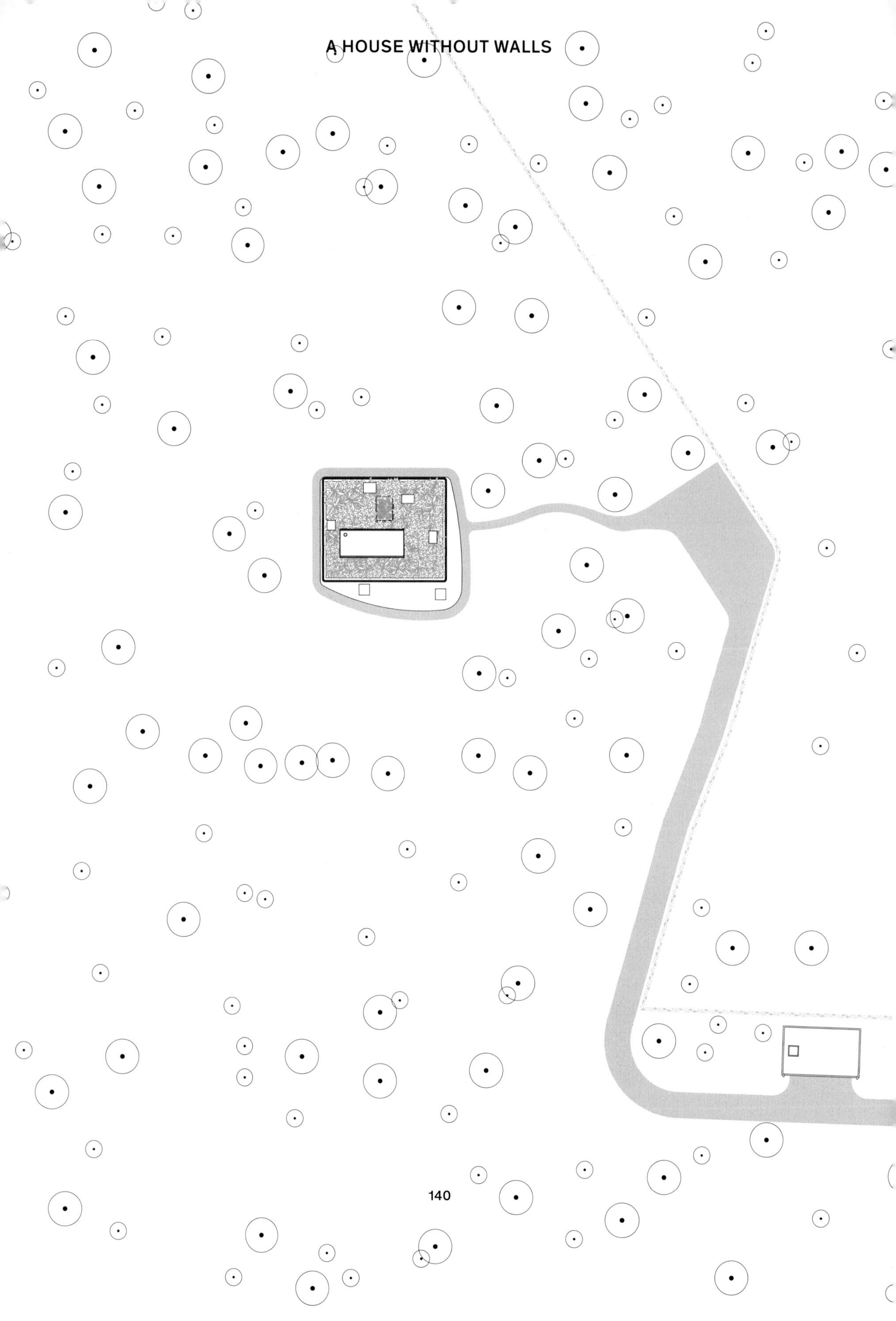

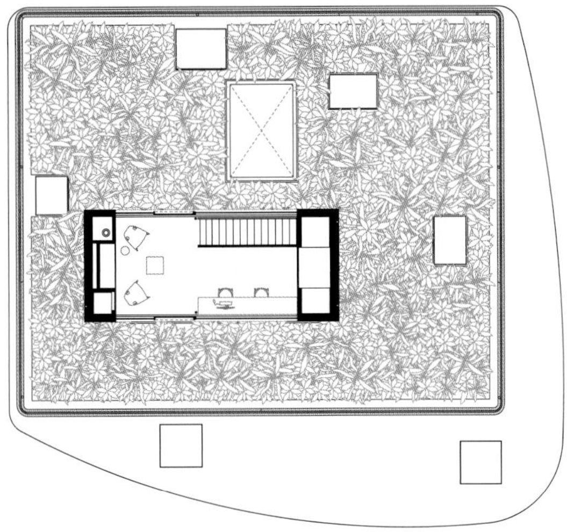

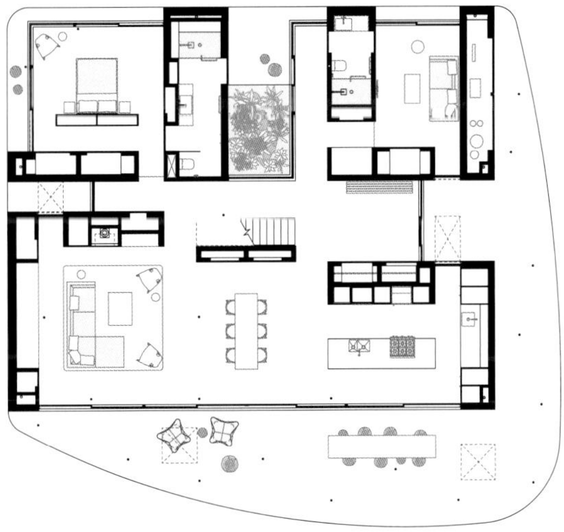

A HOUSE WITHOUT WALLS

The originating metric stories of this house were the open brief and an open hilltop site closely surrounded by tall coniferous trees and stone ridges that course in a parallel bias across the site. The brief contained limited spatial concepts beyond a desire for shelter in- and out-doors and the site offered some inherent view and aspect relationships, though not prescriptive organizational concepts.

There is an undeniable view to the west through tall trees. There is access to the site from the road. There are suggestions of pathways that would extend deep into the 80-acre site that the client assembled in stages from contiguous parcels. This arrangement of natural, but not untouched, elements choreographs occupation and movement in increments. The spatial nature of the site establishes calibrations and punctuations—the dots of trees in plan and the less maneuverable rocks—that one either moves through in a contingent manner, avoiding or alighting on one then the next, or pauses in between.

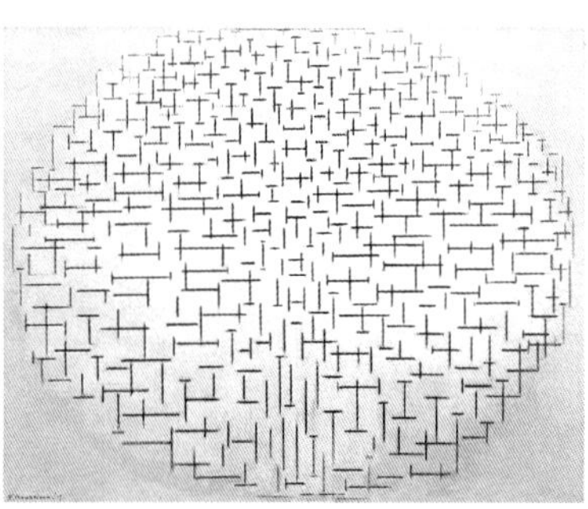

Like the site with its trees and rocks, the architectural metric story of this house, a true open house, is one of intervals between objects and sticks, something like a story you could tell about the 1915 Piet Mondrian painting Pier and Ocean.

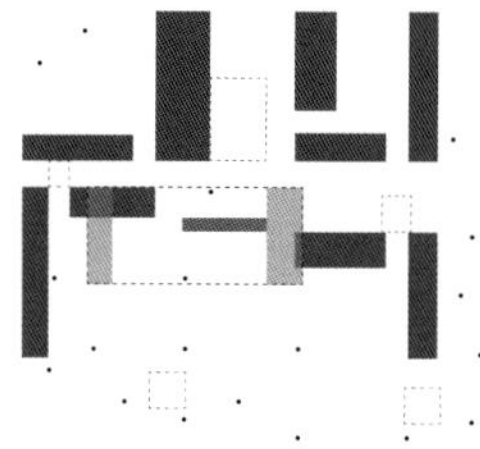

Covered by a flat roof, the spaces of the house are bracketed by solid volumes, alternating in north-south or east-west orientation; and by columns positioned in and out of phase with the activities of the house—and in conversation with the tall trees and rocks on the site. There are no walls—just volumes, columns, and glass. The metric story of this house plays out between the gravity and shear of volumes and boxes, the flat plate of the roof, the plants on this roof, and the open brief that enabled the outside to flow through the inside of the house and the resulting spaces to toggle in alternating patterns amongst tall trees.

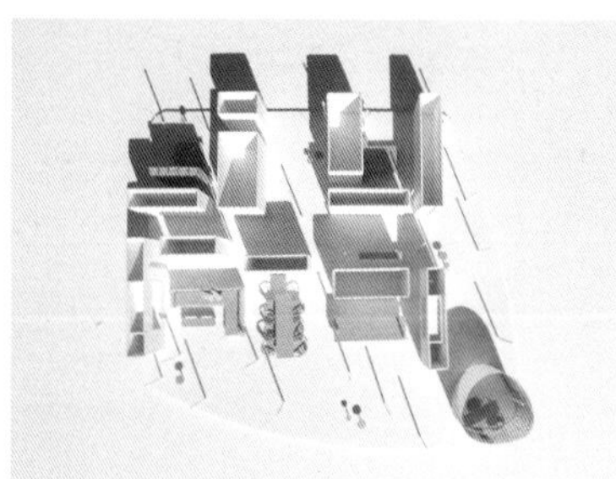

The roof is a 3,500-square-foot plate that shelters inside and outside space and supports an elevated meadow. The volumes that bracket this house's space are all completely enclosed and are 12 in total, ranging from 90 square feet to 30 square feet.

Consistently clad in fiber cement, they contain, in clockwise concentric order from entry to kitchen: the south bedroom room closet, the mechanical room, the second bathroom, the north bedroom bathroom, the north bedroom closet, the living room fireplace volume, the dining room closet, the living room cabinetry and closet, the kitchen cabinetry and the entry closet; and then the chimney and two utility volumes in a small second floor space called "the pop-up."

The pop-up is open on its two long faces and bracketed by its own solid volumes and sits within a 6"-deep meadow planted on top of the roof.

The roof is supported by thin steel columns that only operate in one structural dimension—the up-and-down axis of gravity—while the 10 ground-floor volumes operate in back-and-forth shear as well as in gravity to complete the structural scheme of supporting the flat plate roof. The 23 columns—13 outside, 10 inside—that support the overhang patio roof are 2.5" in diameter and engage the spaces of the house by an irregular placement that is based on the necessities of structure needed to maintain a thin roof and appropriate spans.

To top it all off, the roof is designed as an 8"-thin plane with a 11 1/2" thermal sponge on top. The sponge contains mineral wool insulation achieving a thermal R-value (resistance to heat flow) of 46 and supports 2,000 square feet of sedum—robust succulents that change colors throughout the year and constitute the house plants of this house. The sedum is set on the thermal sponge in 1,000 1' × 2' trays. Energy code does not specify the R-value that the succulents add to the roof assembly, but undoubtedly the plants help cool the house in the summer and warm the house in winter. The other values that the plants add to the house are immeasurable.

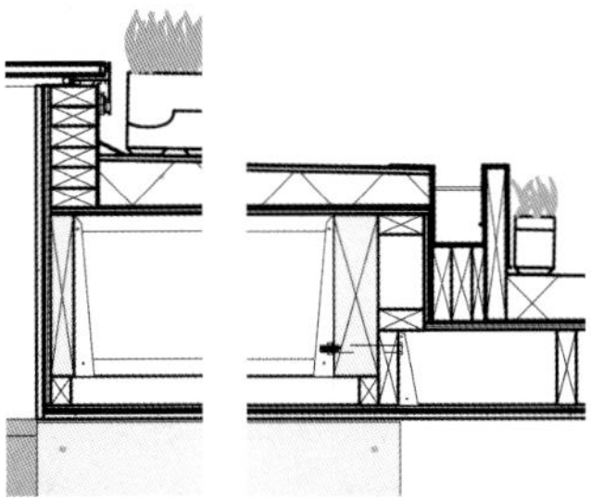

This is a house in a grid.

Located in Hudson, New York, the house inhabits an irregular square grid, on a slope. The house places indoor and outdoor domestic spaces within a stepped-grid frame. Each corner of the house has a differently-shaped open patio, pin-wheeling around the center. Some patios are covered and some are partially open. Each patio provides an equivalent living space to the adjacent indoors: an outdoor living porch, an outdoor dining porch, an outdoor sleeping porch, and an outdoor bathing porch. Indoors, there are two identically-shaped bedrooms and two identically-shaped bathrooms. Freestanding in the middle of the floor plan, the bathrooms and utility room are contained in a floating "pill" that is naturally lit with a constellation of skylights above. Through a series of swinging doors, each bedroom can have its own private bathroom.

Cutting north-south along the house are a series of steps that run through the length of the open square grid. The roof remains flat as the floor drops from east to west: telescoping the rooms towards the open field to the west. This indoor-outdoor raumplan gives this small house an endless variety of spaces and expands the living space to include the outdoors.

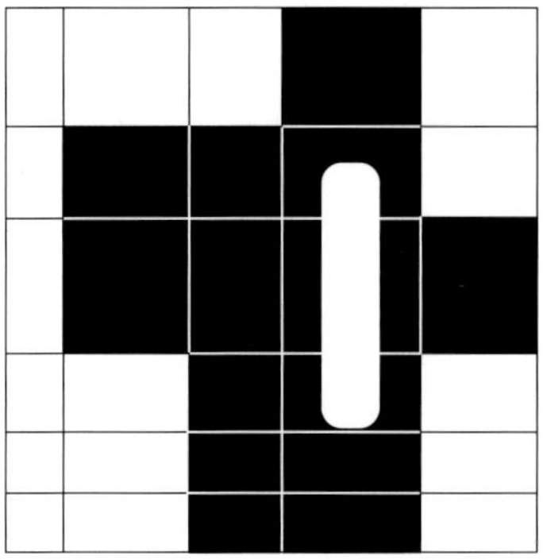

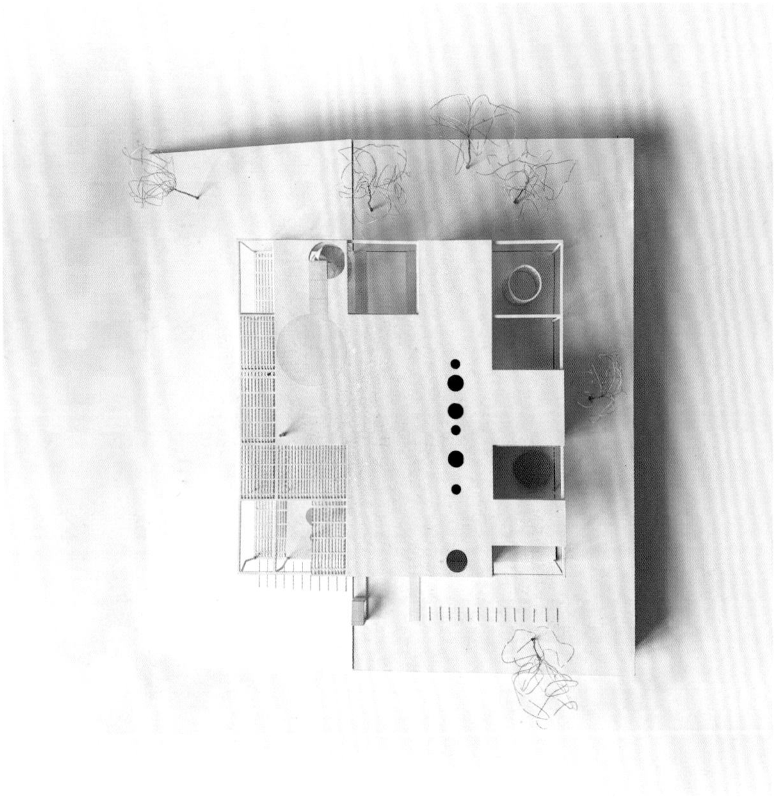

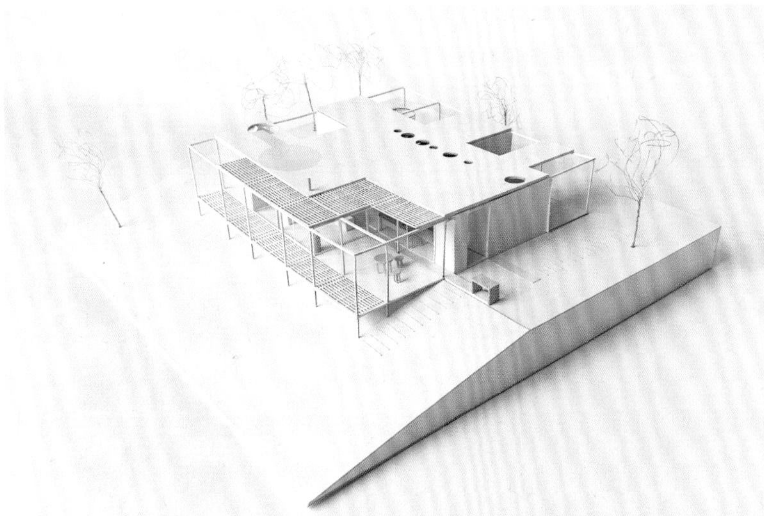

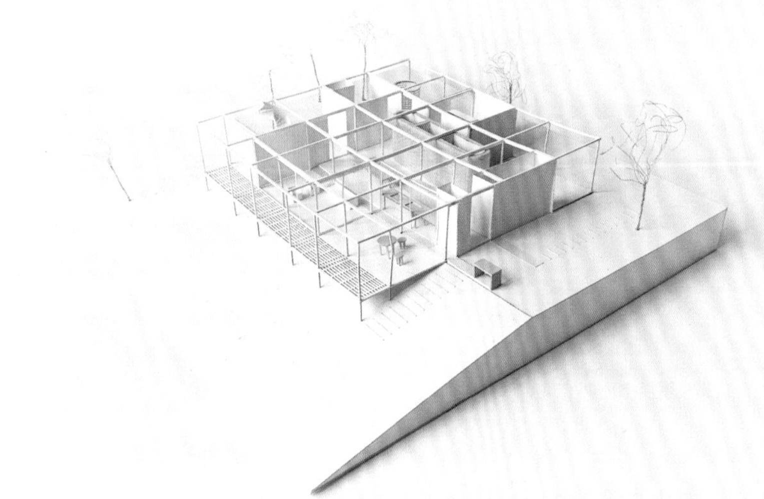

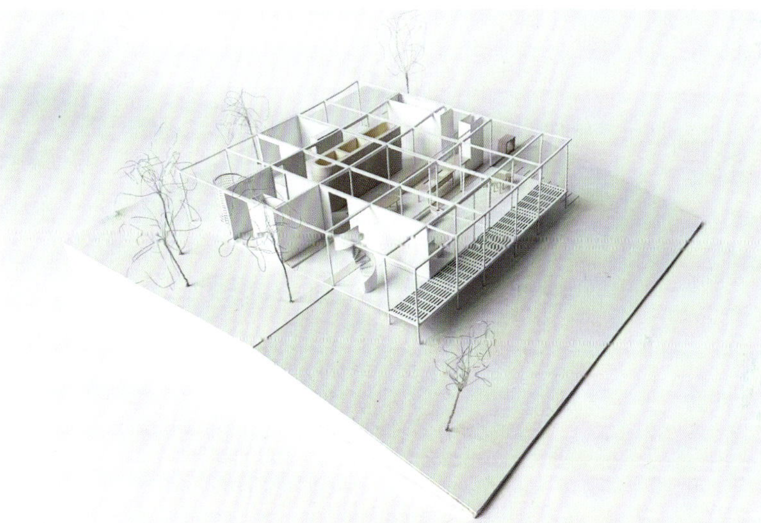

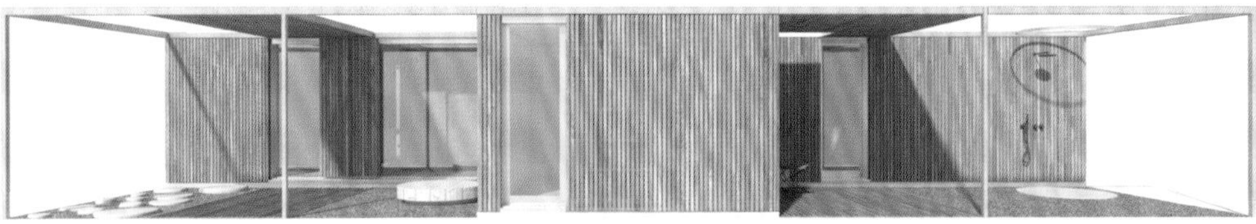

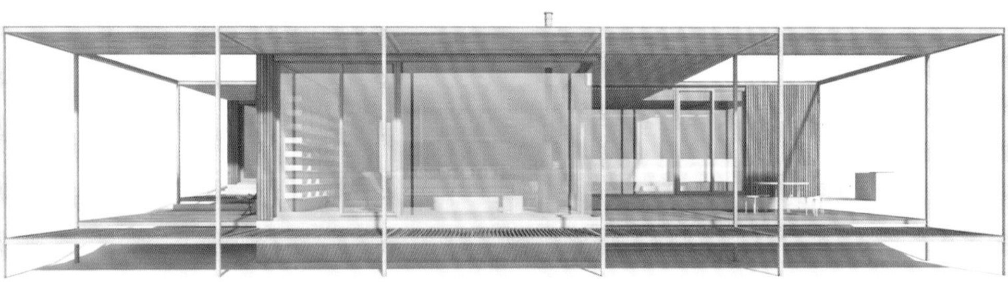

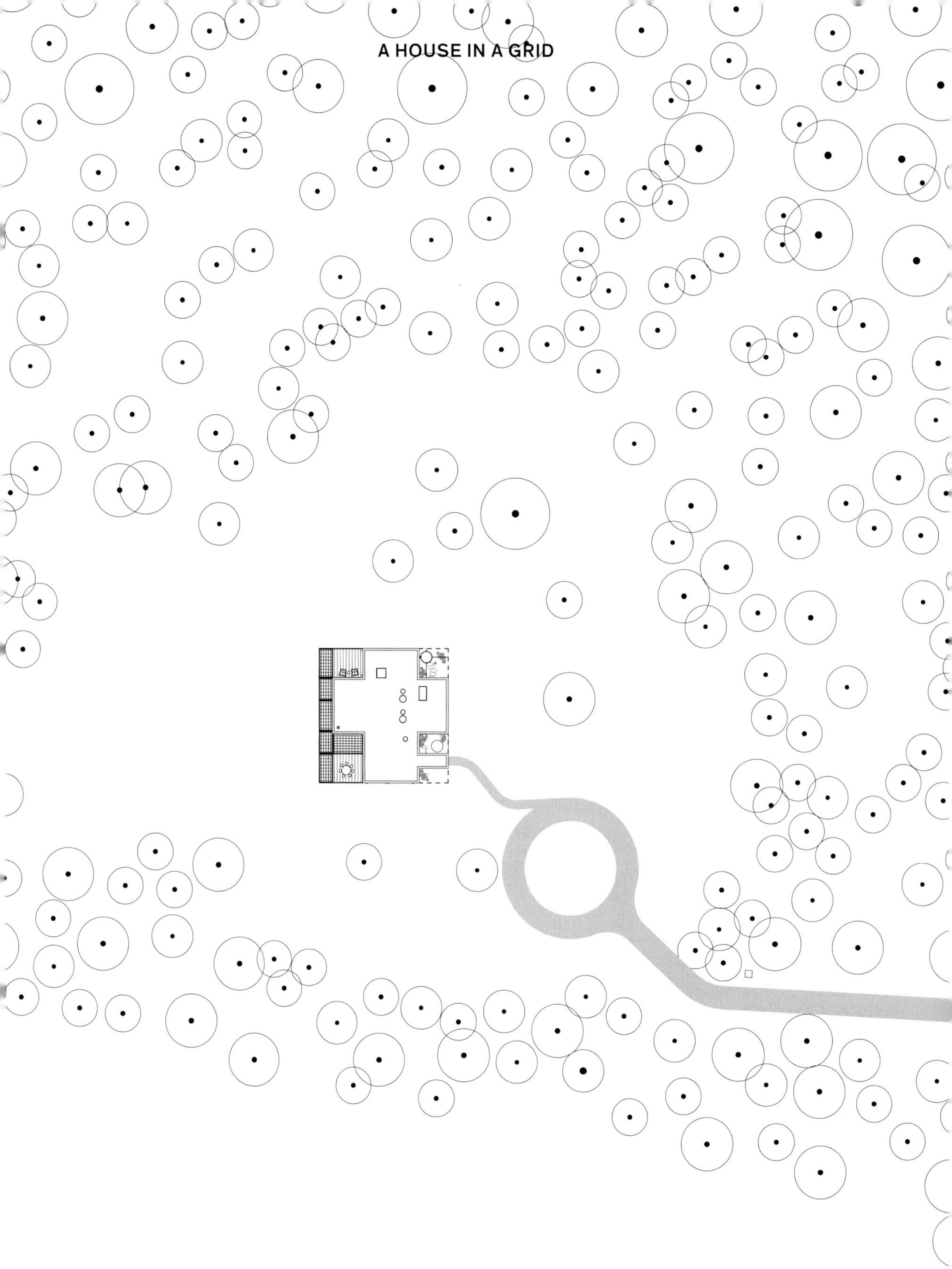

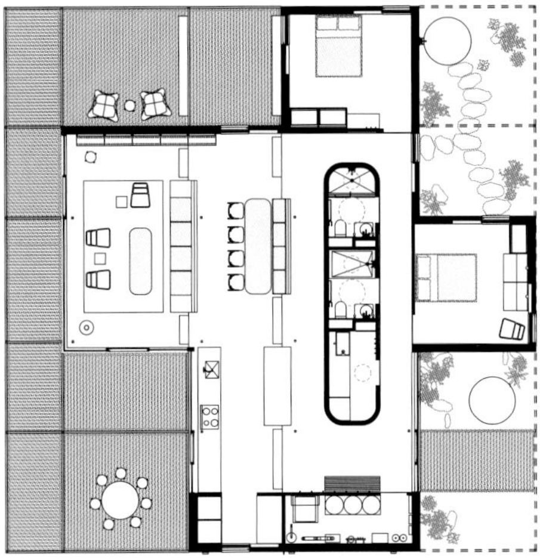

A HOUSE IN A GRID

The 1960s and 1970s saw a radical thinness in American modern house design. The houses of that era featured the traditional fat rectangular plan, but their detailing—the drip edge, the roofs and wing walls—were ever more attenuated. And there was thinness in industrial design: the rounded bulbous forms of cars and motorcycles from the 1940s and 1950s gave way to thinner sheet metal and sharp creases and edges.

The Ford Mustang, the Dodge Dart—and later in the early 1980s vehicles like the Kawasaki Ninja motorcycle and the Honda Nighthawk—sported flat surfaces transitioning into one another across tight radii. To some eyes, this thinness may have signaled an attenuation of imagination, but perhaps as the profligacy and casual optimism of American postwar years drew to a close with the end of cheap oil and the human disaster of the Vietnam War, designers consciously or unconsciously enacted a tighter and tenser esthetic.

The Case Study Houses and the lean mean architecture of Craig Ellwood's swingin' Malibu houses hanging off cliffs—all transitioning beams and impossibly thin ceilings between interiors and exteriors—demonstrated that this design was brashly optimistic in its own way: optimistic about thinness. Architecture could do it all—but just do it real thin, real open and without extraneous burdens, domestic or foreign. This house, consequent to this history, is thin, but finds its thinness through its strategic detailing and contemporary integrated energy systems.

A House in a Grid dispenses with the current questionably effective and unquestionably unhealthy bloated "sustainable" wall section, which puffs up barriers with layer after layer until code metrics are met. Instead, the house uses the dynamic performance of geothermal and solar technology to make a net-zero house whose walls and roof can be thrillingly thin.

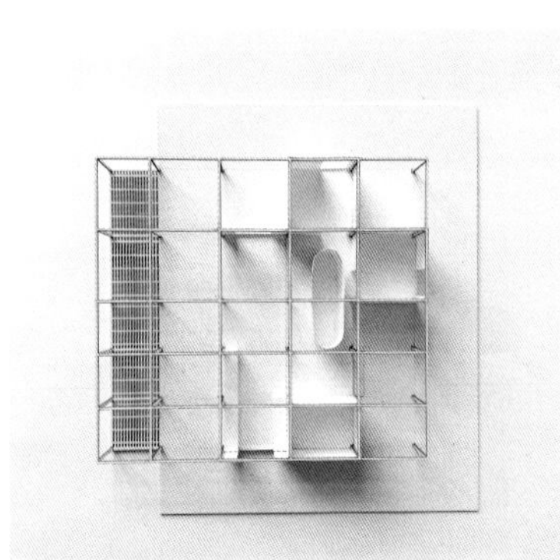

The skinny 56' square galvanized steel frame, made of 2.5" square columns and 2.5" × 4" galvanized steel beams, pervades and peristyles the house, creating short spans and allowing for thin structural members. Living in the house is living within the frame, like living within a glade of trees. The frame is irregular in plan and in section, enabling a variation of scaled spaces based on domestic programs throughout the house. From west to east the grid spacing of the frame is: 6'-0", 13'-6", 10'-6", 12'-6", 13'-6". From south to north the grid spacing of the frame is: 12'-6", 9'-0", 13'-0", 9'-0", 12'-6". The frame is flat at the ceiling but the concrete floor slab falls away in 1' increments as the house moves toward the view to the west. As a result, the spaces transition in height from 8' at the entry and bedrooms and bathrooms, to 9' at kitchen and dining, to 10' at the living area and finally 11' at the westernmost exterior terrace.

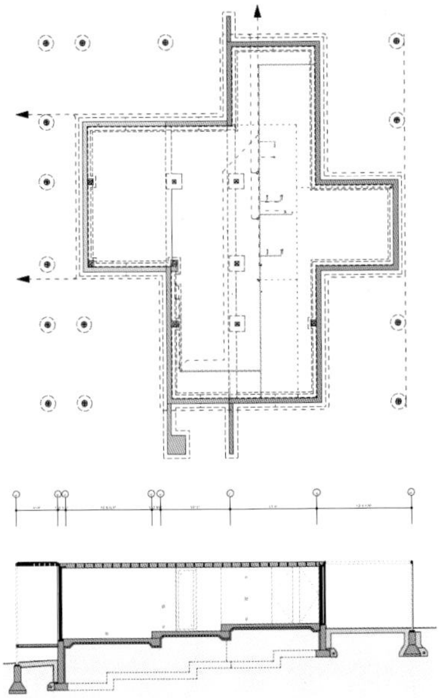

The communal spaces of cooking, dining and living combine the raumplan of specifically functional stepped spaces with the overall free plan by stepping and programming spaces—but dispensing with walls between these spaces, and placing a pill-shaped infrastructural volume to divide public from privates spaces within the house.

Even though the house is in the American Northeast, the walls are conceived as thin membranes, California-style, and interior and exterior spaces are fluid even when walls are solid. Similar to A House for the Next Site, this house has two identically sized 12'-6" × 12'-6" bedrooms. The wall section is an efficient wood frame with a grafted steel tube frame bolted to it—creating, due to the architectural desire for the alignment of steel frame/siding/concrete foundation, a wall section that goes from pared down and efficient to furred out and architecturally varied, visually uncluttered but explicit in its systems.

This is a house of lines.

Located in Ancram, New York, the house was built in the middle of an agricultural field. Long linear grooves, formed by the dimensions of machinery, are etched by years of farming into the rolling hills. These parallel lines inform the design of all configurations in the house: the primary spatial organization, the cladding, and details. Additionally, the cross section of the house follows the contour of the land as it steps up from east to west.

The programmatic spaces of the house are divided between two linear volumes, one wet and the other dry. The wet zone—consisting of bathrooms, kitchen, laundry, and utilities—occupies a long, thin volume; whereas the dry zone—consisting of the living and dining rooms, and bedrooms—exists in a wider volume that provides for more generous spaces. The two volumes slide past one another as they follow the linear farming pattern. Inside, the twenty-foot-long kitchen counter overlaps the two volumes at the ground floor, drawing together the working (wet) and living (dry) spaces, holding a constant datum, as the floor level steps up. Large cutouts in the ceiling and roof mediate the division of space between the first and second floor, while also providing natural light and ventilation.

The horizontally oriented corrugated-metal siding; patio paving patterns; plantings around the house; and the attenuated retaining walls, which are extensions of the long walls of the foundation, all define the exterior spaces of the garage, entry walkway, and patios, and extend linearly into the landscape.

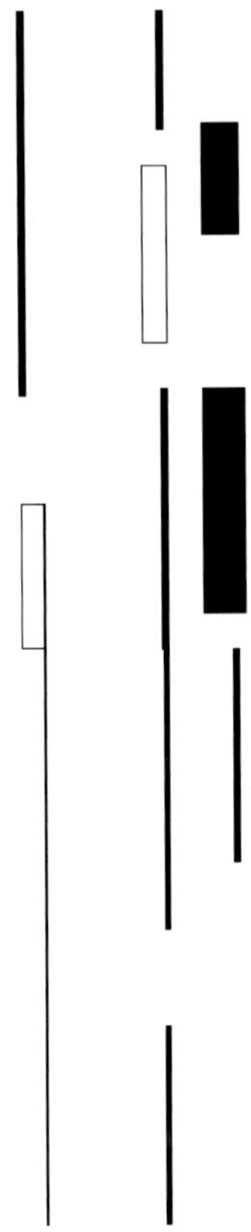

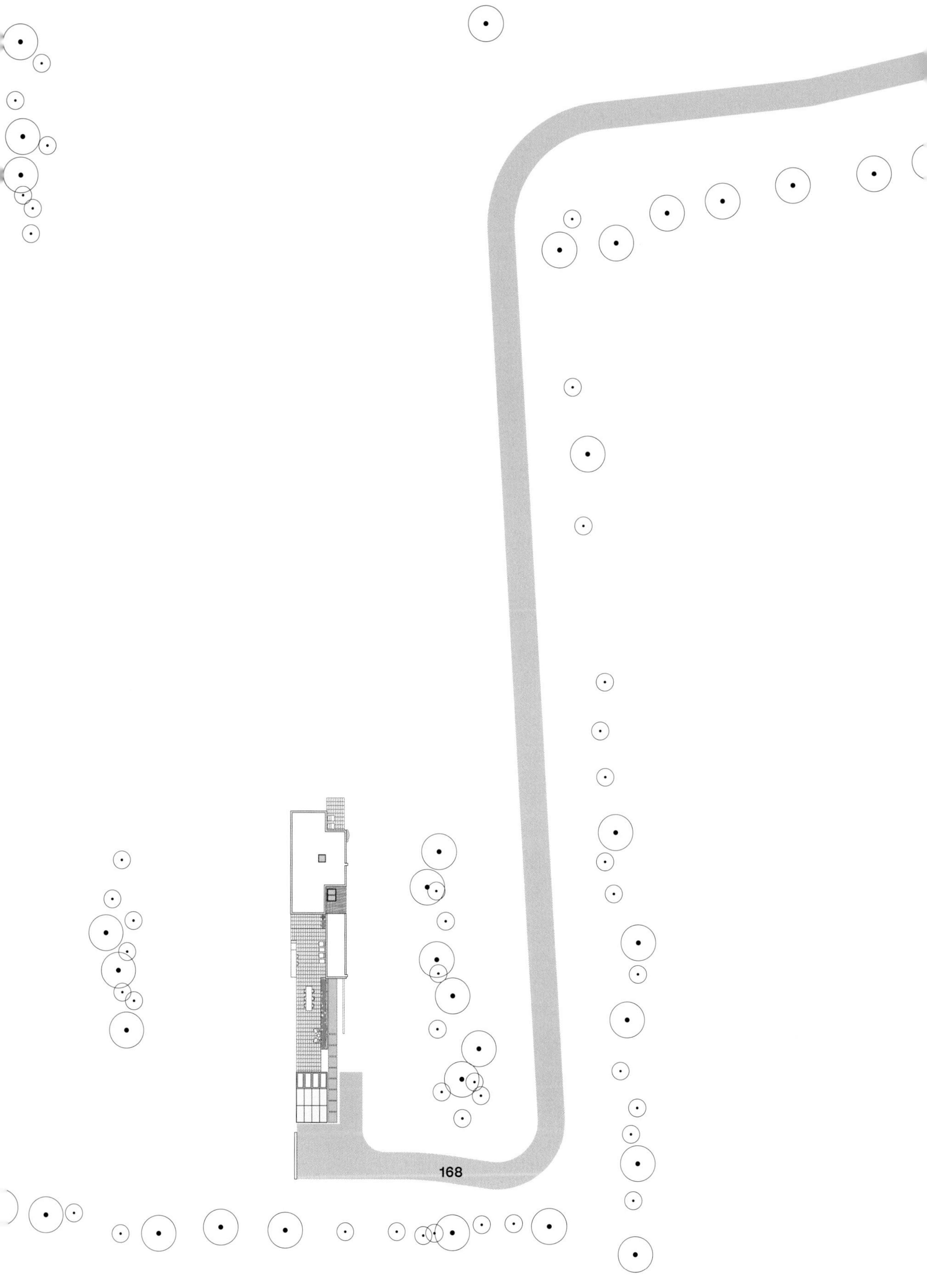

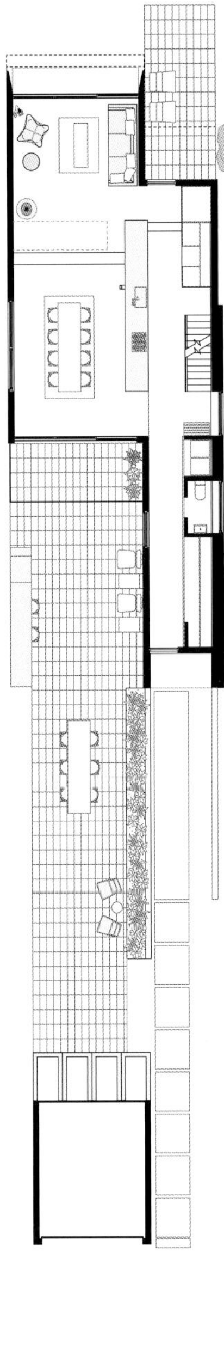

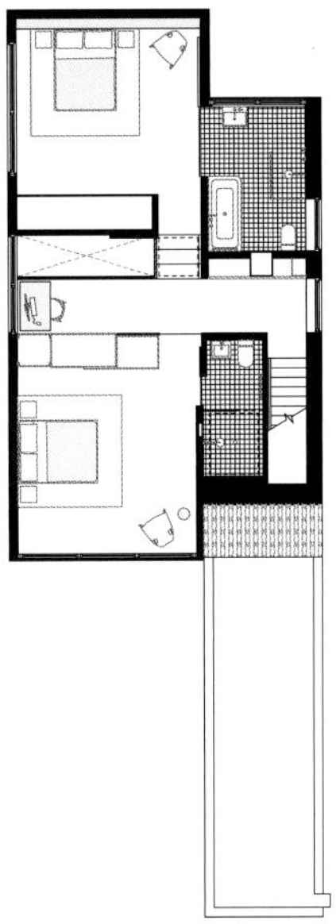

A HOUSE OF LINES

Tractor wheels are typically set at 60" to 120" wide—depending on the furrows to be plowed and the types of crops to be planted in them. Having planted corn and rye on the site, the farmer next door, for whom the property received an $8,000 agricultural exemption in 2004, had 8 acres of linear cornrows coursing across the site.

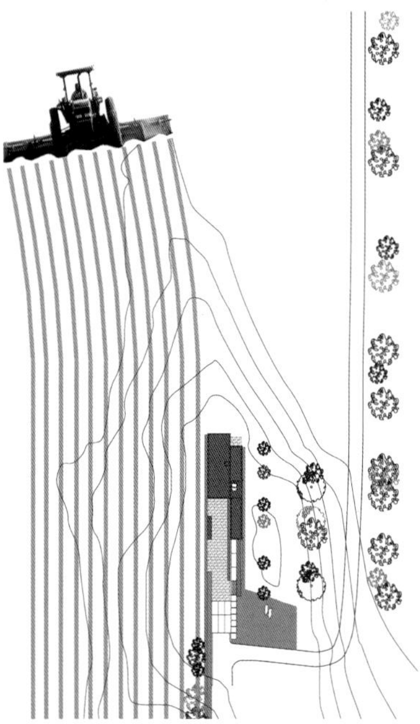

This house now occupies this site, and these furrows in parallel stripes that aggregate into volumes: a 16'-wide "dry" volume and an 8'-wide "wet" volume.

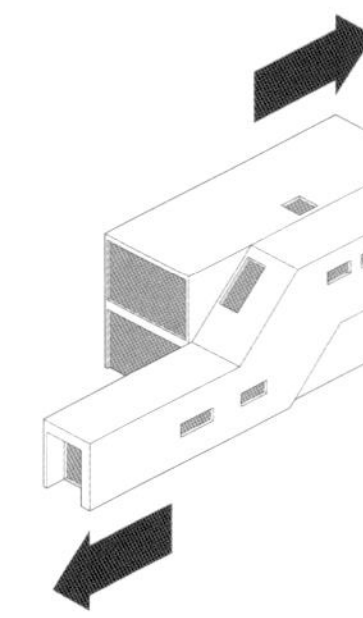

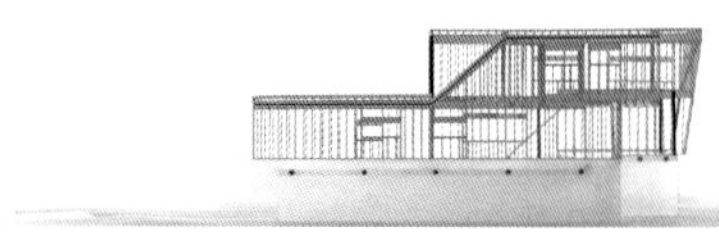

Along the overlap between wet and dry sits a 20'-long white box, like a piece of chalk: a white solid-surface cabinet poised on top of an upper platform containing cooking and cleaning elements and infrastructure: gas, water supply, waste, and electricity, all needed to run the cooktop, the sink and two shallow drawer-style dishwashers that hover above the floor.

A rectangular steel column shifts out of the way so that the overlap is occupied by the central kitchen counter, not the structure needed to support a 12" deep flitch beam carrying dead and live loads at this critical structural juncture in the house. The structural metric is provided for, but its clarity of support is secondary to the assembly of 8 to 12 people who can cook and assemble around this piece. The column simply slides south by 24"; the longitudinal span above, that appears to be 30' long, is comprised of two beams that are carried by saddles bolted to a lateral beam spanning from north wall to the shifted column in question.

Since the short ends of the house are open to glass while the long ends are more solid, moment frames are needed to resist the lateral loads. The house is primarily wood-framed; but steel, such as the beams and saddles just described, is needed to achieve spans (gravity) and resist lateral loads (shear).

While the white floating counter hides its infrastructure, an aluminum frame—fully on the wet side of the house—that carries the sink in the bathroom exposes its plumbing. The 1/2" aluminum flat bar frame bolts to the walls and floor, the 30" × 16" × 5" sink sits on top of the frame, and the bottle trap and hot and cold supply lines run from sink to floor—unashamedly exposed.

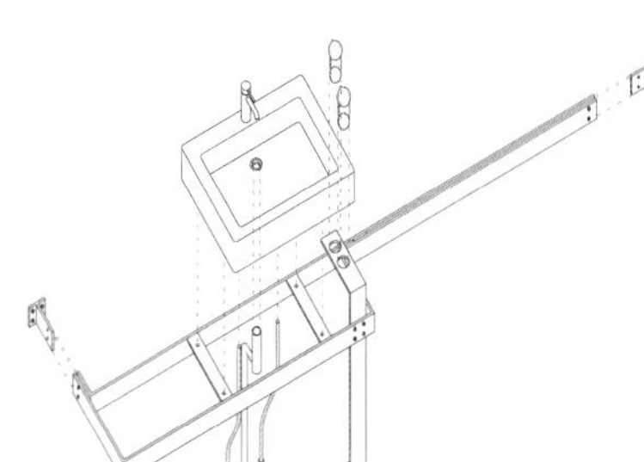

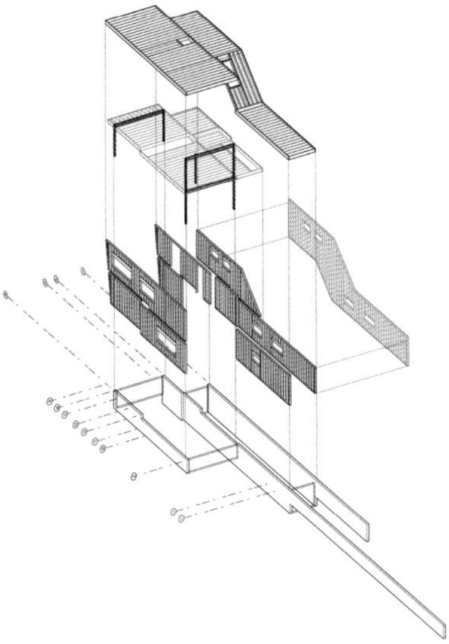

This house is a new and an old house.

Located in Stone Ridge, New York, this house was first built in 2005 and then added to nine years later. The house sits at the crest of a ridge and steps down with the steep topography toward a stream below. The house is comprised of a series of large stepped landings, enabling the passage down the ridge toward the stream.

The stepped house slides its upper volume of the house along and past its lower volume. This shift creates two exterior spaces: a covered parking or recreation area at the ground floor, and the main bedroom deck at the second floor. Inside, a linear organization of storage boxes runs lengthwise through the house on both floors. This double-height-storage volume, a figural spine in the floor plan, is also the infrastructural zone, containing areas for laundry, ductwork, and plumbing.

The interior of the house is organized by prioritizing views out towards the trees and the stream. Beginning at the entry and continuing through each room, the local focal point is always oriented outward. As one enters a space, a window or door is placed on axis, framing a broad view of the landscape or a single tree.

The addition containing two bedrooms and a garage is connected by a glass-enclosed bridge. The cube-like volume of the addition picks up on the large, square entry and second-floor window. Each room of the addition has a square window and a square skylight. With the addition, the finish on the wood-clad exterior of the house changed from light to dark.

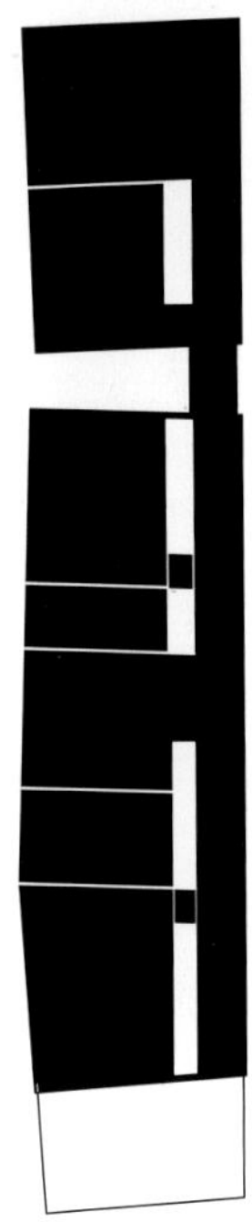

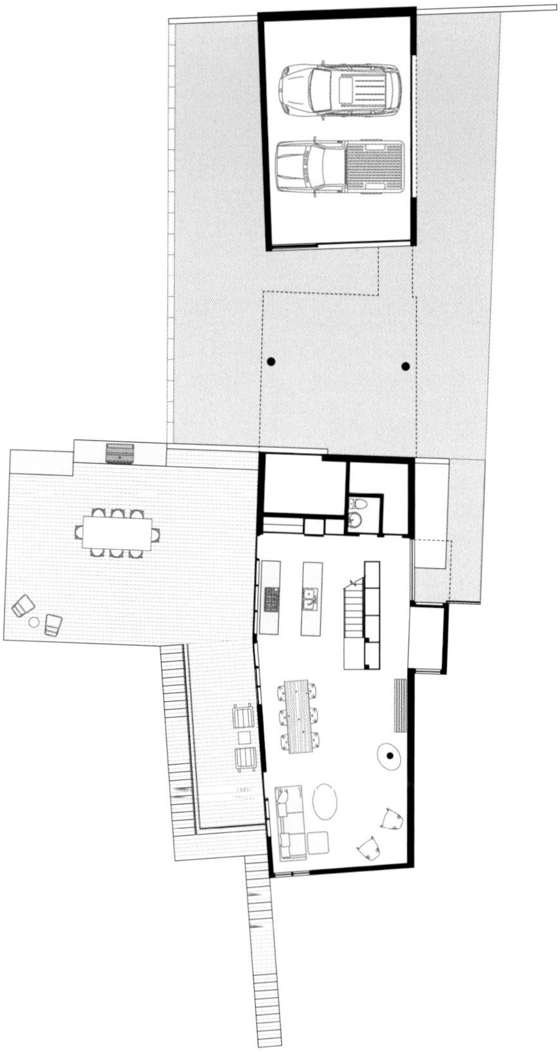

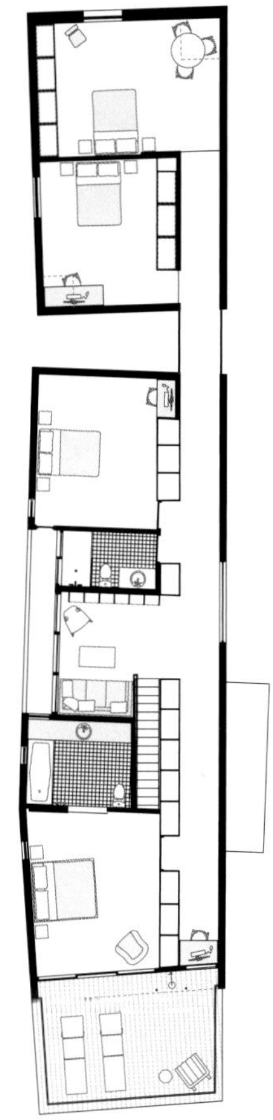

A HOUSE AND A HOUSE

On the site of this house, trees compete with neighboring trees and those still standing give one another space by what feels like somewhere between 10' to 15'—less in a thicket but enough room for canopy and roots to spread. When a forest is cleared to make room for a building, the resulting clearing, no matter how small, changes the perception of space. The difference between 15' and canopied and a view to the sky and, let's say, 20' clear all around, is dramatic. The former keeps you moving and the latter, the clearing, makes you stop and think about things.

Slope (which dictates speed), like stairs or steps in a house, is another element that changes your perception of space. A 5% grade slows walking speed from 4 mph to 2 mph, changing the experience of space over time. When your heart rate increases from 60 bpm to 120 bpm, your perception changes with the increase in oxygen and the alteration of the position of the head relative to ground. The first house started with ideas about perception of a place relative to the time it takes to get there and to move through the landscape of the site: the two-hour passage to the site, the 12-minute walk down the hill, the plateau in the middle of the walk and then the 15 minutes to walk back up.

In the first house, the metrics of site play out as topographic landings. The house is a stair unto itself containing domestic experiences that are directly related to the experiences that the landscape affords. There are three concrete landing pads—4"-thick tapering concrete platforms, each not more than the code maximum 30" above ground, and 4'-wide × 5'- to 8'-long—that you walk on when moving from the parking plateau to the front door. Parking is 18" above the front door sill height. Inside the front door, you are on another platform, an extension of the three pads outside that lead you to the main level of the house. You step out and down onto an outdoor wood platform—a deck that leads to stairs and landings down to the water, or out to the landscape with its myriad levels and clearings.

The upper level of the house is like a treehouse platform. It hovers above the land, especially to the east where the slope falls away. To the west, the platform almost touches the ground as the land slopes up. You could have almost jumped to the ground and upper slope. But that was all before the metrics changed—when we dug into the hill nine years later, added to the western end of the first house, and opened up a larger clearing for a House and a House.

If the metric story of the first house was about perception and speed of movement in a topographic wooded landscape, the metric stories of the second house revolve around how an extended house can be linked and how the experiences of the site and the house itself can be newly maximized.

The first house was 2,400 square feet, organized linearly and comprised of large square apertures on the north side while the addition was 600 square feet and a study in square spaces—albeit still bisected by a spine of volumes that establish storage on one side and the division of hallway space and room space on the other. The DNA of the first house travels through the new house in the linear extension of these 30"-wide Douglas fir plywood-clad infrastructural volumes that contain storage, plumbing, and chases for future utilities as well as the primary ways that you circulate through the house.

The linkage between original and addition is a thin 8-foot long × 4-foot-wide glass bridge—perhaps of no material—in order to link houses but also to distinguish them, at least formally, from one another. The immaterial thinness of the bridge is contrasted against the solid cedar clad walls of the two flanking phases of the house.

With the addition, the house also underwent a palette transformation to create the unified whole. The first house was clad in untreated 4" cedar shiplap siding on the second floor with light gray 10' × 4' fiber cement board panels below as cladding the first floor. A House and a House dispensed with the lighter palette above and was unified by black stain on new and old cedar siding boards creating a dark floating 100' volume above, split by the thin immaterial bridge. This light-to-dark transformation sets off the house as an object in the woods, as opposed to the first house that was an object of the woods.

This is a house with three wings and three yards.

Located in Amagansett, New York, the house divides a 1.25-square-acre lot into three yards: re-configuring the typical suburban lot organization of front yard with driveway and back yard with pool. Instead, in this house, each of the three yards is programmed according to its activity: a recreation yard facing south, with a pool; a garden yard facing southwest; and an auto yard for cars, motorcycles and bikes. The house becomes a three-spoke intervention that frames the outdoor rooms that are each yard. The driveway cuts straight through the center of the house, with a back-facing garage that opens to the auto yard.

At the intersection of the three spokes at the second floor is an outdoor amphitheater for sunbathing and movie-watching that doubles as steps up to the roof deck with views to the ocean. At the ground level, the space below the amphitheater is the drive-through breezeway that provides access to the garage and auto courtyard. On the upstairs second level, the ends of each spoke cantilever out from the house's ground-level base. The braced-steel structure is designed to resist gravity loads as well as the intense lateral wind loads that occur near the beach. Through the large glass sliding doors at the ground level, these structural elements are visible throughout the house.

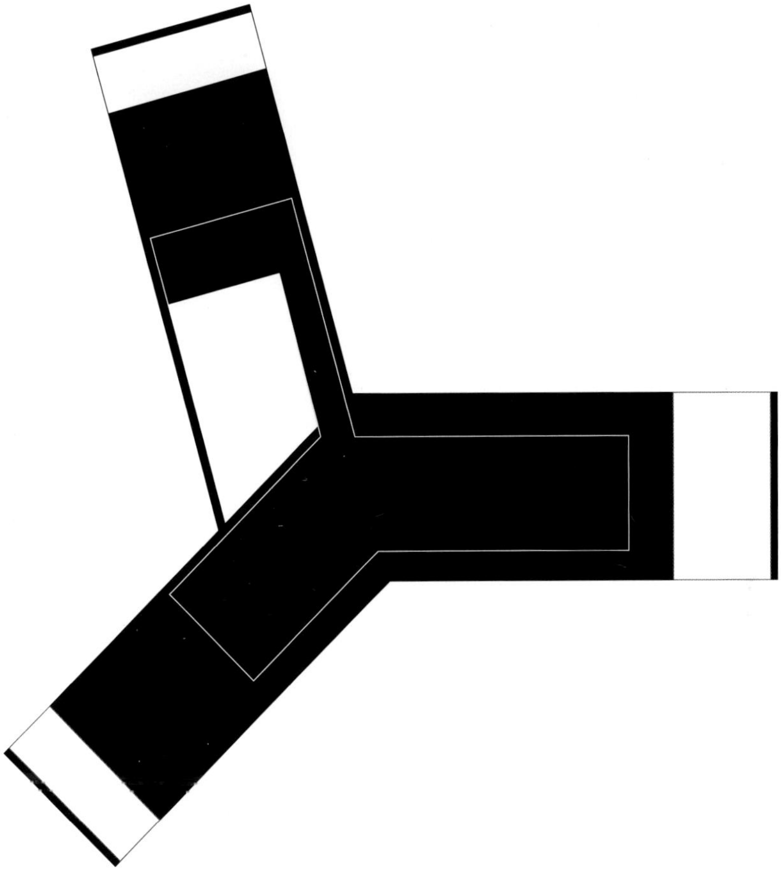

A HOUSE WITH THREE YARDS

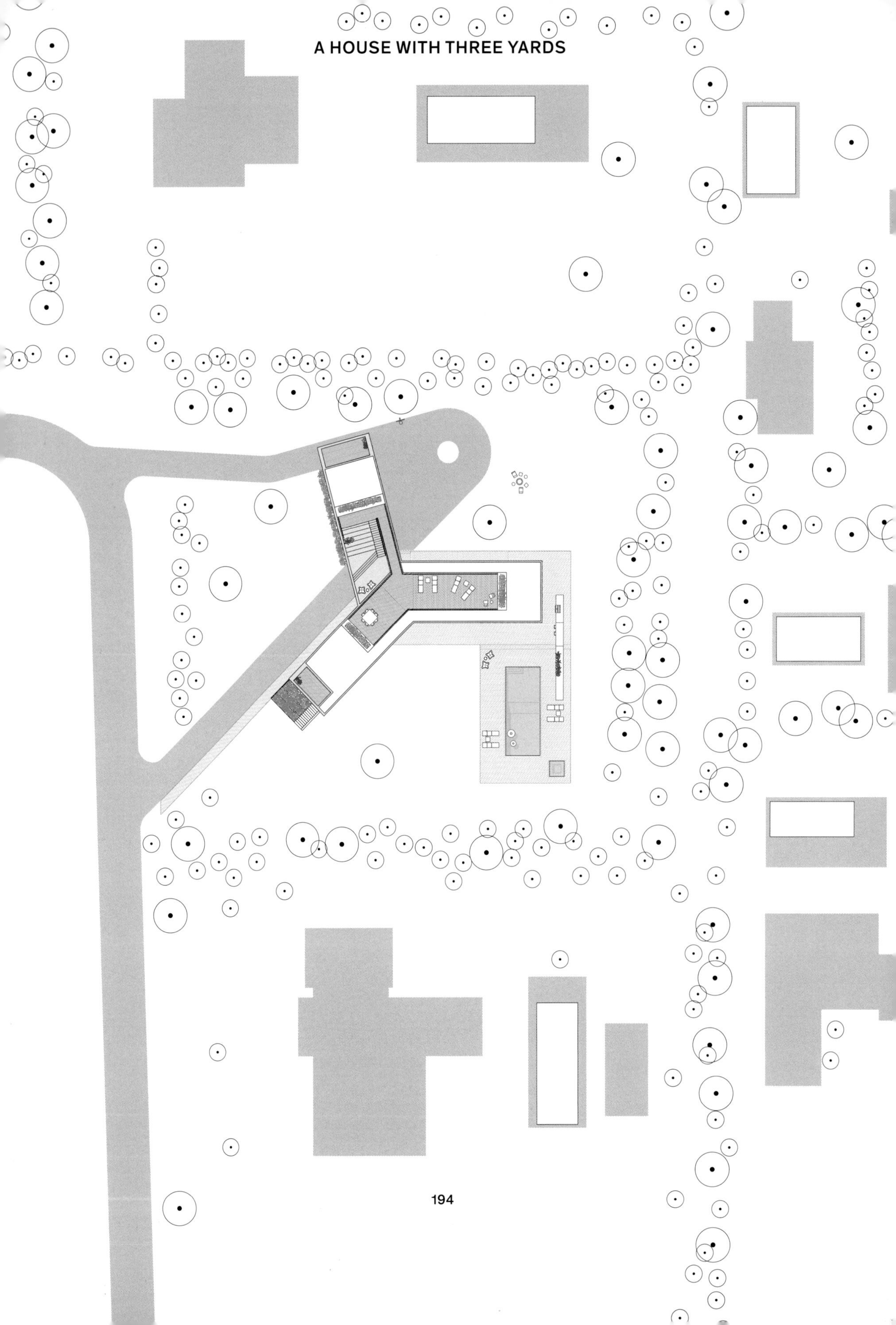

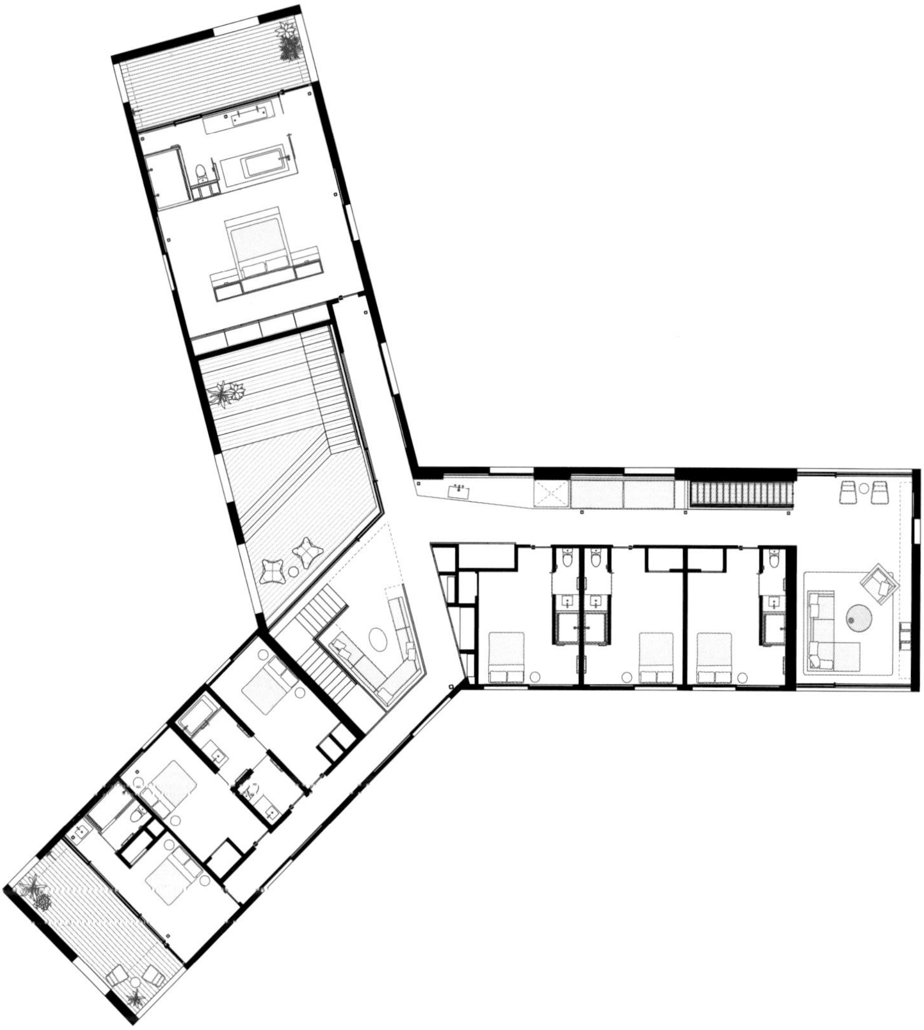

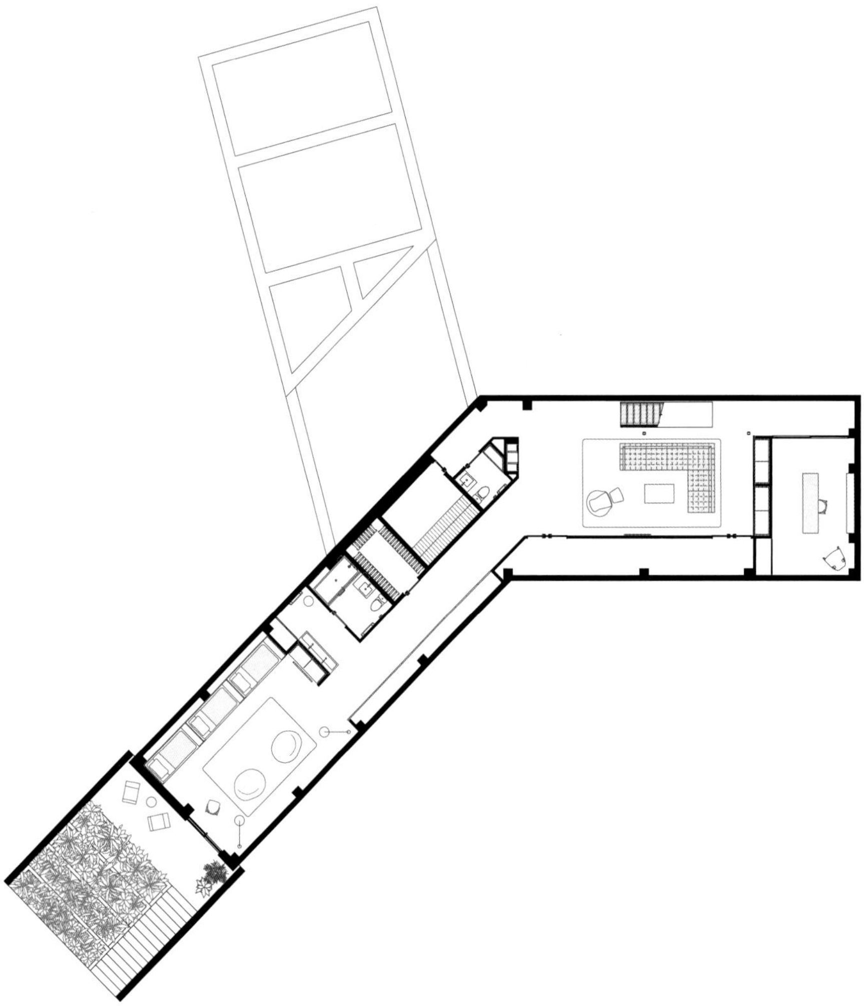

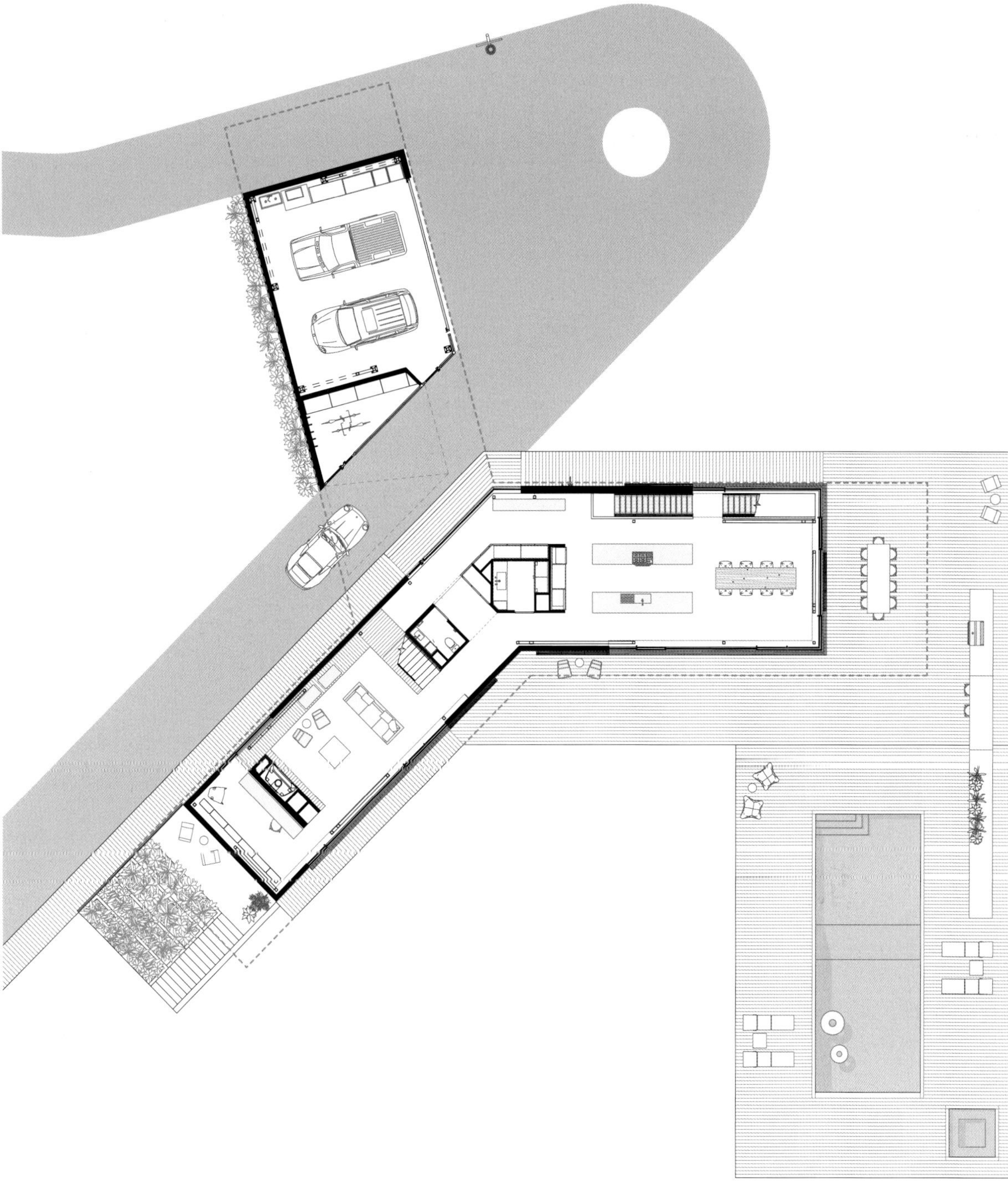

A HOUSE WITH THREE YARDS

The metrics of this house are grounded in the solidity of materials and structure. The clients had initially asked us to design a scheme to add to and renovate the modest 2,800-square-foot 1980s contractor modern beach house that they owned. The beach house was thin, we designed the added bulk they needed for their growing family—achieving some degree of solidity—but what they really wanted was a new, big, bold, solid house that they could engage actively, where they could entertain friends, play sports, work on cars, and launch to the beach to surf. But this was long before they found the last unbuilt parcel of land in their beach town to build on.

In 2009, they called and said that they had just purchased an acre and a quarter "pile of dirt" and asked if we were we still interested in designing them a house (and were we!).

We focused the domestic metrics of this house toward solidity—but not in a grounded house, and not in a small house, but on a heavily grounded but lifted house. Another foundational metric of the house emerged when we mentioned that the house could actually be smaller than usual for the area—maybe 4,000 or 5,000 square feet—but feel even larger by being strategically open to its landscape. The response came back, "But we want a big house." So, big it became—as in 8,000 square feet of enclosed and conditioned space big, and on a 55,000-square-foot lot. This house is the largest house presented on these pages, but sits on the smallest parcel, and features the most bathrooms (eight) in a single house that we have designed to date.

Design meetings were boisterous and the models too were big, 3/8"=1'-0" big. When designing a big house, or any house for that matter, that contains the desires of a family unit, whatever its constitution, and the domestic elements and open possibilities—the ways of looking at a house, the advantage (and joy) in seeing space take shape in a model of robust scale—all this leads to further investigations and resolutions of material, space, and activity.

This house, like old big houses, has wings—like a Shuriken Japanese throwing star (an early formal and formative diagram); three wings above the ground floor at 1,500 square feet each, joined at the middle at a void, atop another void where cars drive through to turn around the 30'-diameter circle and park, and/or be lifted for service in the three-car garage.

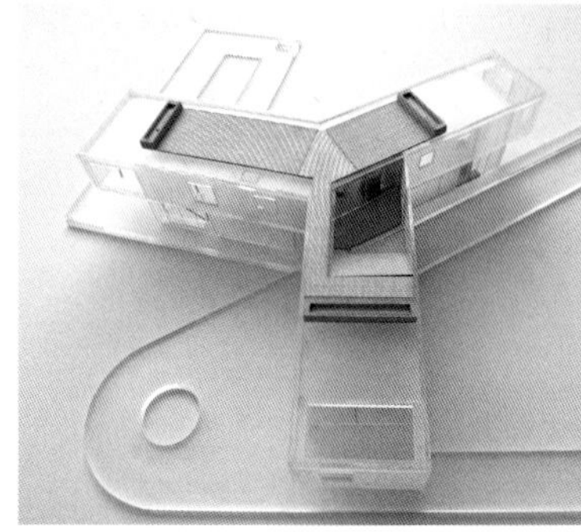

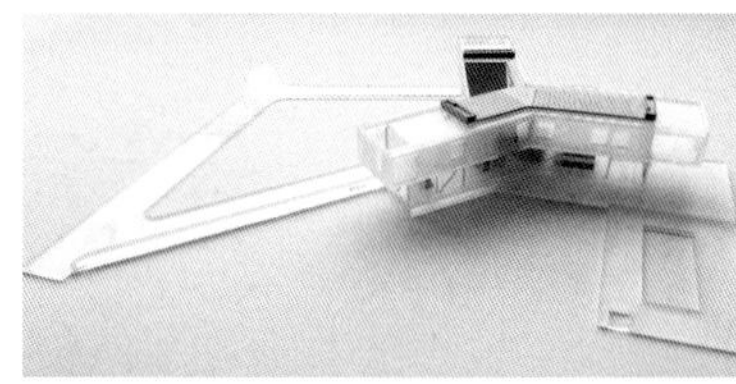

These three spoke-like wings of the house divide the square lot into three yards, all brought to life by their own activities, and in direct contrast to the typological suburban metric of a front yard, back yard, unused side yards, and the house in the middle of the lot. The resulting spaces around the spokes are a pool-focused yard, an automotive and sports yard, and a garden. There are no side yards as such. The spaces of the three spokes travel from basement consisting of bunk room, TV room, and studio; up through public spaces on the first floor; bedrooms and outdoor decks on the second floor; and a triple-spoked 2,400-square-foot roof deck that addresses the ocean to top it all off.

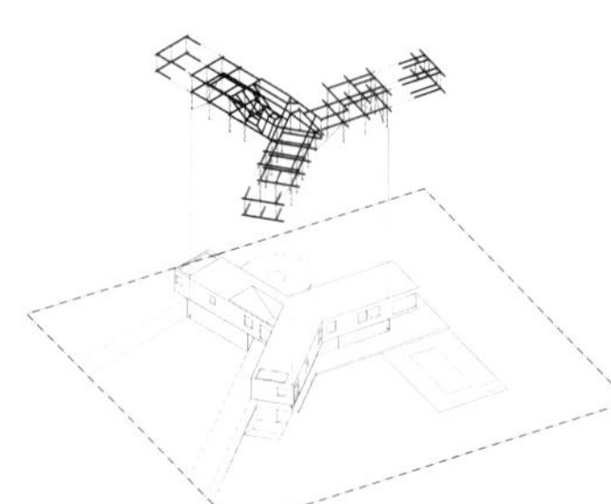

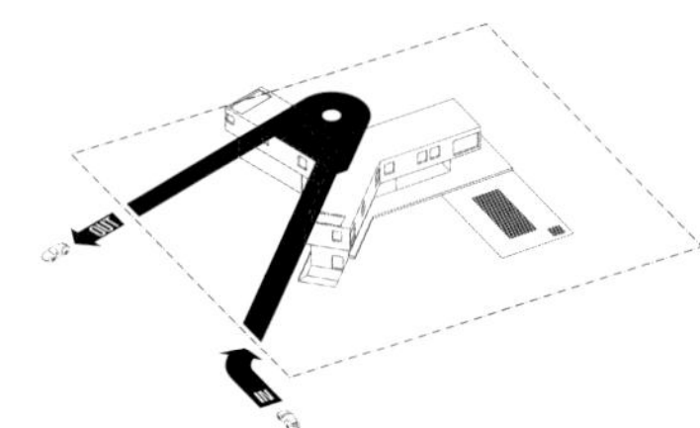

The wings have cantilevers at the second floor, two at 12' long and one at 18' long. Because these three cantilevers are designed to resist 120 mile-per-hour winds, speeds not quite a Miami Dade hurricane code metric but forceful enough to require carefully calibrated steel and concrete working in unison with the concrete for the foundation, where the forces needed to be resolved, and which was designed for 4,500 psi.

The structural metrics of the house above this foundation are addressed through a hybrid wood framing and steel frame, but primarily through this highly tuned steel frame—working in concert with the strong concrete foundation—where the cantilevers are bolted onto two-story columns in star-shaped bolt plates. Wood is employed as infill and to aid in shear.

Solid materials are exemplified in the concrete foundation that is exposed at the lowest level of the building. Traveling up in the house at the main level, the building is clad in 1.75" thick glass fiber reinforced concrete panels (GFRC)—the solidity of concrete becoming thinner. Then at the floor above, 5/16" fiber cement panels clad the wood framed walls. So, the material is robust—a must at the beach—but the degrees of solidity modulate as they travel from ground to sky. Topping off the composition of materials are 1/8"-thick perforated aluminum screens that slide over floor to ceiling glass windows and doors. The screens are both thin and strong—aluminum having a high strength to weight ratio—and protect the glass in a storm.

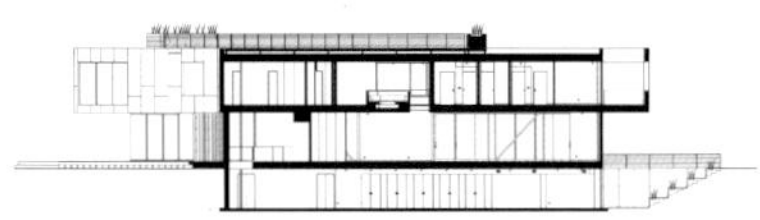

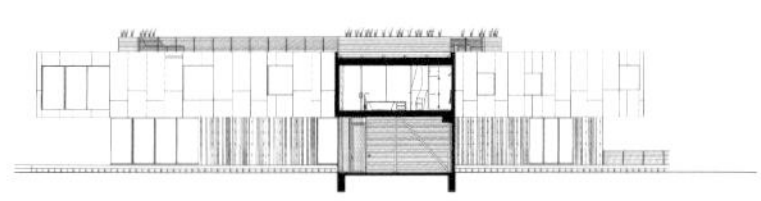

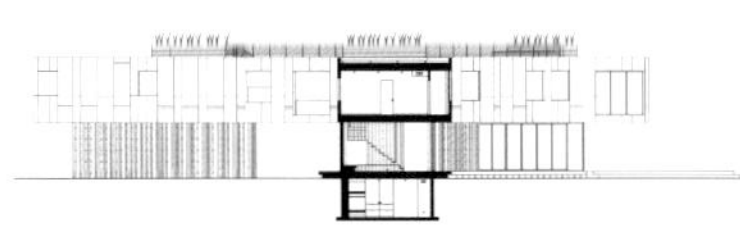

This is a house whose floor plan is in the shape of a snail.

Located in Ancram, New York, the house is a 400-square-foot structure. It reduces the elements of domestic living to the bare essentials. It includes places for sleeping, bathing and cooking, plus a small storage closet. The living space is outside—partially covered and partially uncovered.

The house is located in an open field next to a pool. A perforated concrete-block wall wraps the simple volume, creating enclosure for privacy. At the center of the spiral is the most private space: the bedroom and bathroom. As the wall uncoils, it opens up the living space to the more communal area at the pool.

The perforated concrete blocks are assembled at angles along the spiral, creating different degrees of visual enclosure and privacy, along acute and oblique lines of sight, while allowing for breezes and filtered views out towards the surrounding landscape.

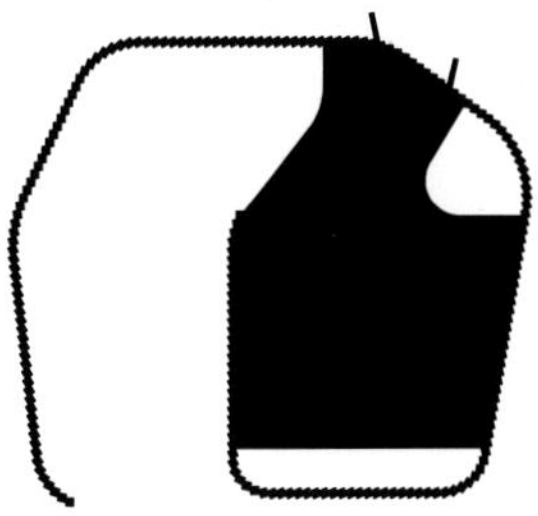

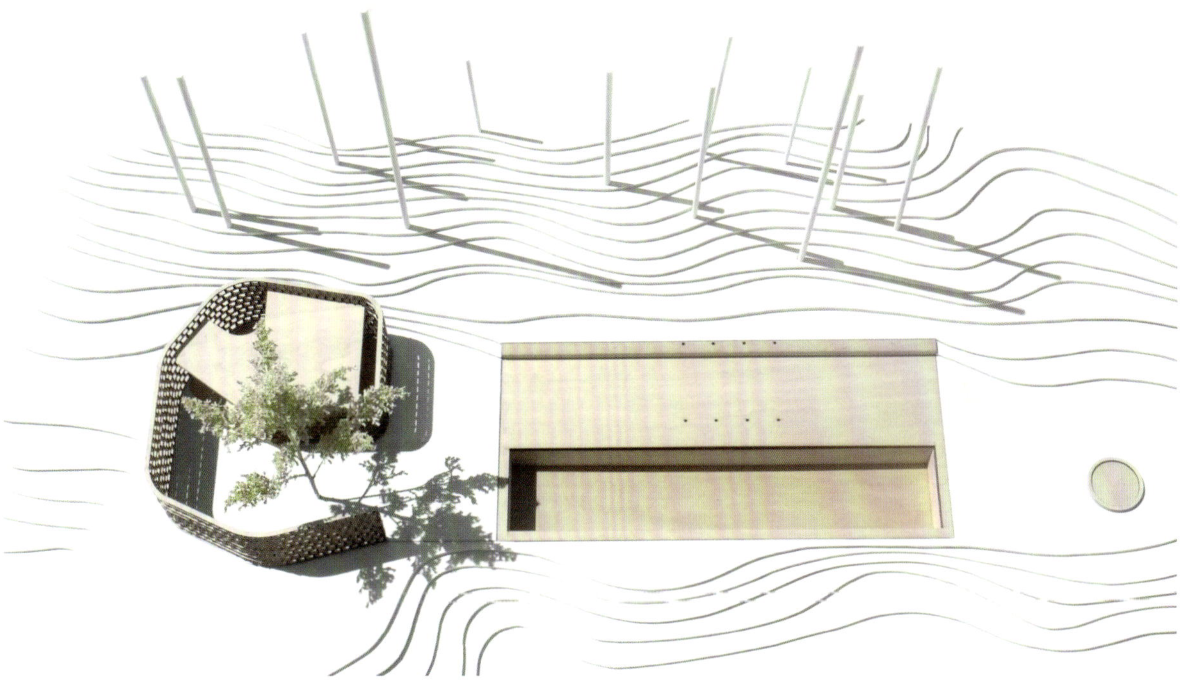

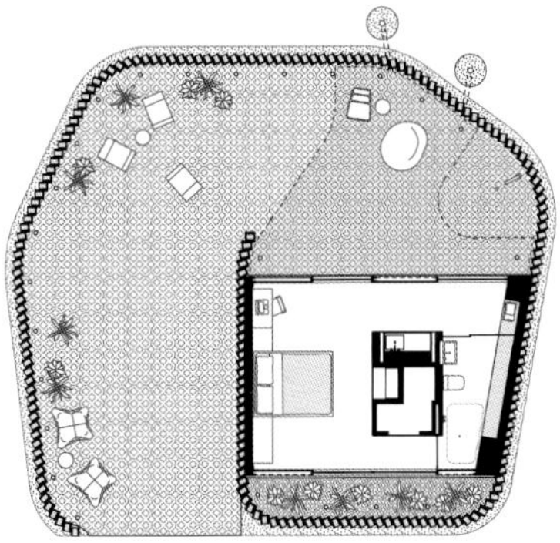

A SNAIL HOUSE

Snail shells play out the metrics of the animal's growth in logarithmic spirals that are described by the mathematics of the Fibonacci series or the Golden Mean—the genius of nature and cellular growth. The shell grows successive chambers through which the developing resident can progress forward over its lifecycle, making a dynamic house that grows with the snail's expanding size and behavior. In the case of the common garden snail (Cornu aspersum), tectonics, growth, and survival are all intertwined.

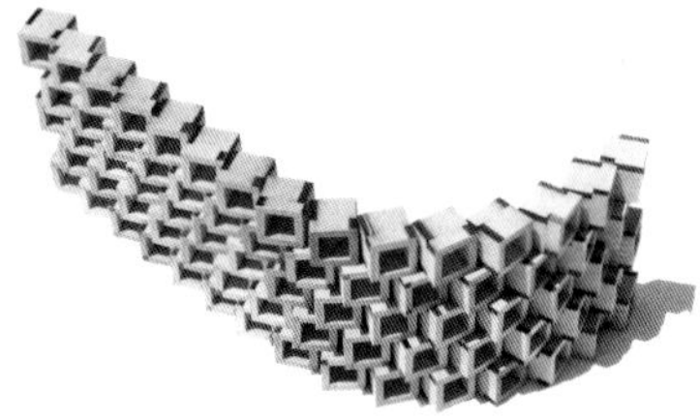

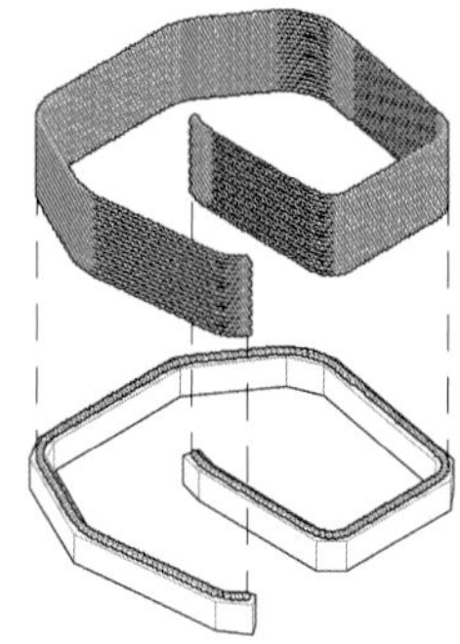

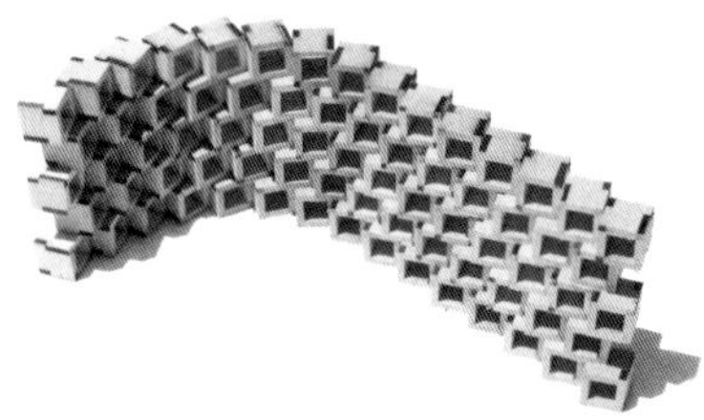

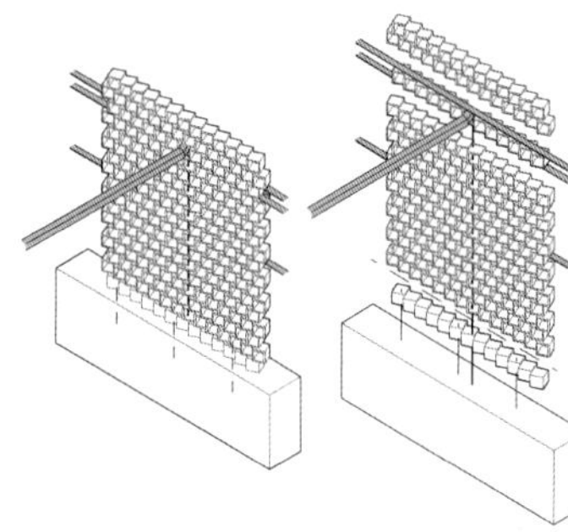

This house plays out its metrics in the nesting of spaces and their successively increasing dimensions, from the smallest and most central and internal spaces to the exterior spaces that reach out to the site beyond. Spiraling from smallest outward are: the mechanical closet and clothes closet, the bathroom, the bedroom, the patio, and pool deck (which is outside the parameters of the snail, but a close cousin in this house).

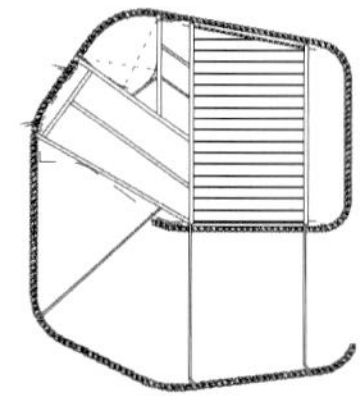

Unlike the snail and its shell, this house does not grow dynamically after it is constructed. Architecture is suspended growth. The metrics of this house's pared down inhabitation are based in the successively nested geometries that expand from the 3' × 5' mechanical closet for heating equipment up to the 12' × 24' patio all wrapped by coiling walls made of 8" × 8" × 16" shifting and pivoting concrete blocks. These blocks, the central tectonic metric of this house, are made of ground-face concrete masonry units (CMU for short).

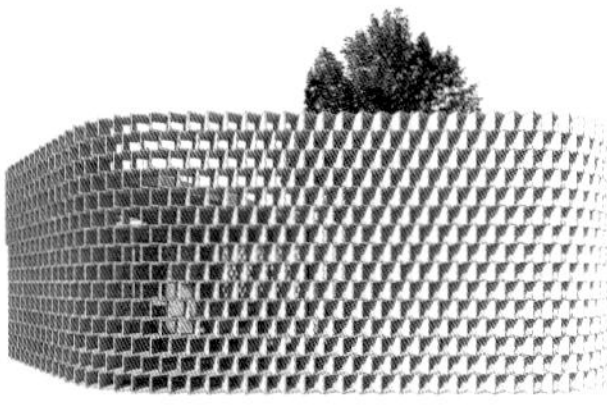

The blocks are laid up sideways, 90 degrees to normal concrete block construction, to reveal their internal voids and make the wall perforated, with varying degrees of visible porosity as you move around the house or inside the interior outdoor spaces. The 90-degree set of the block constitutes two curving and not-at-all parallel screens that afford the graduated degrees of privacy and mediated views out. Similar to the curve of the Fibonacci series and the nested rectangles therein, the metric of the block is the wrapping unit that constitutes the curved walls wrapping the rectangular spaces.

This house, the smallest in this presentation of houses, boasts the thickest wall sections of all houses in this book. At 8" plus 4" of continuous mineral wool insulation and another 8" of insulated block, the walls width is 20" thick at its thickest—a real thick shell.

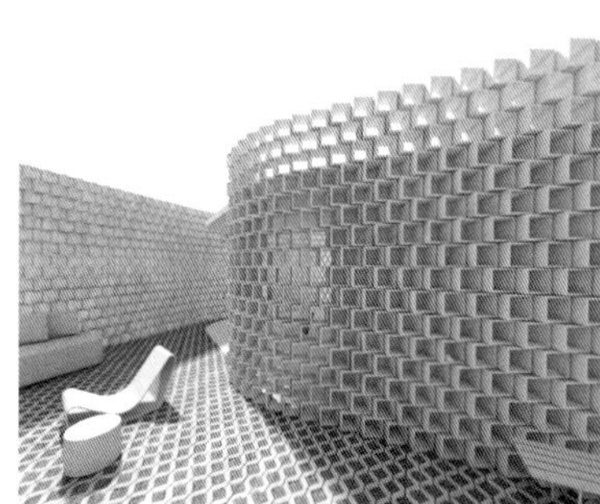

This is a house-shaped house with no front door.

Located in Taghkanic, New York, the house consists of two volumes placed side by side. One volume is for the communal living spaces and the other volume is for the private bedroom and bathroom spaces. The two volumes shift past one another, creating two porches: one at the north and one at the south. The north porch faces north and east, off of the kitchen and dining area. The south porch is covered and faces south and west, off of the living and studio space. At the center of the house, the two volumes connect and create a cross-cut view east-west through the house.

Large square sliding doors and windows align across the two volumes, providing views through the house. Because each face of the house is equipped with large doors, you can enter the house from any point—eschewing any formal front or back door. Each façade offers a way into the house, depending on what direction you are coming from.

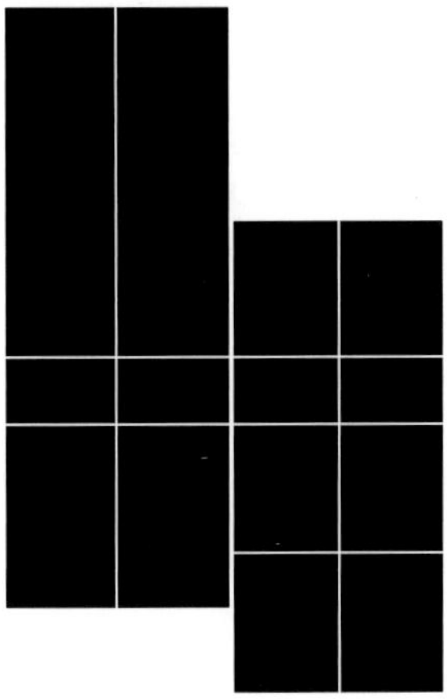

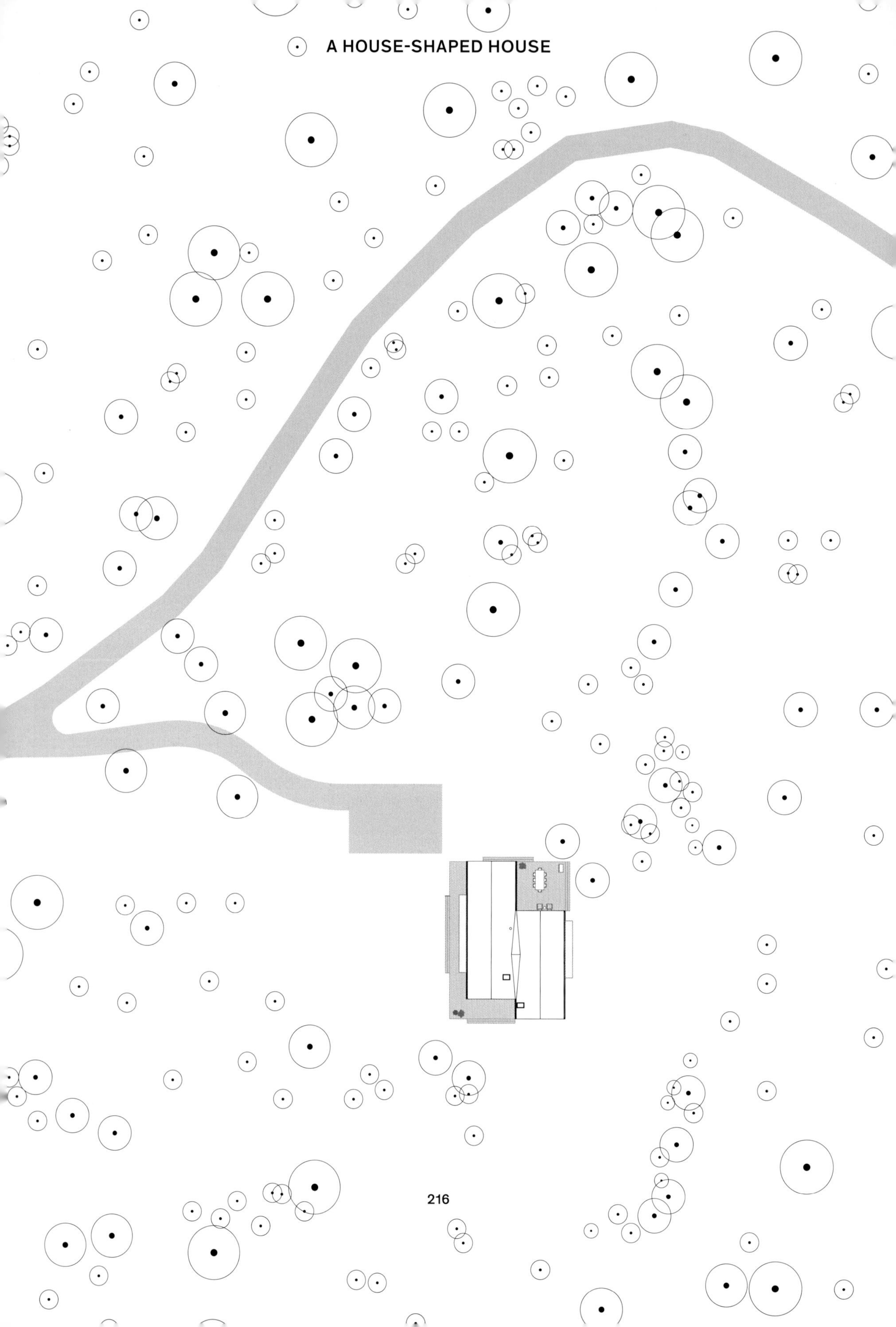

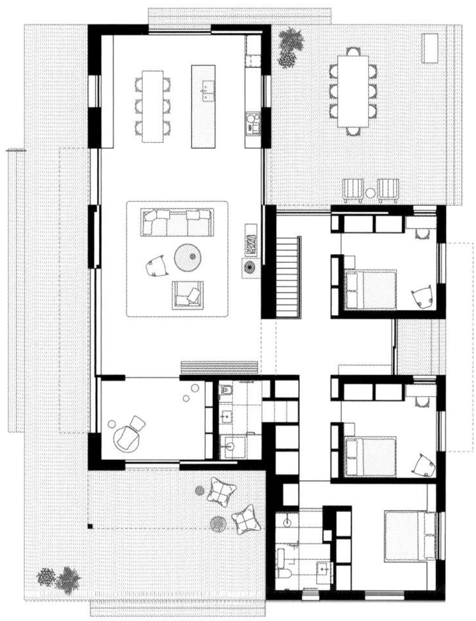

A HOUSE-SHAPED HOUSE

Some architectural metrics are less organic than others. The brief of this 2,400-square-foot-house plus 1,200-square-foot basement was delivered as a desire for a predetermined form of a house—the archetypal gable-ended box (in the shape of a "house," of course), but doubled to form two gable-ended boxes shifting past one another in plan.

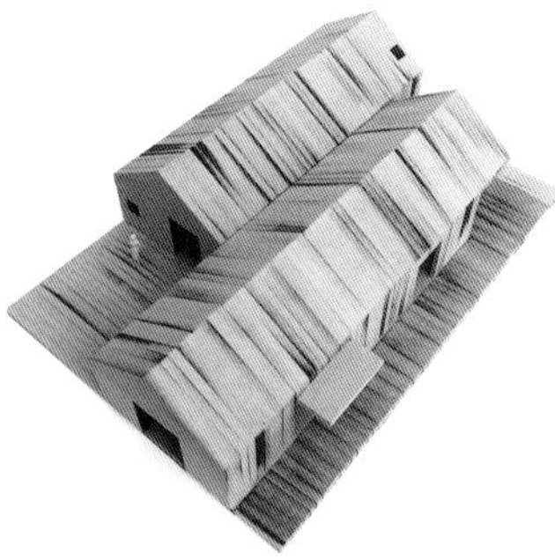

The plan of this house is coincidentally the same planimetric diagram as in our House of Lines (and with its own pedigree in architectural history, notably in Frank Lloyd Wright's Robie House of 1909). Living areas were to occupy one gabled box and private areas the other.

Our metric response was to make the two volumes identical in size, 42' × 22', to shift the volumes past one another so that each gable has its pure autonomous form—a technique that Robie House blurs by covering the forms with an extended roof and eaves—and to make all windows and doors squares. Sliding doors are 7' × 7', casement windows range from 5' × 5' to 3' × 3' and 2' × 2', and skylights in bathrooms area also 2' × 2'. The received figure of the gable form, rendered abstract with no eaves or trim and the relentless squares conjoin to address the given brief through an abstraction of the house form, times two.

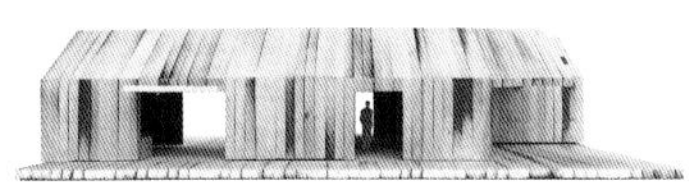

The metrics of water and drainage drive the architecture of the autonomous gables and the wall section of this house. Gutters at 4" wide are needed to remove water from the two 1,052 square feet of 6:12 sloping roof. A large cricket is needed by the intersecting gables to divert water into gutters embedded in walls. In order to not have one gutter impinge on the drip edge height of the other gable, and to not have that gutter widen the appearance of the gable next to its neighbor—a condition that is doubled on both sides of the house at the shift—a simple shift in the roof plane ensures drip edge heights and gable equalities, and that water does not run back into the cricket valley. The house's wall section is a study in non-structural thickness. Thickness derives from continuous insulation applied over the cavity wall and from running leader pipes inside the walls, behind the siding. A simple wood-framed house with 2" × 6" studs contains 12"-thick walls with integrated 3" leader pipes and gutters hidden behind the 4" cedar siding boards and furring—all this ensures the purity of the gable, unencumbered by gutters grafted to the outside surfaces. Square sliding doors likewise do not interrupt the gable surfaces, and use the thickness of the section to slide into hidden pockets inside the walls.

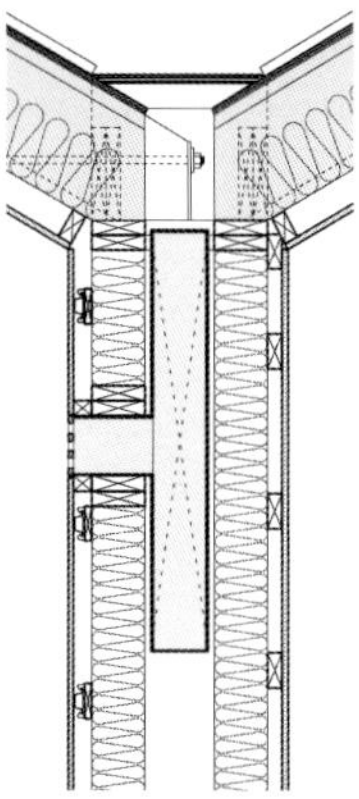

This is a house in five shapes—five versions of an open courtyard house.

Located in Taghkanic, New York, the houses explore the possibilities of the open courtyard through five distinct shapes: an oval, a rectangle, a right triangle, an isosceles triangle, and a trapezoid. The site stays the same. The house changes shape.

Oval House has a soft, rounded oval roof with an off-centered circle courtyard in the middle. Rectilinear walls and volumes sit below the rounded roof. The off-centered courtyard allows for a variety of room sizes.

Rectangle House has four bars of varied width, each differently programmed, with pitched roofs that rotate around a rectilinear open courtyard. Open-roof deck spaces are accessed from second-floor bedrooms.

Triangle House has three bars of three different widths. The open living spaces are located on the legs of the triangle and the bedrooms are placed at the corners. There is a lower level that opens to the field below.

Isosceles House has three bars of three different widths, two bars have the same length. There is a "pop-up" room above the main space overlooking a planted roof garden.

Trapezoid House has an arch-shaped open courtyard in the middle of a trapezoid volume. The courtyard space steps down to the lower level, opening up the section of the house and allowing light and views deep into the lower level. At the roof, an oval "pop-up" room overlooks a planted roofscape.

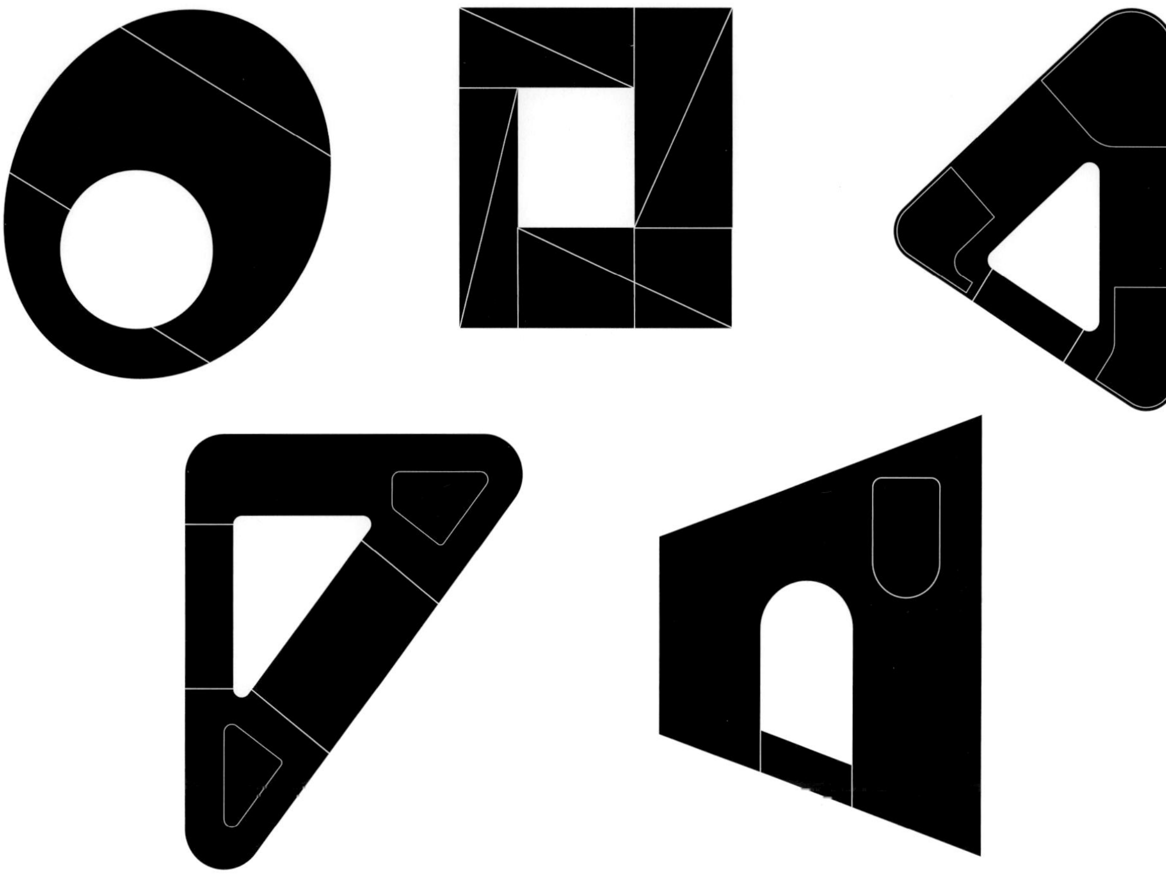

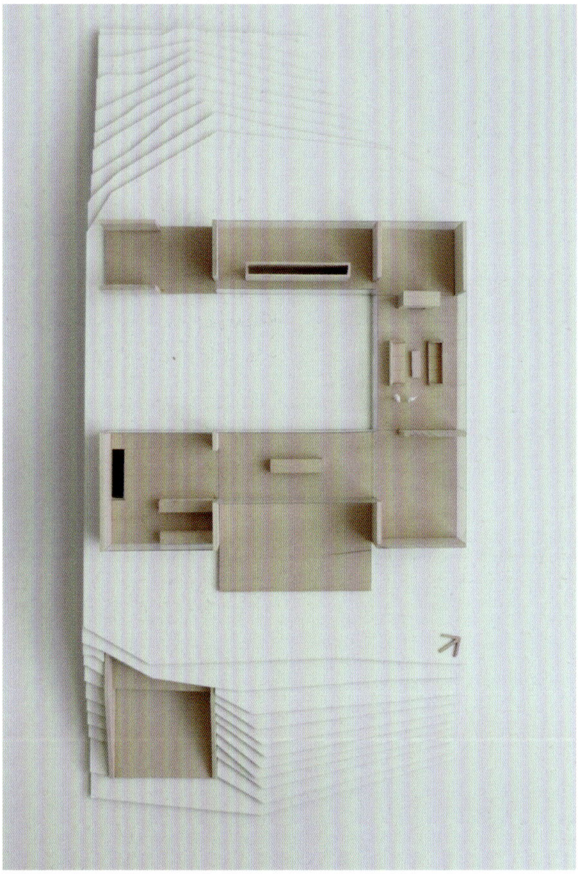

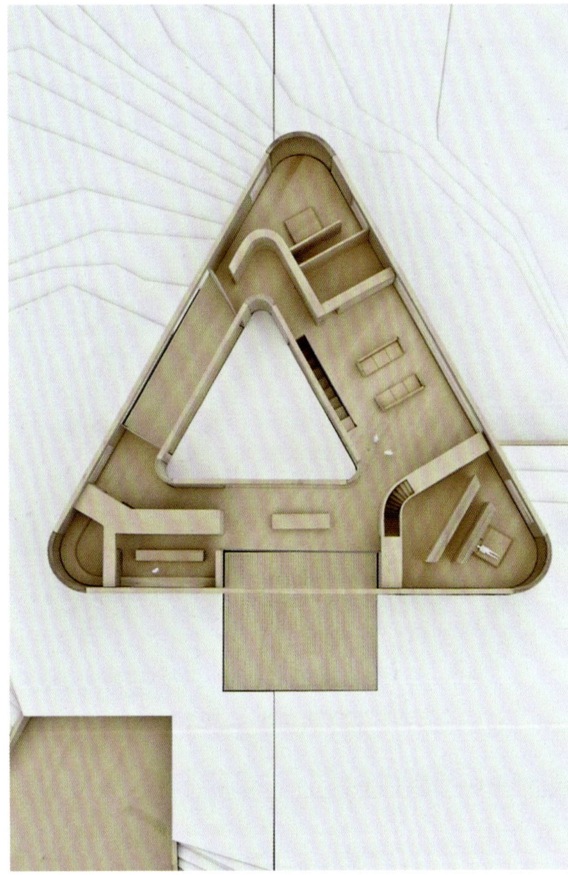

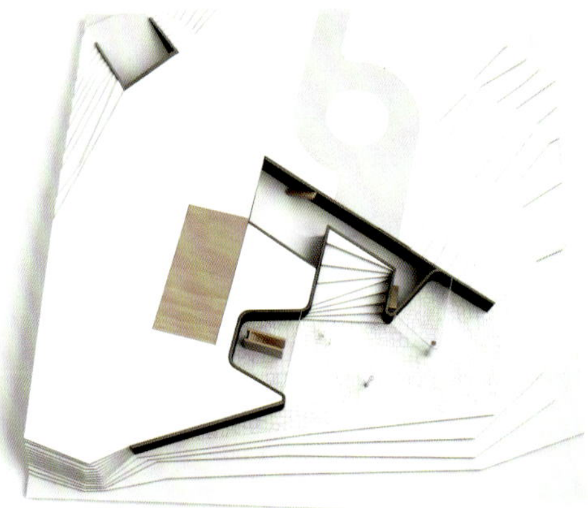

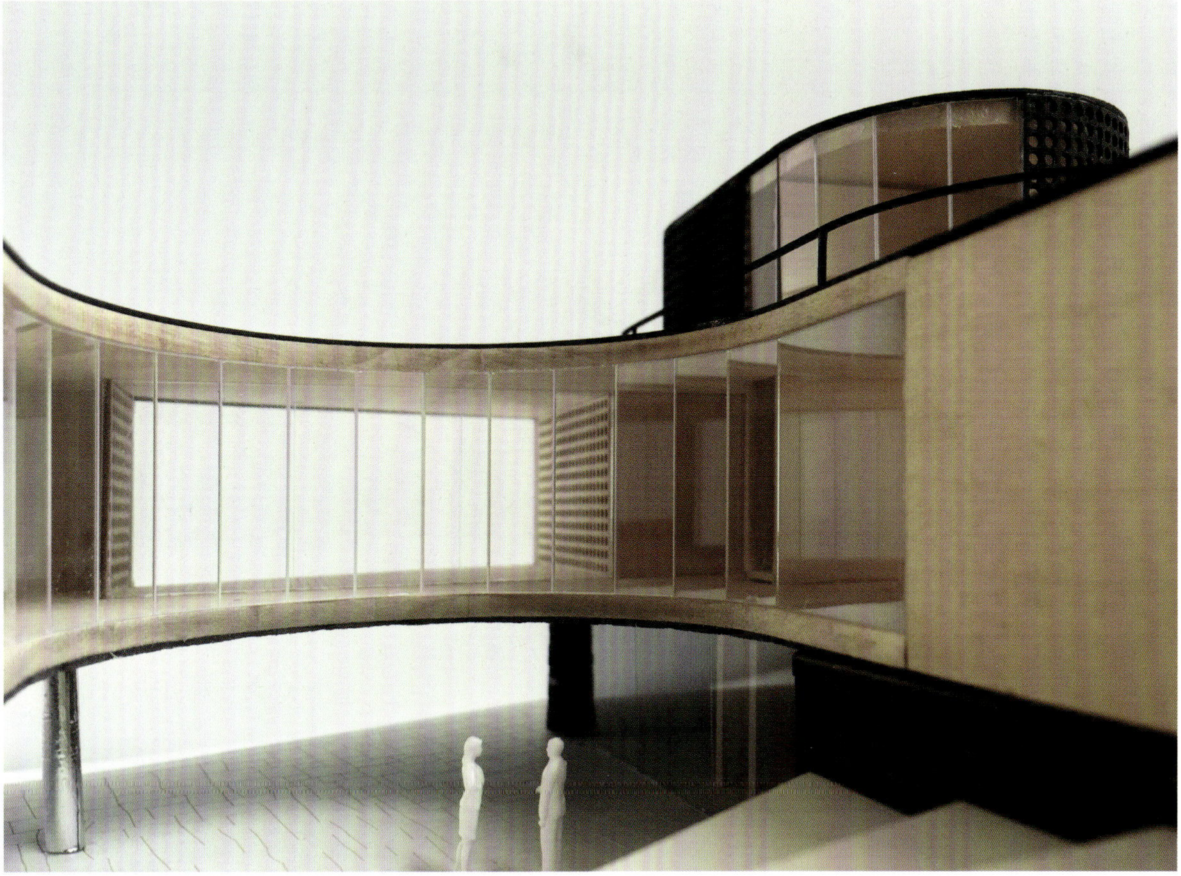

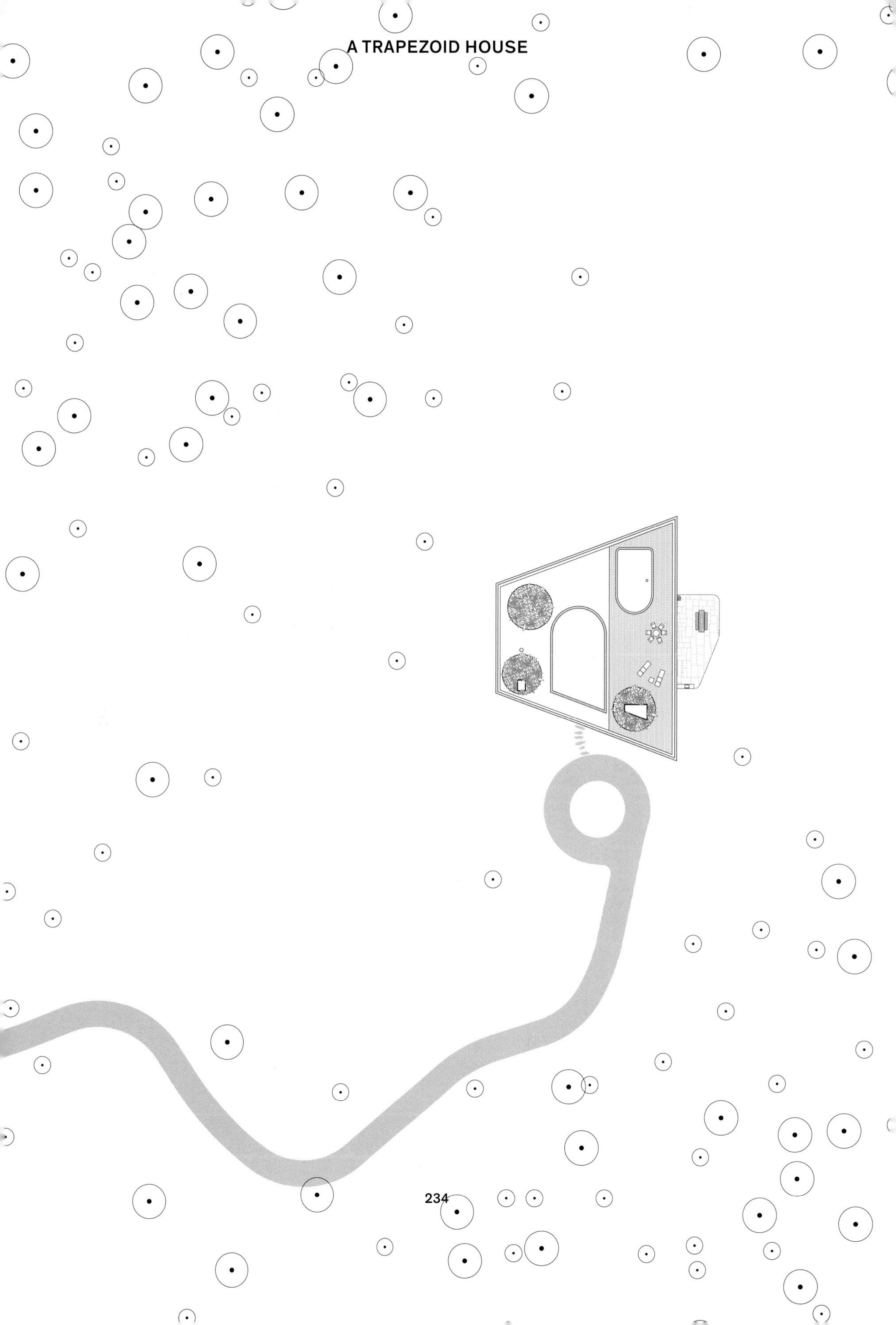

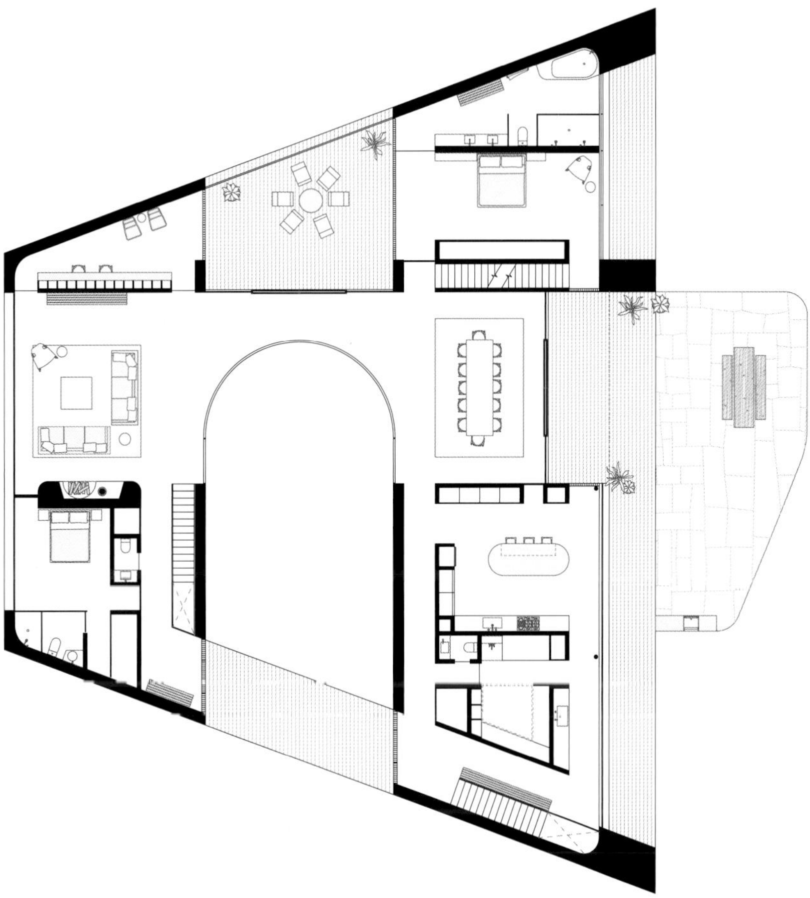

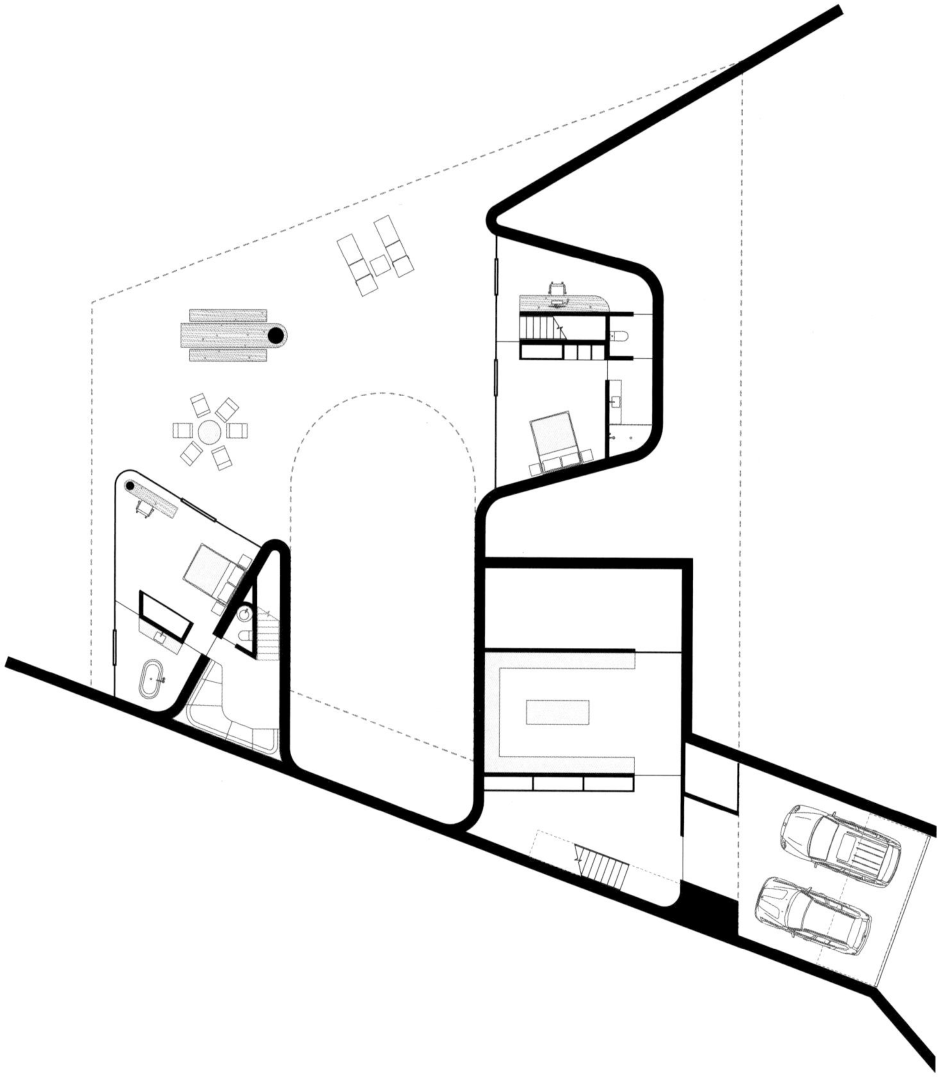

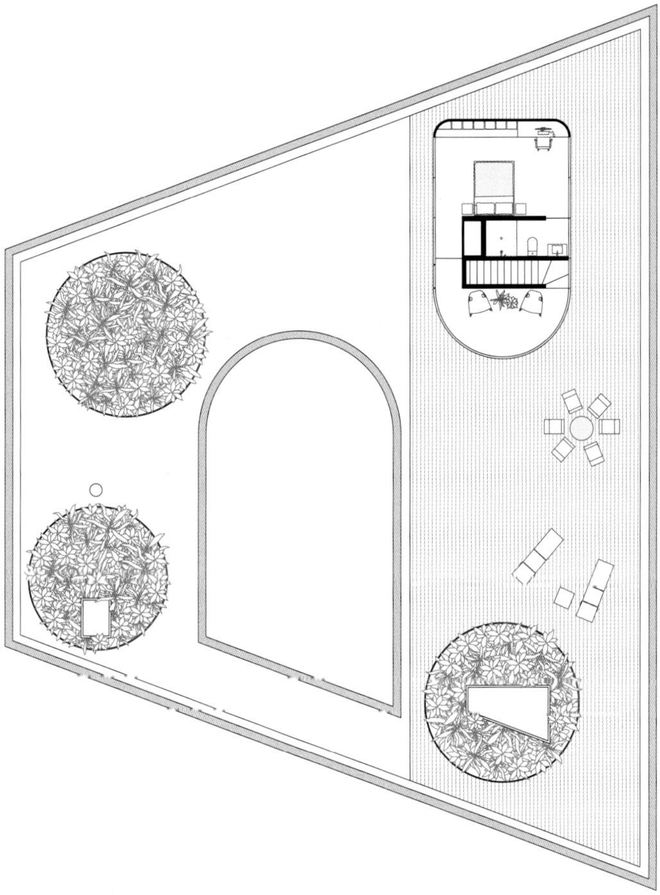

A HOUSE IN FIVE SHAPES

These houses—five unbuilt alternatives for the same site—occupy the top of a hill with almost 360-degree views. The hill has two viewsheds: one west and 35 degrees wide and another, the larger view, east and 270 degrees wide.

The metrics of the 360-degree siting established a geometric framework that five distinct shapes address in different ways. Each shape responds to the 360 degrees but occupies the site such that views, whether short or long, framed or expansive; points of access in plan and section (another metric in these houses); and open indoor and outdoor spaces all inhabit geometries that enable the oblong nature of the of the site and its occupational opportunities to be maximized.

Sitting on top of a hill, although expansive in its feeling of command and consumption of the view, can also make you feel inadvertently exposed. So, a right-sized and right-shaped courtyard provides protection on top of the perch. The metrics embedded in each geometric shape are particular to that geometry; and each enables a series of unique domestic spatial organizations and experiences.

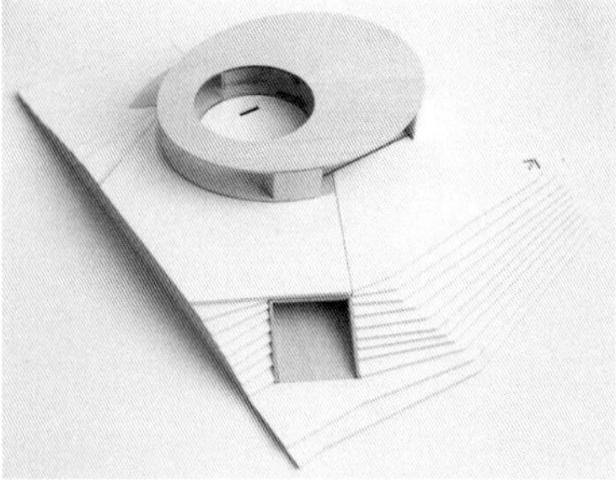

For example, the oval, while seemingly passive in its geometry, is a circle that has actively stretched to broaden the long, wide view to the east of the Berkshire Mountains.

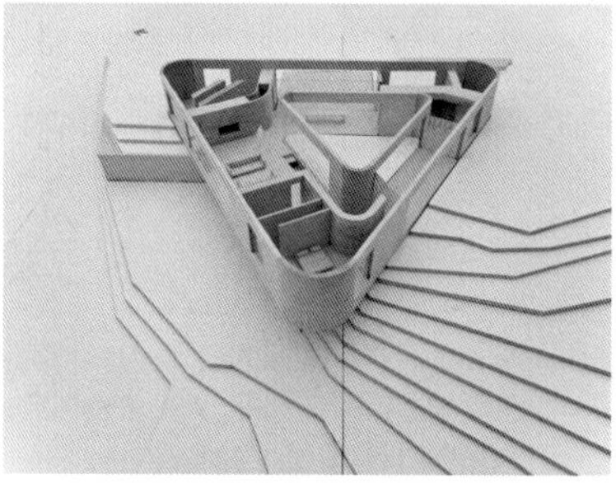

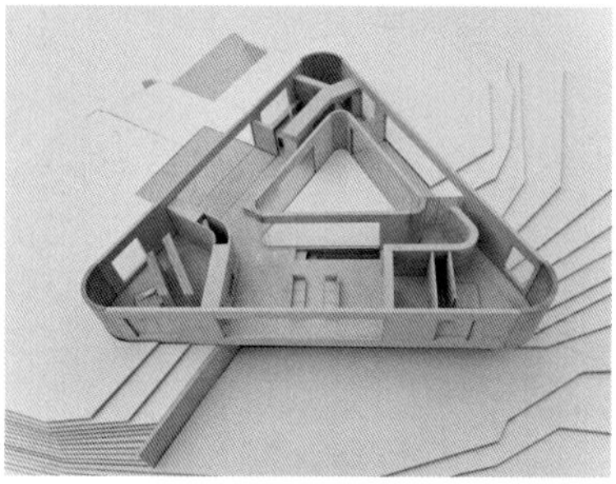

The isosceles triangle, with its two equal and one unequal sides, affords three open indoor/outdoor relationships and an idiosyncratic occupation of the knob, similarly stretched like the oval.

The right triangle presents a 90-degree corner upon entry, but the hypotenuse veers away connecting the living area to the bedrooms and dining bar while maintaining the view toward the Catskills to the west.

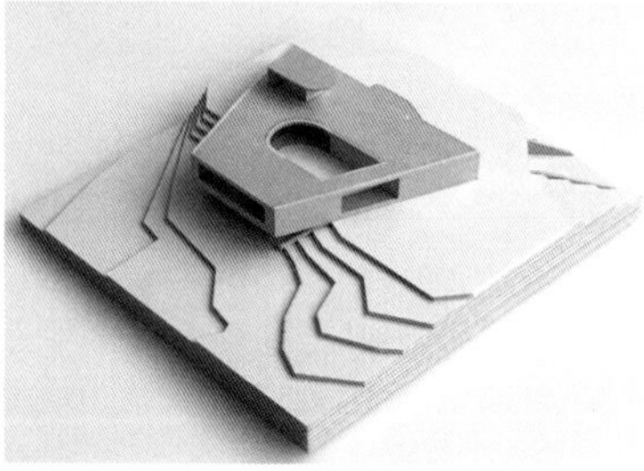

Very similar, but decidedly harder-edged than the oval, the trapezoid establishes a domestic organization most akin to the site's viewsheds in that a series of spaces can be stacked along the wide view while the narrow end of the shape focuses the long view that is framed by bracketing trees.

Similarly hard-edged like the trapezoid is the rectangle, but this symmetrically centered shape contains an internal logic that may be the least site-driven but that still maintains a protected courtyard and an open ground floor. The rectangle is formed by four bars, each of which contain a discrete second-floor space. Each shape reduces itself down to the shape of the courtyard it contains—the oval a circle, the isosceles another isosceles, the right triangle a right triangle, the trapezoid a smaller trapezoid with an arc (the rule breaker!), and the rectangle a rectangle—and sets up a protective metric that focuses in different ways on the center of the house.

The sectional metric of each differently shaped house plays out in the relationship between the Bruce-Wayne-like arrival of the car below the house. The driver, caped crusader or not, emerges up alongside the courtyard, and the section of the courtyard itself. The trapezoid plays this section to its best advantage, sliding the courtyard downslope and under one of the angled sides of the shape, creating a cascading outdoor space that is framed by a 20'-long bridge. The four courtyards of the four other shapes are flat-bottomed and contained by the linear bars of each shape.

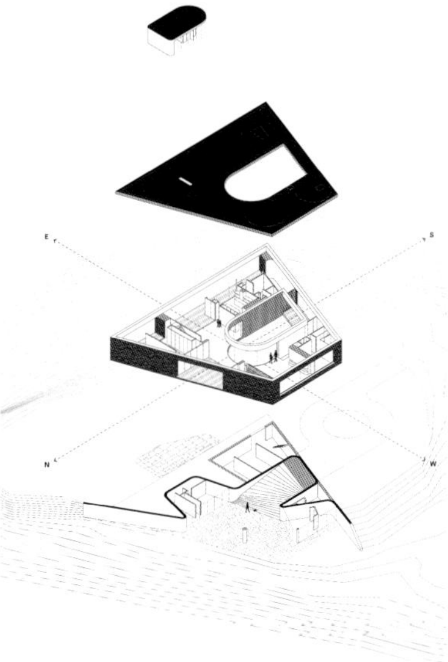

This is a garden in a house.

Located in Princeton, New Jersey, the house is organized around a central square-shaped courtyard. This central courtyard functions as both an interior enclosed living space and an exterior protected garden—providing both natural light and ventilation deep into the middle of the house. The kitchen, living, dining and library spaces all spiral around the garden courtyard. At the north end of the courtyard, along a large window, a stair runs up to the second-floor bedrooms.

Every room has a window and every window is a square. The windows are located in relation to views outward towards the landscape and inward toward the enclosed garden. Each window is placed at a height that aligns with an activity on the inside of the house. So a window next to the dining room is lower (for viewing at a sitting position) and a window at the kitchen is higher (for viewing at a standing position). The sizes of the windows vary and are determined by the program inside, degrees of desired privacy, the direction of the sun at different times of the day, and desired views.

A layering of interior and exterior spaces occurs as you look through windows from inside the house through the courtyard to the outside and then again to another interior space. The garden courtyard acts as an outdoor living room, sheltered by the house yet opened to the elements.

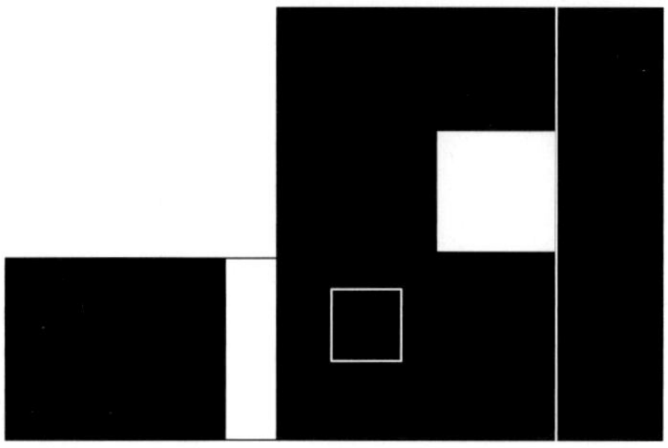

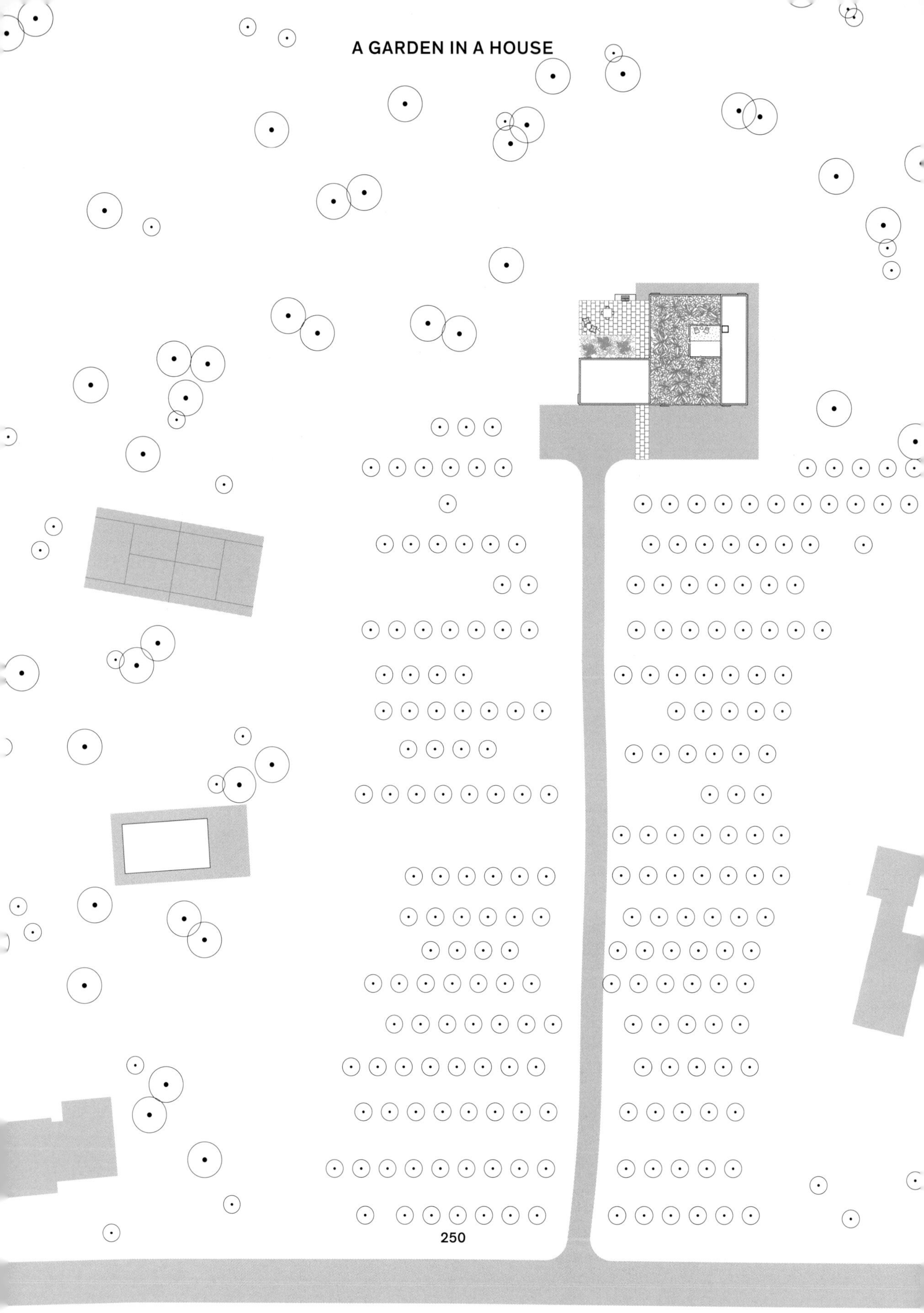

A GARDEN IN A HOUSE

The metric stories of this house revolve around plants and the classic exercise of budget reduction.

The site as originally found contained 100 or so pine trees planted in a shifting grid and spaced at approximately 12' on center—the vestiges of a former tree farm that backed up to a constellation of hardwood trees running into a protected wetland deep into the site.

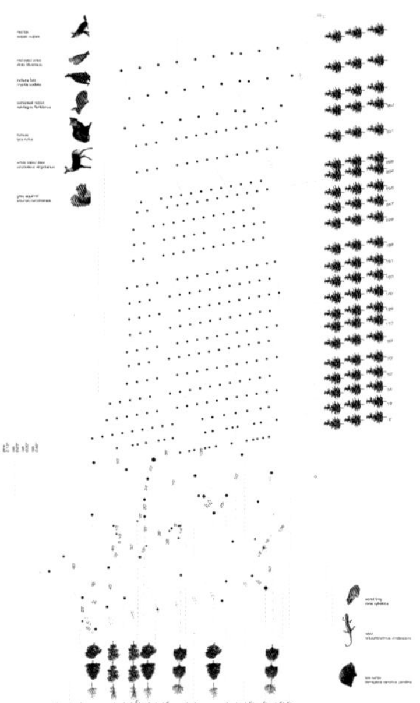

In a previous design, the house was organized around a courtyard and was to be lifted to allow airflow into its center, and to allow the house to hover and spiral up within the canopy of the trees. This first scheme played fast and loose with the famous metrics of the spiraling ramp of Le Corbusier's Villa Savoye—unwinding the ramp of the iconic modernist house around the courtyard in the center.

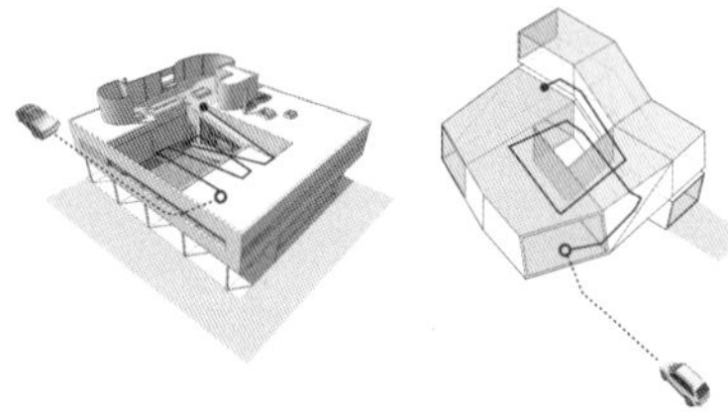

One member of the client family, an avid gardener, had always planned to plant ambitiously around the house. And when the design evolved to include a central courtyard and for plants to be installed at the primary roof level, plantings were to go into and onto the house as well.

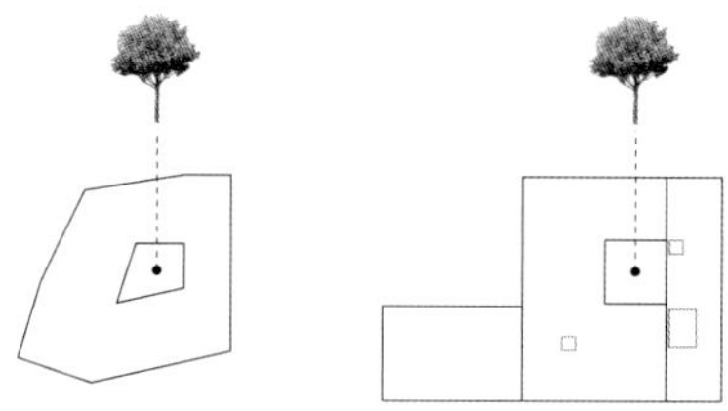

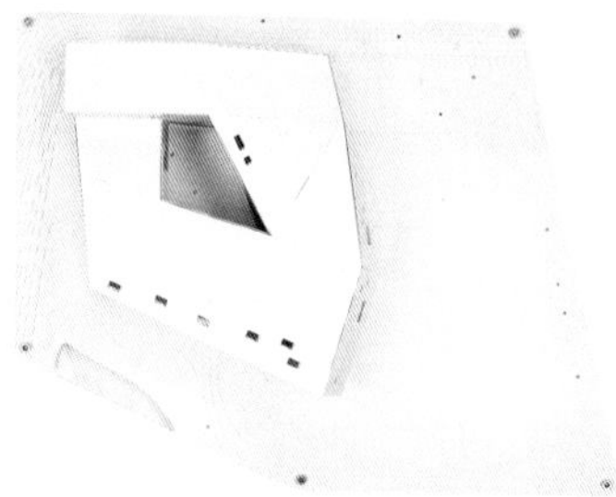

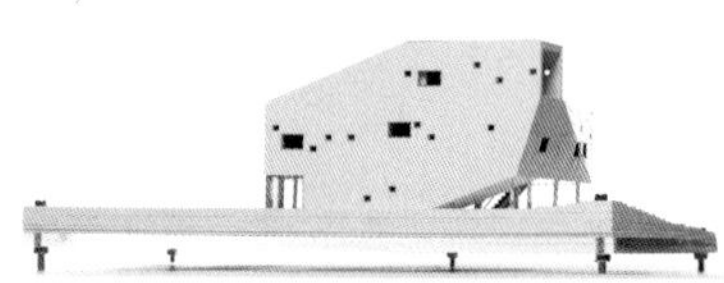

After the first budget came in higher than hoped, the building came back down to earth, dropping 9' lower from its raised level and set onto the site.

The nine columns that previously suspended the raised house above the ground were replaced with a 40' × 40' slab on grade with a 12' × 12' hole in its middle. Windows remained essentially in the same positions but became rationalized into 19 square windows of three sizes: 2' × 2', 5' × 5', 8' × 8'—all positioned in direct relation to the height metrics of the adjacent activities at the windows and the exterior views that they afford. Trusses and cantilevers in steel became a platform frame in lumber with no steel spanning beams, albeit with steel cladding. The once hovering tree-house became a classic courtyard house. All houses begin as castles in the sky. This one literally fell to the earth, but the framed view of the sky remains.

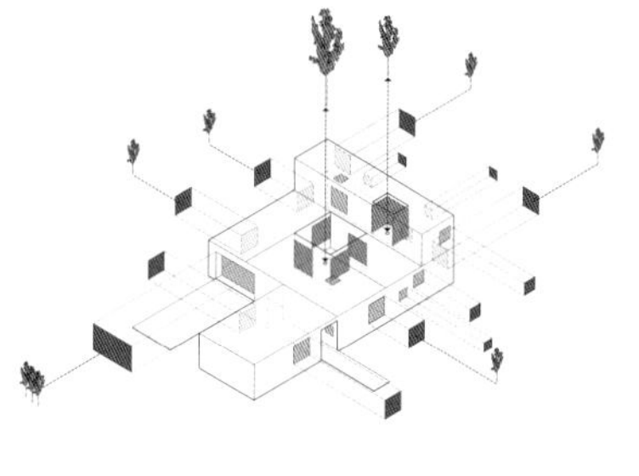

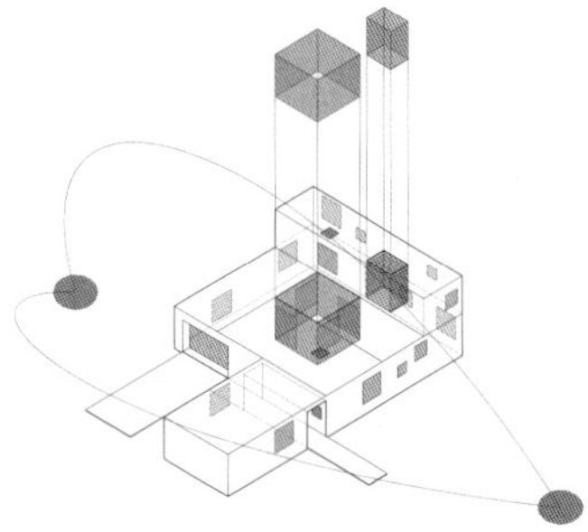

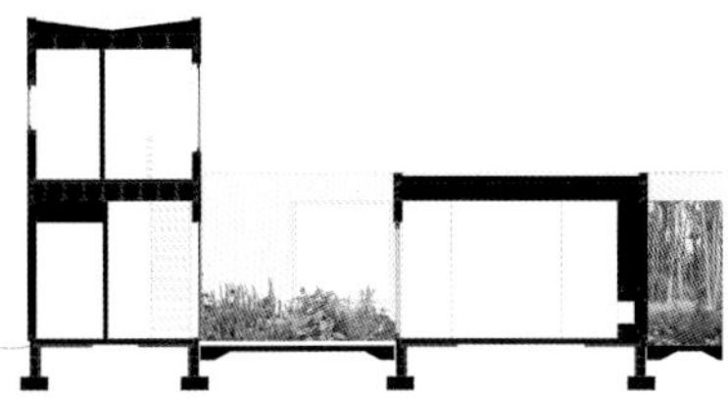

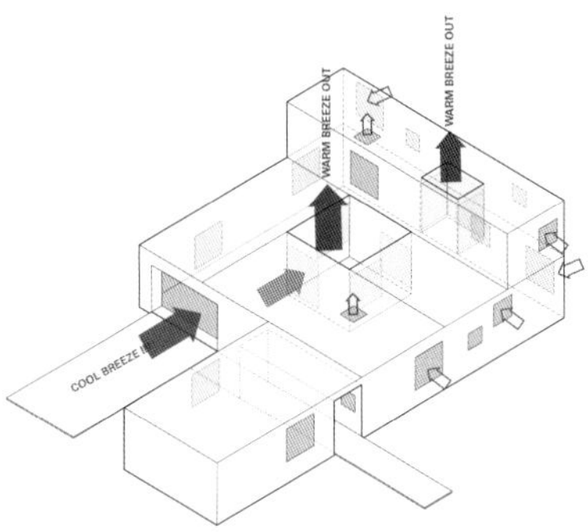
WARM BREEZE OUT
WARM BREEZE OUT
COOL BREEZE

Tyvek

This is a house for the next site.

Located somewhere in Connecticut, the house is a prototype for a house that provides for adaptability and adjustment to future site conditions. Commissioned prior to securing a piece of land, the house locates entry, bedrooms, kitchen, and garage off of one large central living space. Conceived as a kit of parts, the house is comprised of a series of rooms that are discrete volumes. The configuration is a pin-wheel organization that allows for rooms to move and snap to other corners when a site is determined. Depending on desire, rooms can move from facing east or west, north or south, but the main living space remains in the middle with views in all directions.

This organizational strategy not only provides for maximum flexibility, but also eliminates the need for corridors, since all rooms are adjacent to the living room. Because the central-living and dining space is a large space with dimensions greater than any one adjacent volume, the living space always provides for large open windows and doors that have views north, south, east, and west.

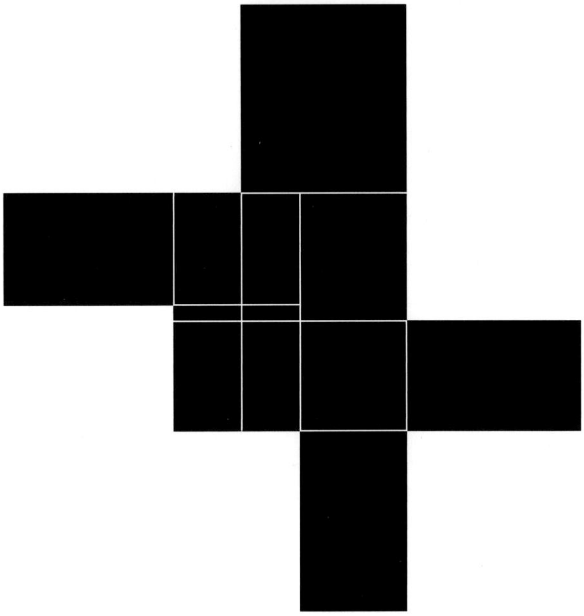

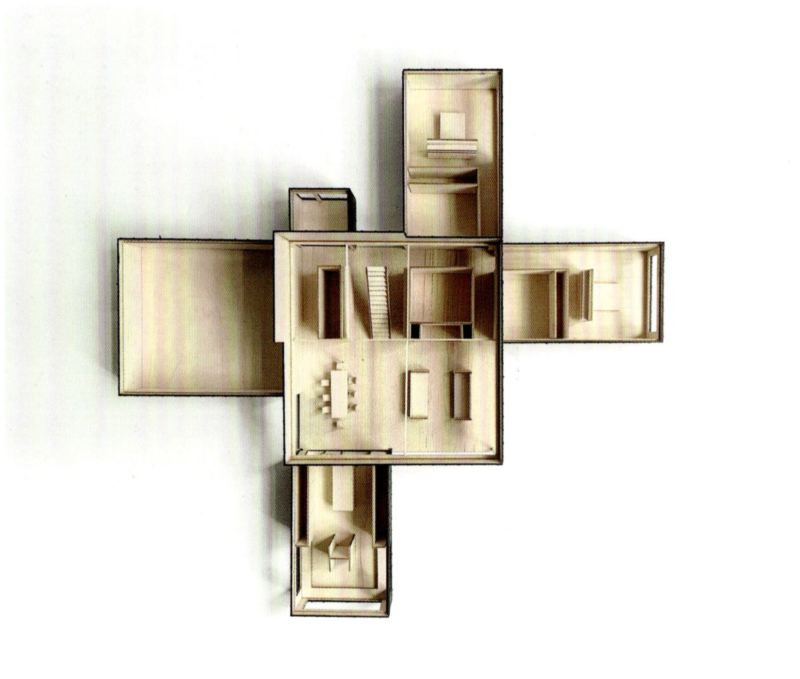

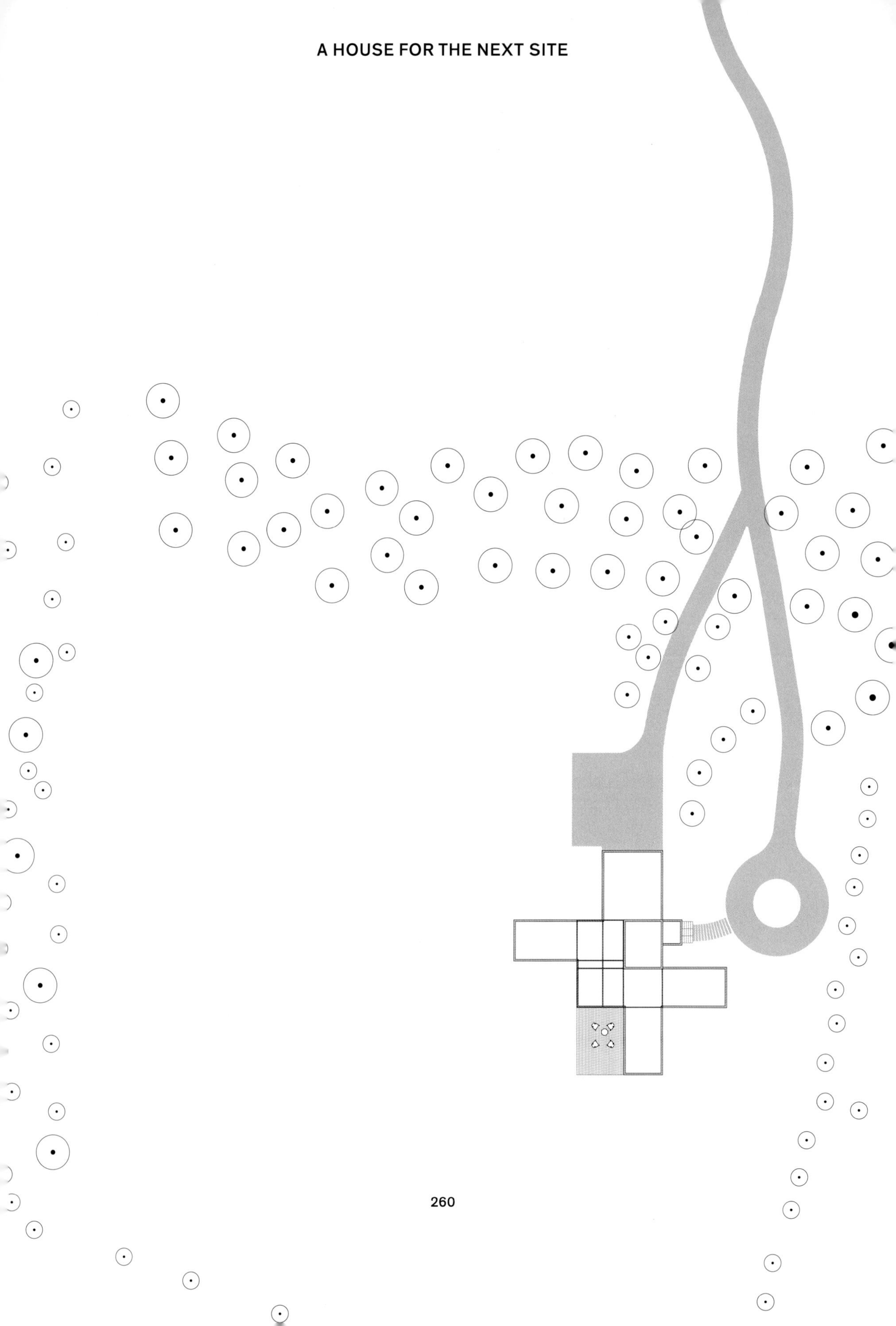

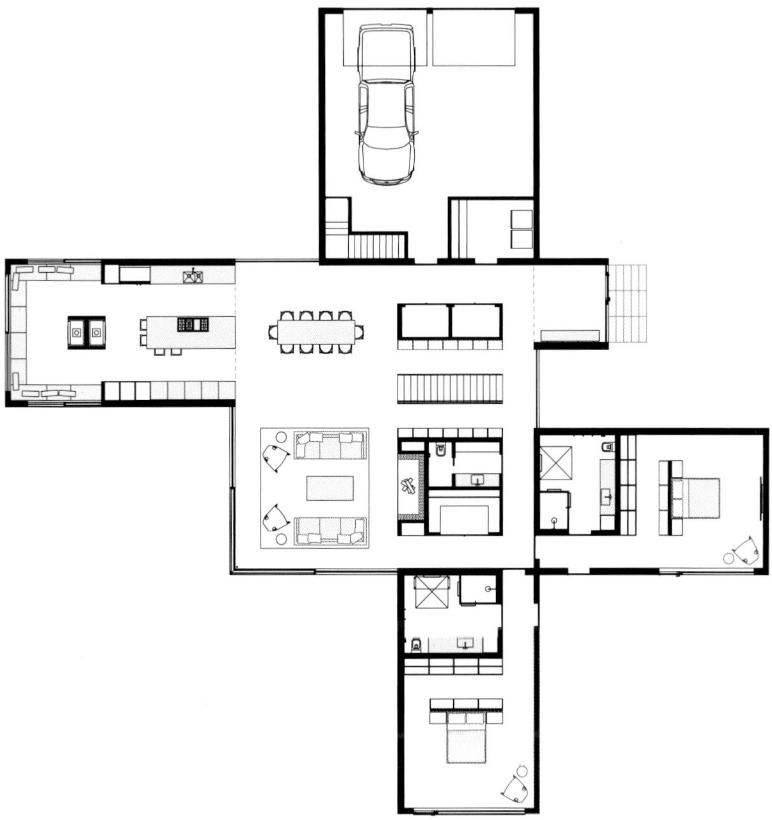

A HOUSE FOR THE NEXT SITE

Like a paper doll, this house has appendages that attach to a central body. Unlike the doll, the house may swap the positions of these appendages—a very exquisite corpse whose legs arms and head can interchange.

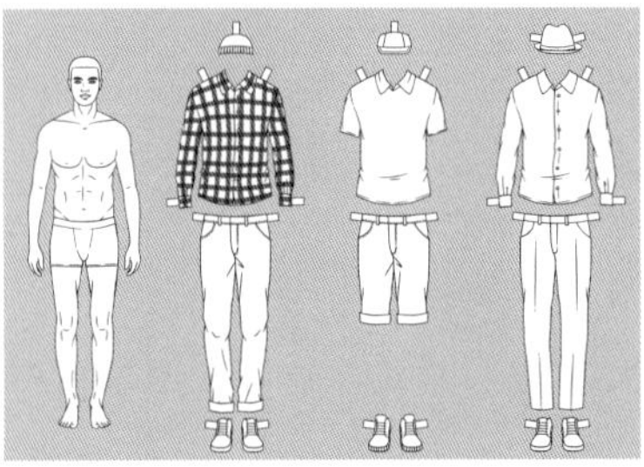

And this is how the metric story of this house unfolds: this commission came from a contractor who had built many complicated houses in their career, including some for us, with the prompt to design a house, that was simple to build and could be "easily" tailored to any site in the Hudson Valley/Western Connecticut region. The land hadn't been found; the site was undefined; the house was to be light on frills and simple, direct, and affordable to construct.

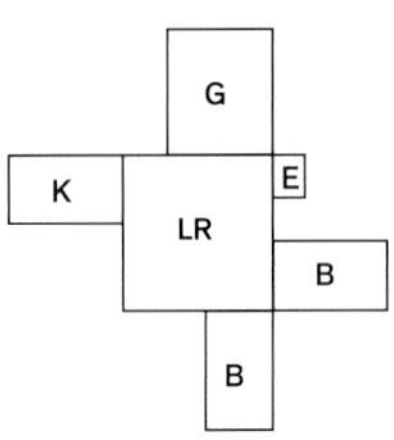

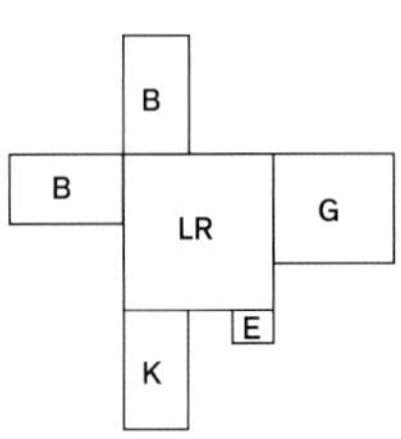

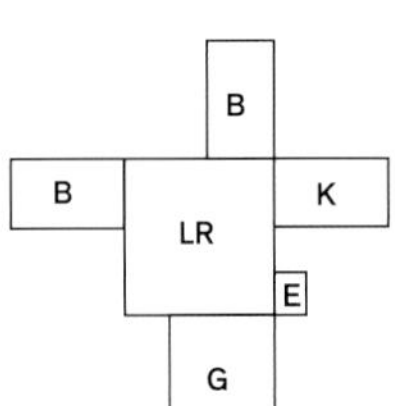

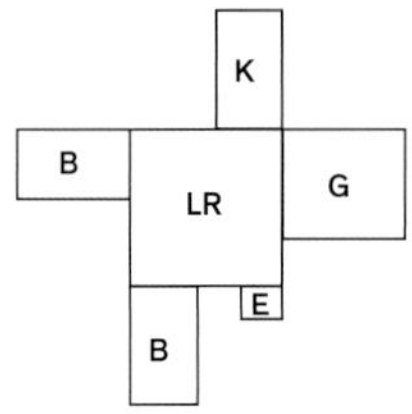

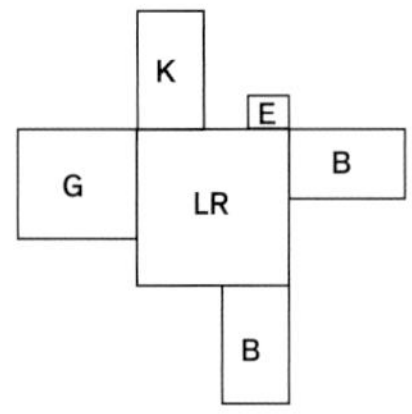

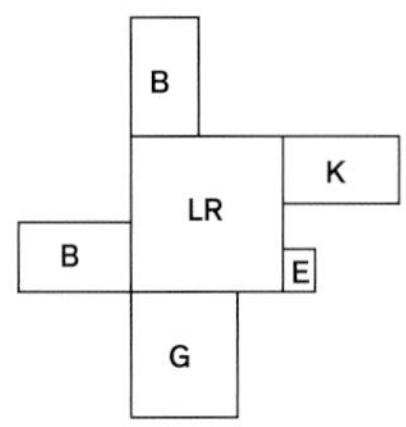

Of course, after the initial design process and the parcel was secured, the site and the sun necessitated an alteration to the scheme. The locations of the appendages on the site around the central space was all wrong. So, a swapping of appendages that was built into the DNA of the scheme was undertaken. The swap was even easier than expected. A simple flip of the entire scheme, a mirroring, was all it took. The 36' × 36' central tall square volume remained in the middle; the 18' × 30' kitchen moved to the other side of the volume; and the two identical 16' × 24' bedroom/bathroom volumes simply flipped to the other side of the volume. In (Paul) Rudolphian fashion, along the 2,100 square feet of surface area of the façade—where the appendages aren't—there is only glass, accentuating the paper doll composition of appendages attached to a larger body.

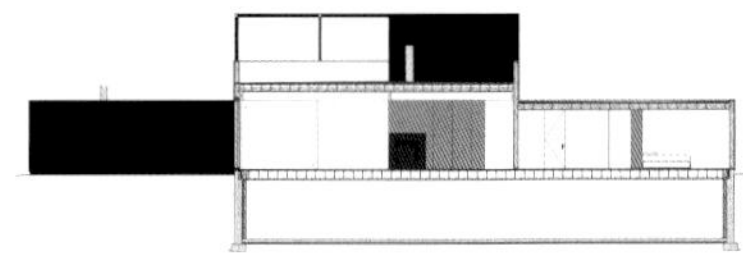

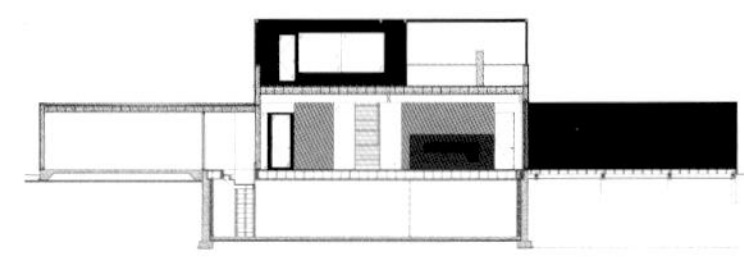

The structural metric in this house plays out as a long-span tartan grid with short-span fringes. The central volume is crisscrossed by 16"-deep engineered lumber beams and the appendages are spanned by 11 1/4"-deep TJI's (truss-joist-I-beams). The deep beams of the central space frame a stair to an upper room and a trellis on the roof traces the tartan lines. The cladding of the long and short span structure is a metric of 17"-wide stripes, black standing seam metal vertically oriented from roof to sill. As with a paper doll, you fold along the dashed lines, flip out the rooms, leaving only glass between them. Then you apply the formal black clothes along the seams and play the game.

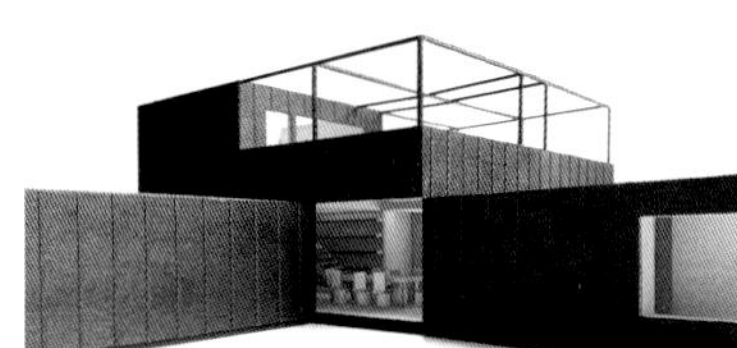

This is a house with a swerve.

Located in Hudson, New York, the house consists of two separate rectilinear volumes that are offset from one another but connected by a continuous roof that swerves in the middle.

Like a dogtrot house, the swerving central patio, sheltered but open-air, offers a breezy outdoor living space that joins the kitchen, living, and bedroom volume with the laundry, bath, and guest room/study volume. At the north and south ends are open covered patios that are additional outdoor living and bathing spaces.

The house is long and narrow, stringing out the domestic spaces one to the other like cars in a train. The narrowness of the width provides for easy cross-ventilation lateral to the living spaces and gives a sense of living intimately with the outdoors.

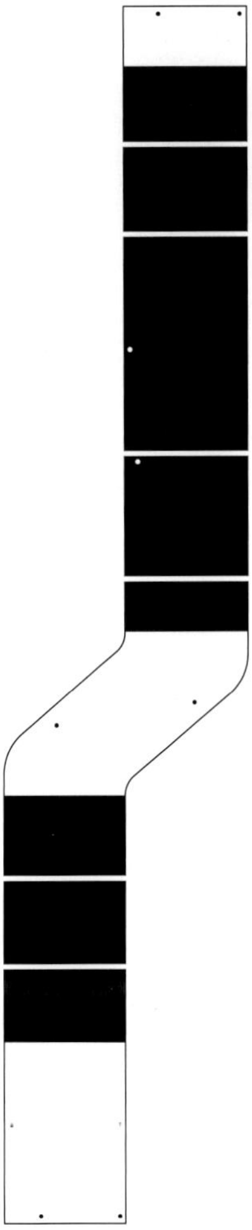

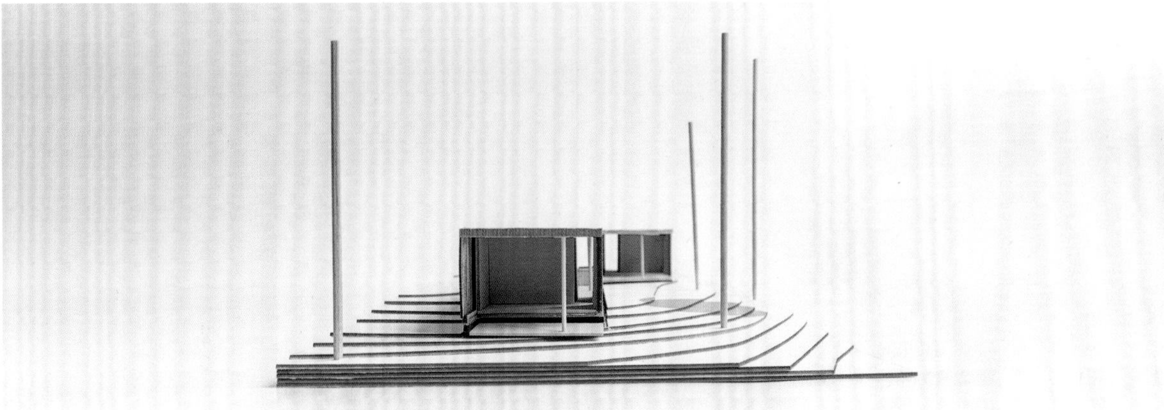

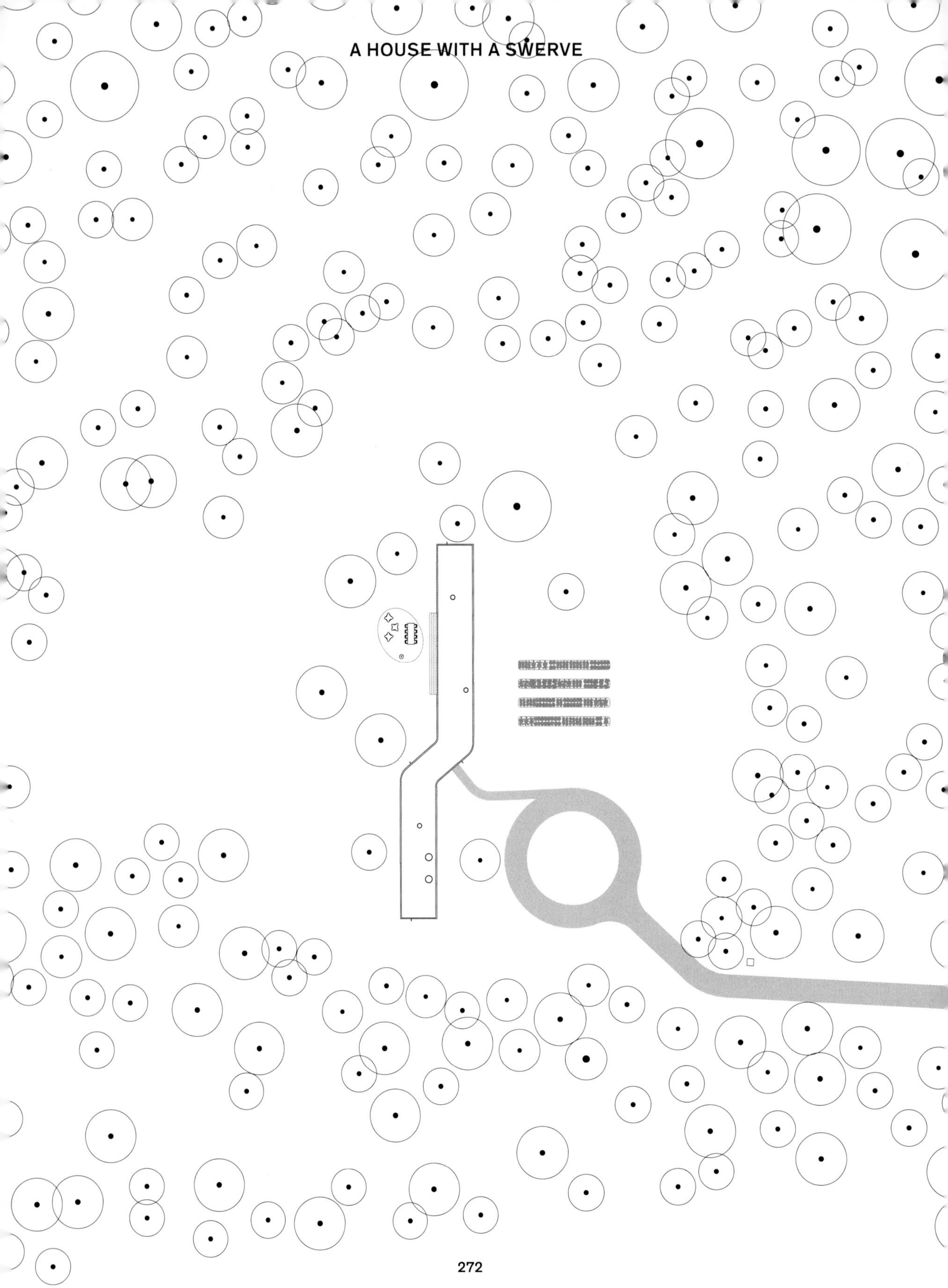

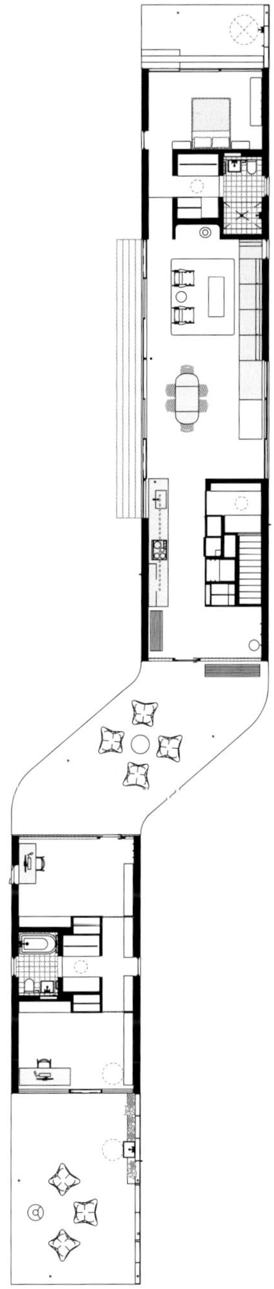

A HOUSE WITH A SWERVE

According to Lucretius, atoms swerve slightly as they move through space, just enough that it could be understood that their path has changed. Expounding the Epicurean philosophy of first-century CE Rome, Lucretius also asserted that the attainment of happiness and pleasure in all human endeavors is the highest good.

This house swerves just slightly, just enough to move out of its own way, to open up the spaces of the long linear structure to an understanding of what could not be perceived beyond the ends of a long and unerringly straight house. The swerve operates on several key metrics that range from site conditions to the activities that occur within the house. At the crux of the swerve is a tree, a 70'-tall white pine with branches that spread out 40' in diameter. The tree both shades and sets up the swerve, but the swerve is also comprised of two railroad-style boxcars of domestic activity: kitchen; dining; living; bathroom; bedroom; patio to the north and studio/office/bedroom; bathroom/laundry; studio/office/bedroom; patio to the south that shifts in plan off of one another along a centerline. At the middle, the tree-inflected swerve constitutes the shaded outdoor space, where the two bars and groups of people meet at various times of the day for meals, drink, conversation, contemplation, and enjoyment, all evoking Epicurean Hedonism at this point of atomic trajectory.

This house constitutes a metric ratio of indoor and outdoor space: 1,700 square feet and 1,000 square feet respectively, in a classic dogtrot house configuration, albeit in a Hudson Valley climate that gets far cooler than the Southern vernacular dog on its trot. The house alternates indoor to outdoor spaces along its length from north to south: from 8'-long patio to 80'-long enclosed space to 22'-long swerve space to 32'-long enclosed space to 24'-long patio. At 166' long, the house is also thin. A 16' exterior-to-exterior width enables ample cross ventilation and very close experiential connections with the spaces outside that are directly within the parameters of the long swerving bar and directly adjacent in the landscape. Accentuating the length and ruling the surface at the swerve are 1,062 vertical lines made by 1.5" knotty cedar boards set at .375" apart to form a rainscreen. As in a graphite or charcoal drawing, the lines will silver with time and the knots will punctuate the surface.

The metrics of structure, energy performance, and the roof are integrally bound in this house. The span across its width is easily handled with conventional lumber. The conventional kiln-dried 2" × 10" roof joists accommodate more than enough roof load (including copious snow load of 40 psi) and more than enough insulation. The house not only exceeds energy code for U and R factors but perhaps makes energy code irrelevant in that it is net zero for energy consumption through its onsite solar energy production coupled with a ground source geothermal heat pump system. So the roof remains thin—accentuating the overall attenuation of the long house on the site, the house remains thin, the building uses no fossil fuels, but it is thick with its swerve and its Epicurean matter and spaces.

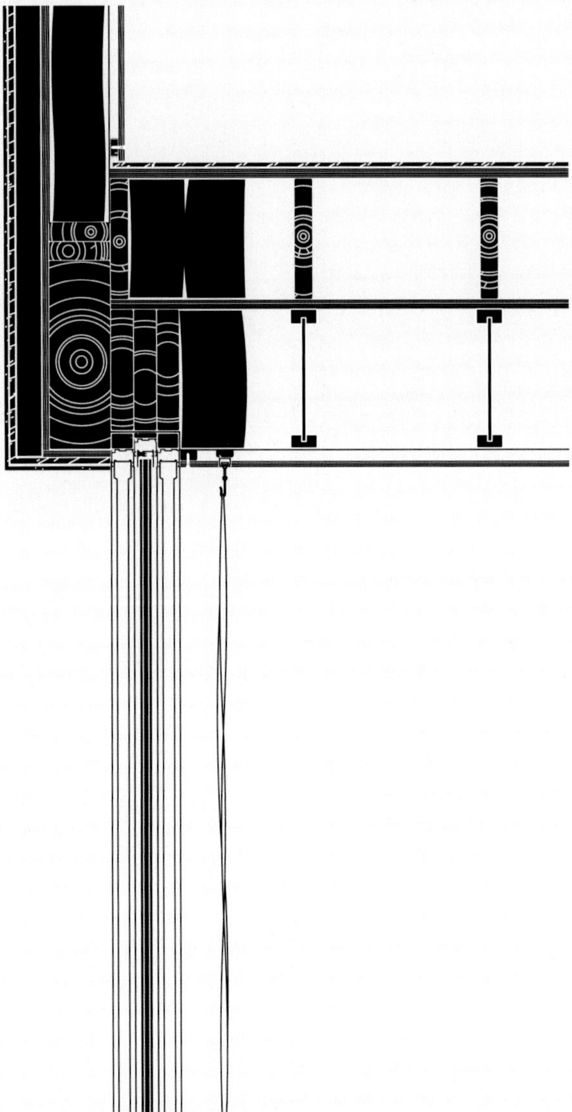

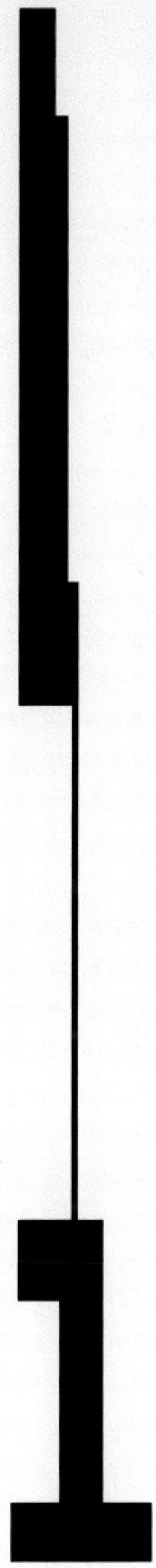

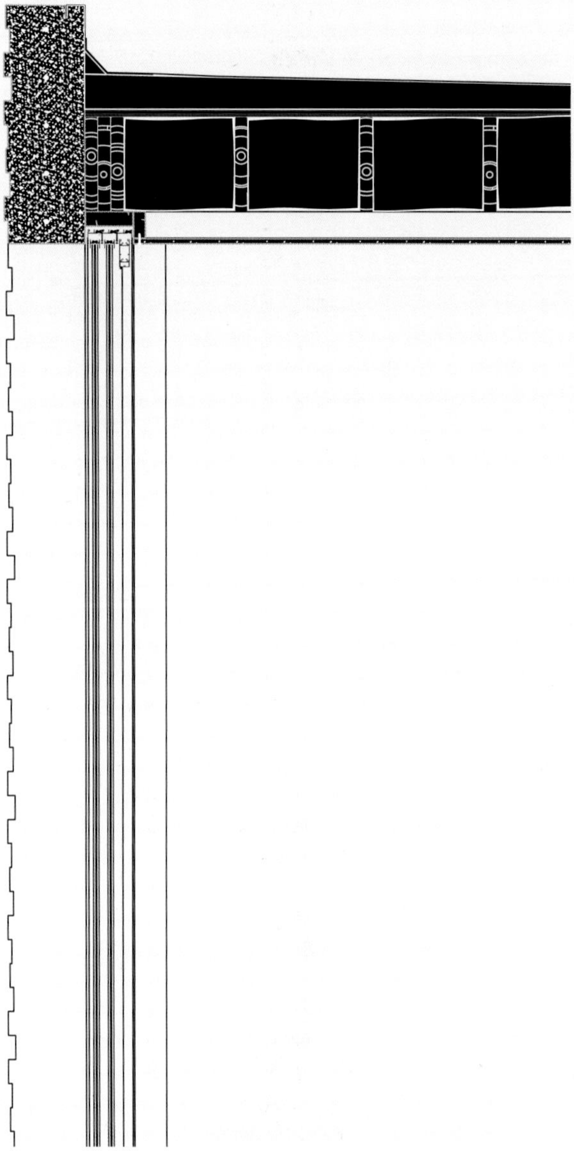

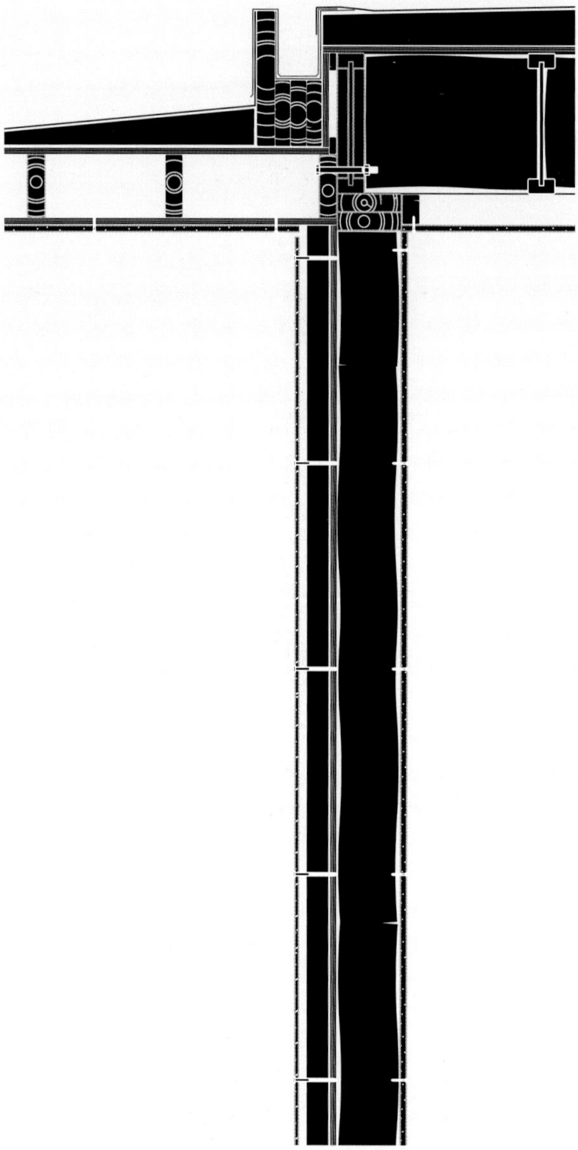

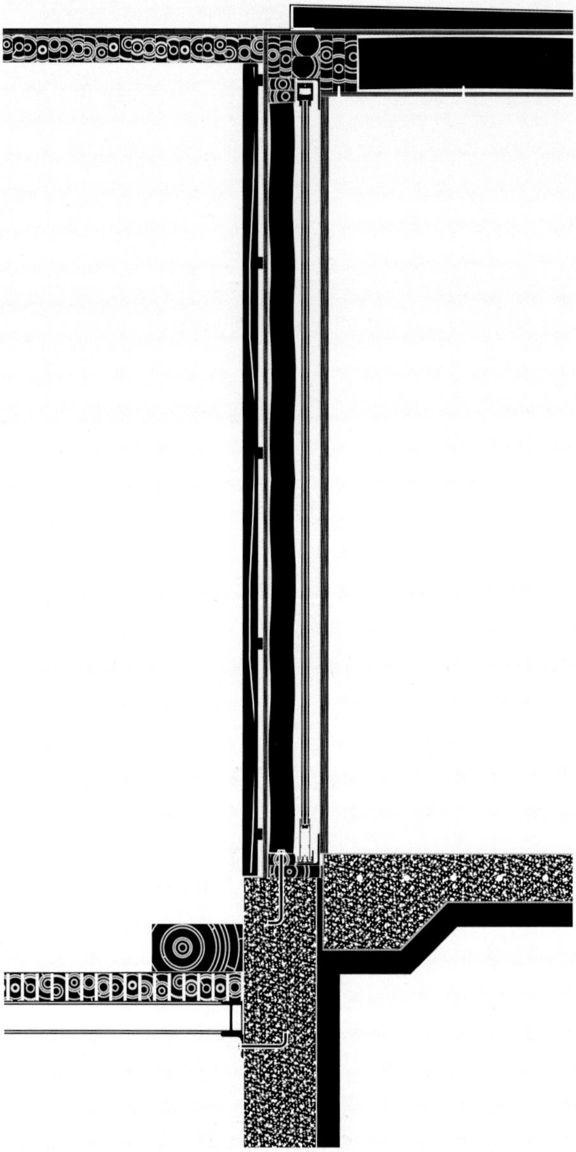

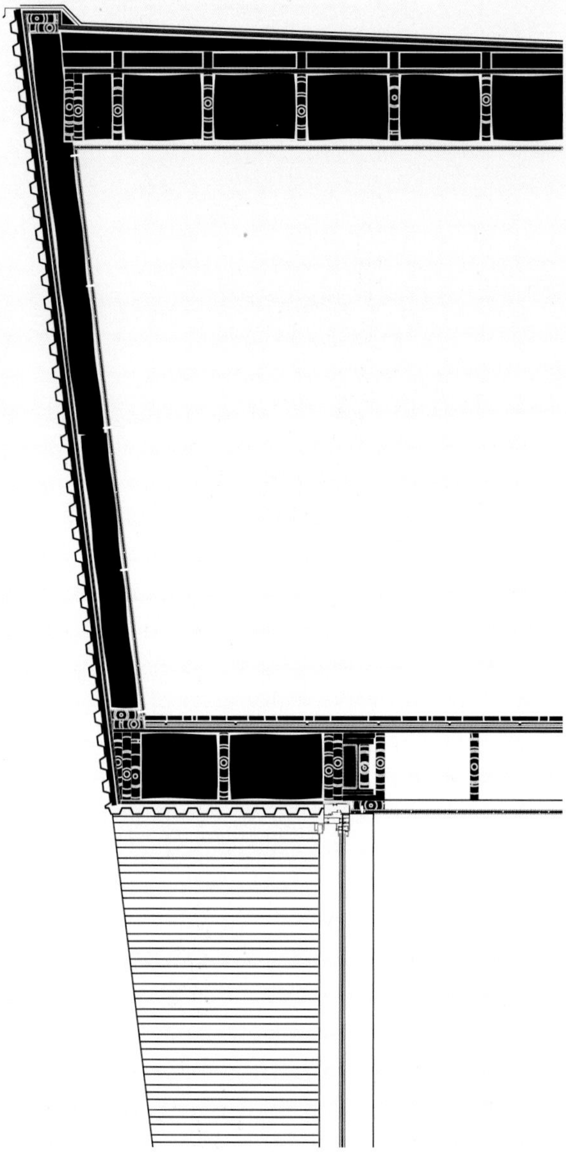

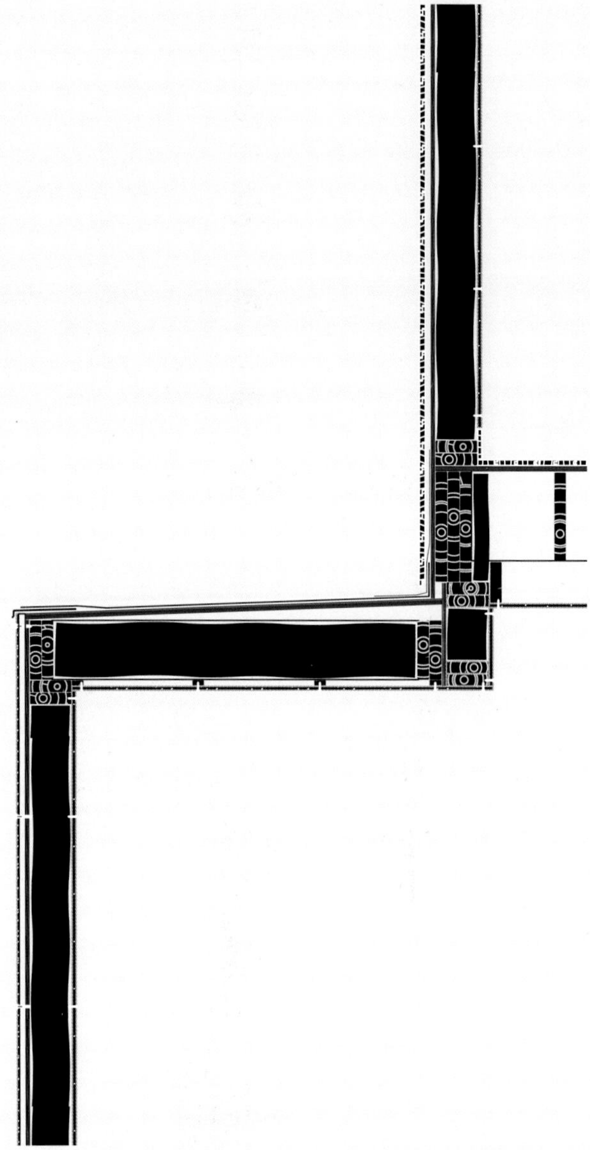

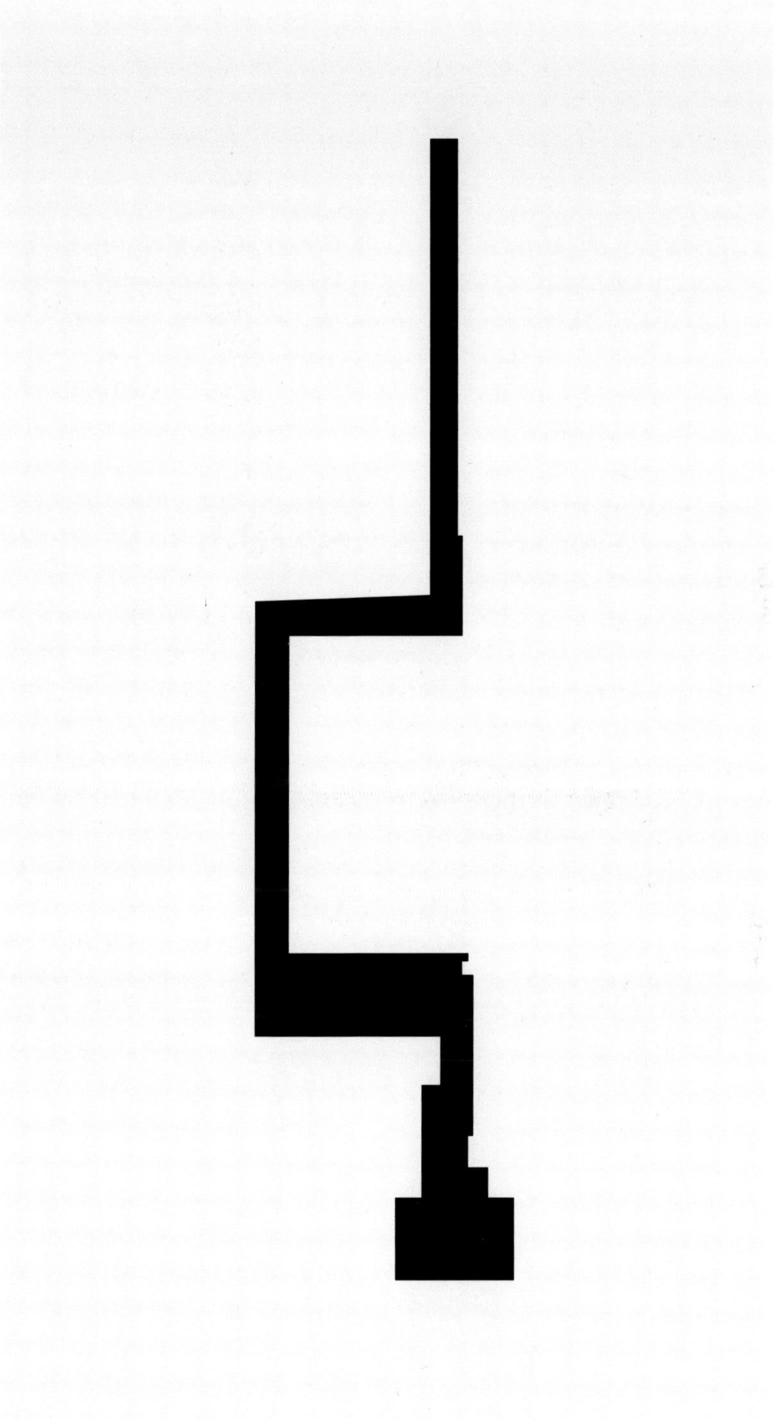

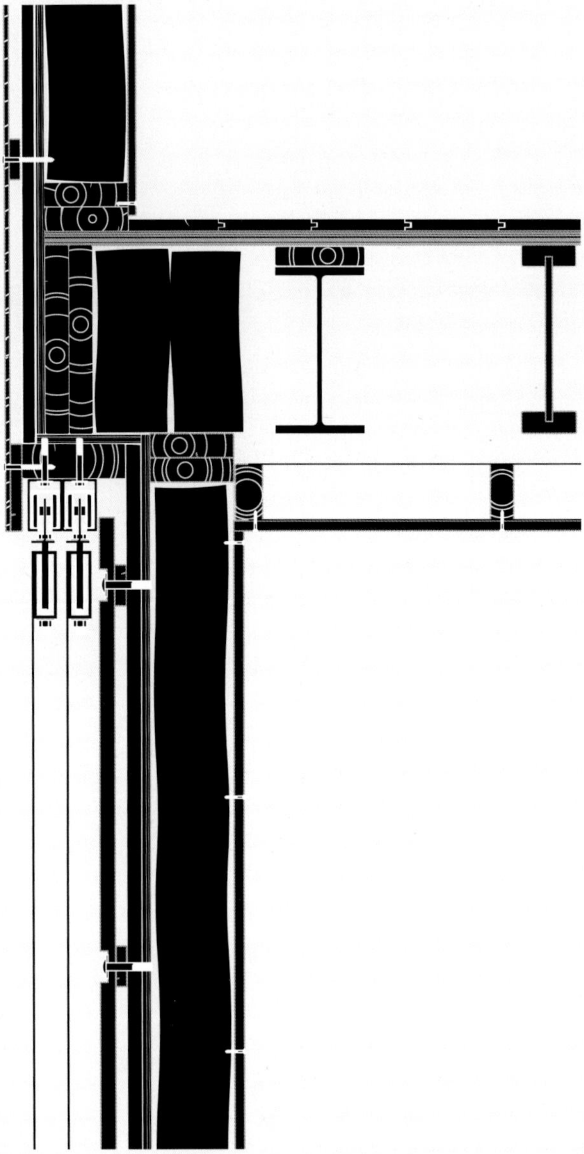

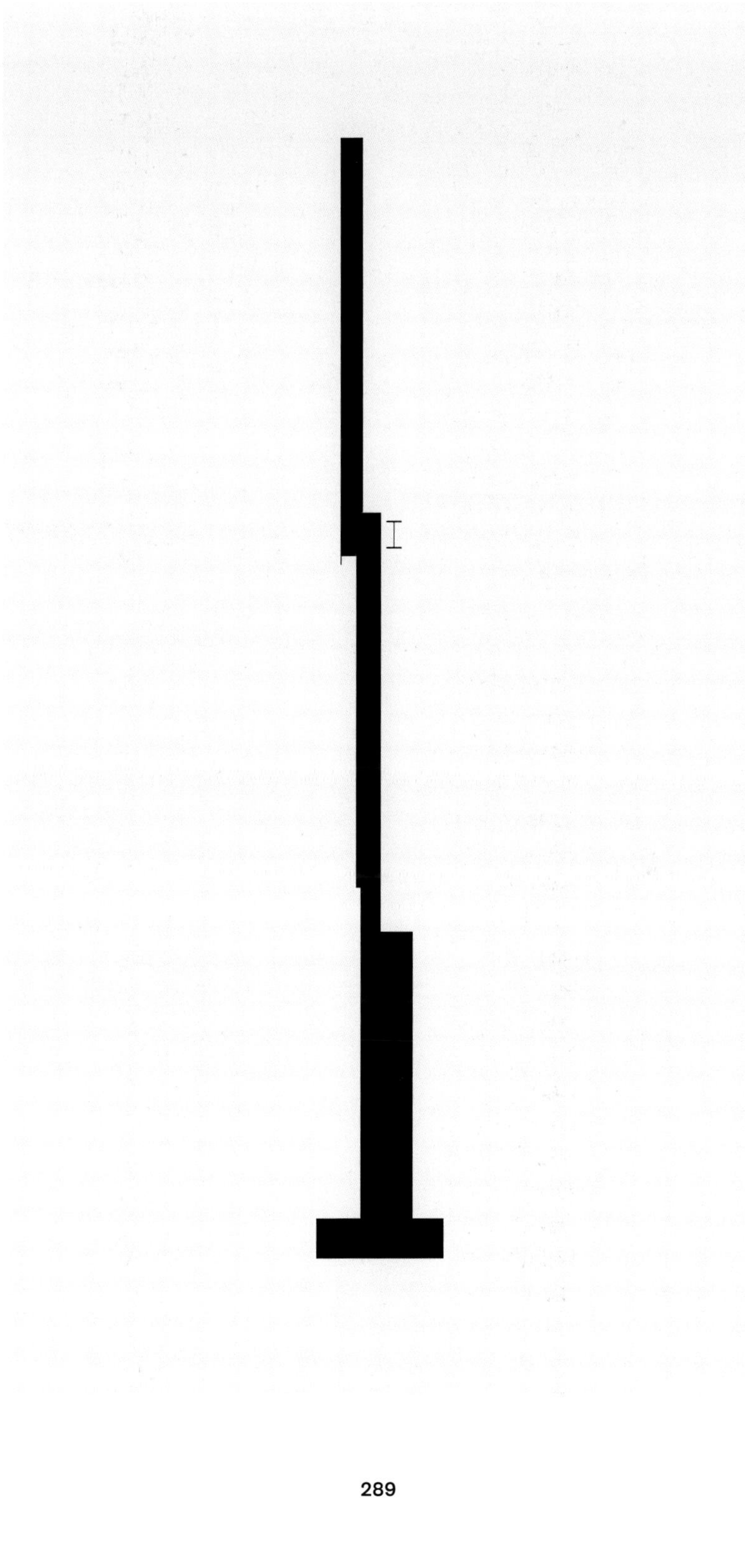

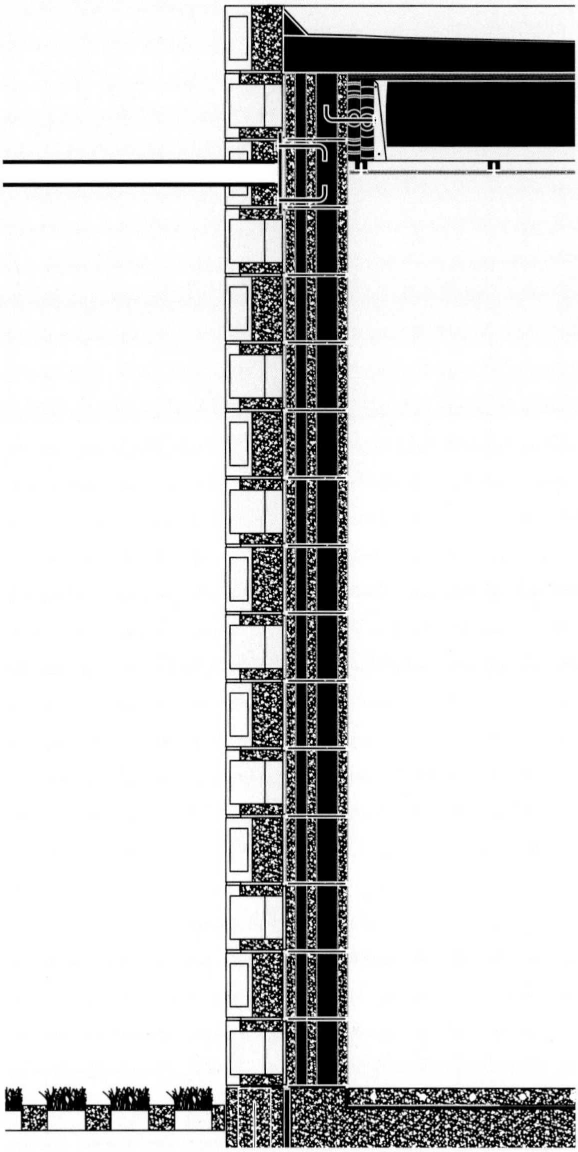

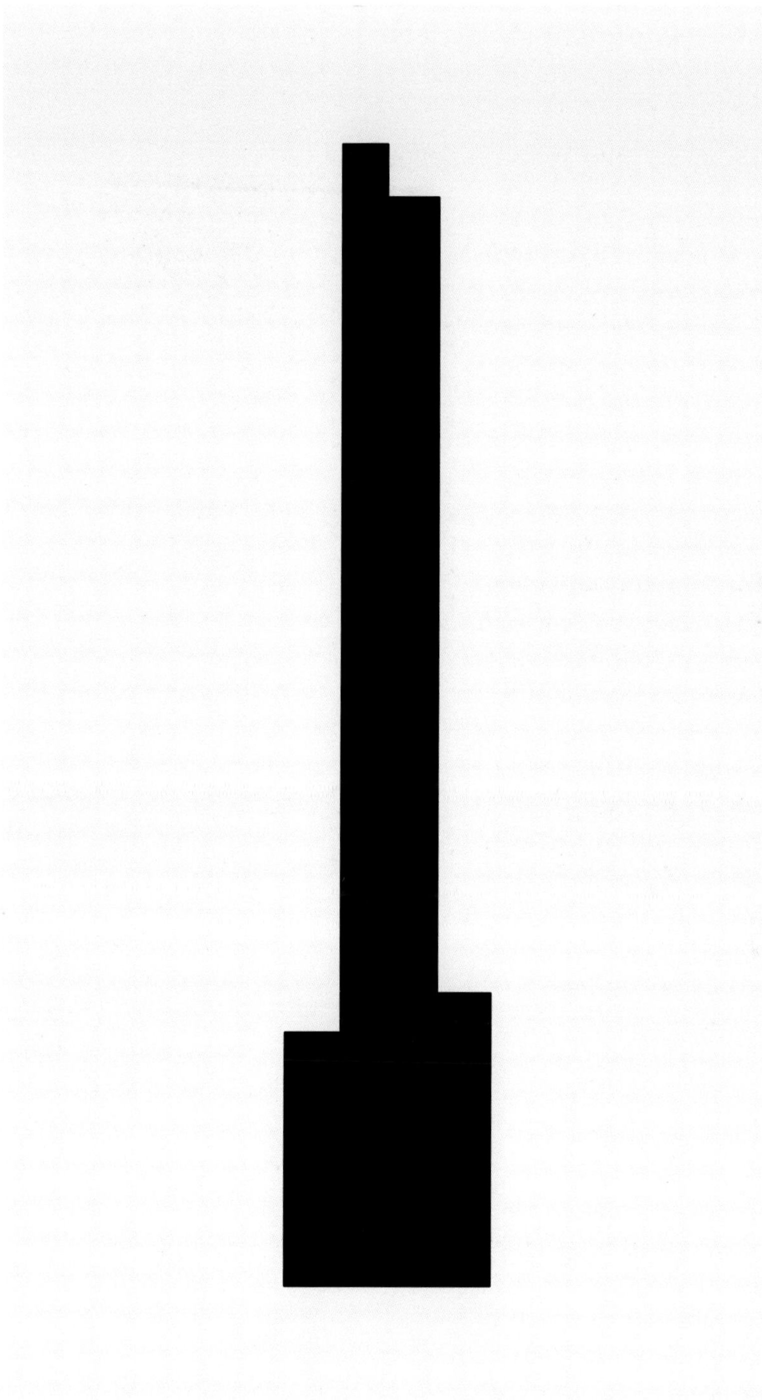

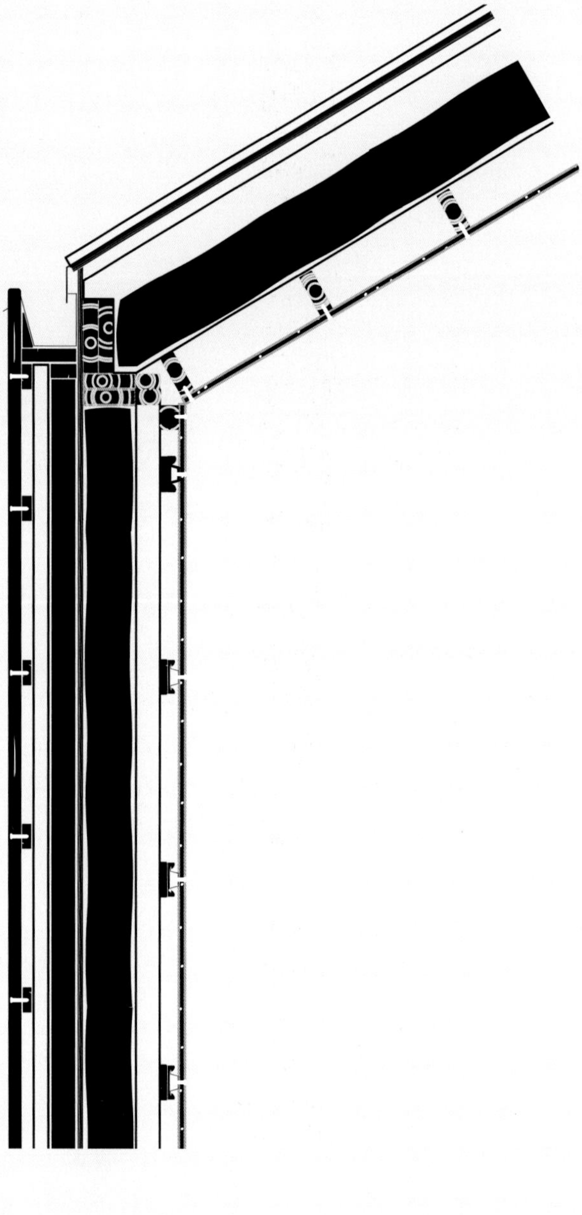

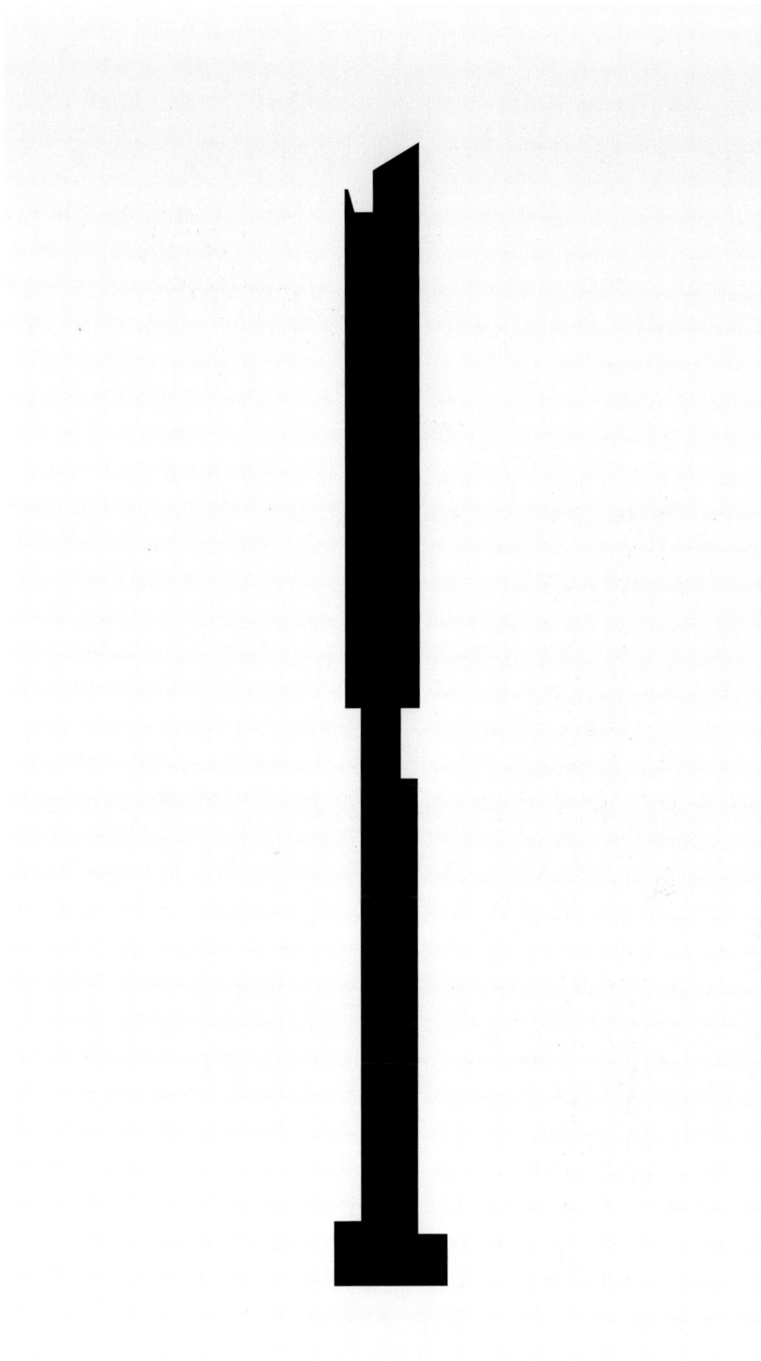

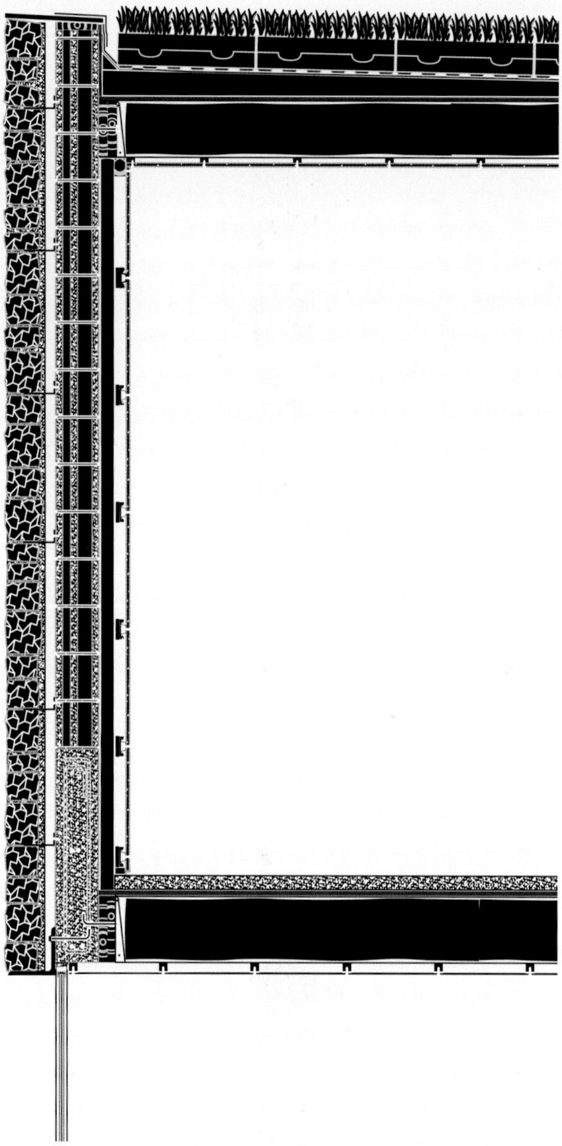

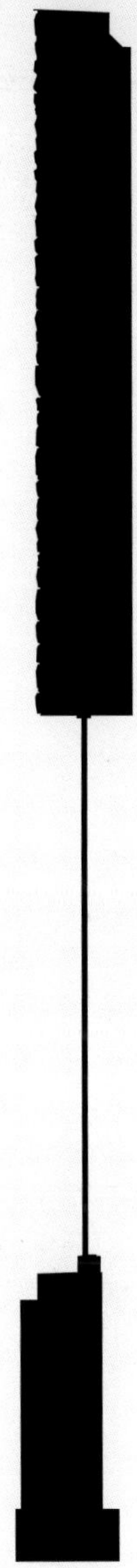

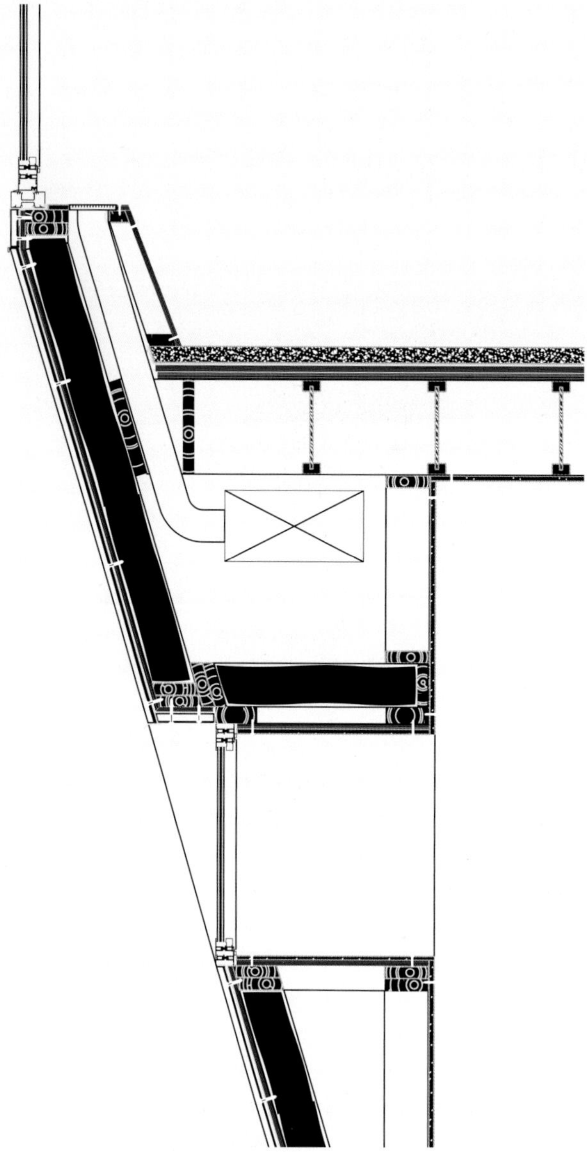

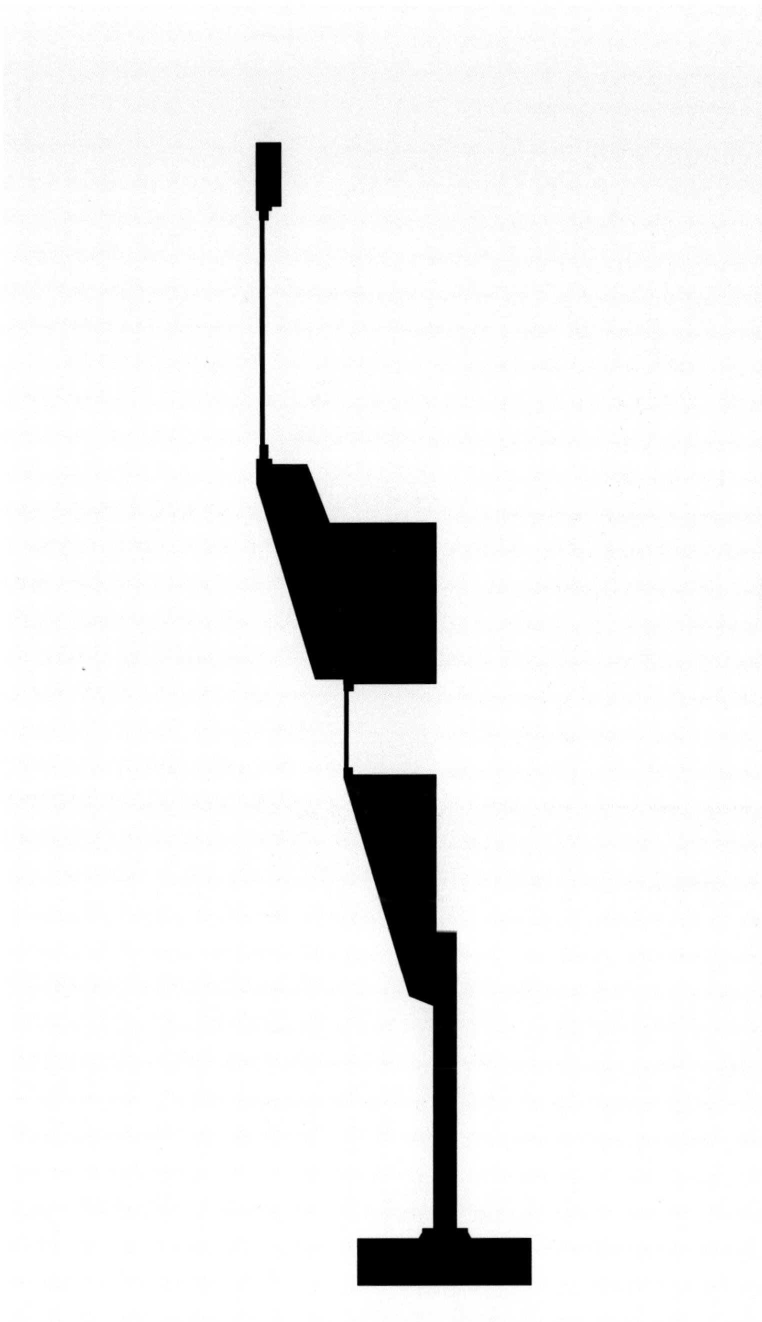

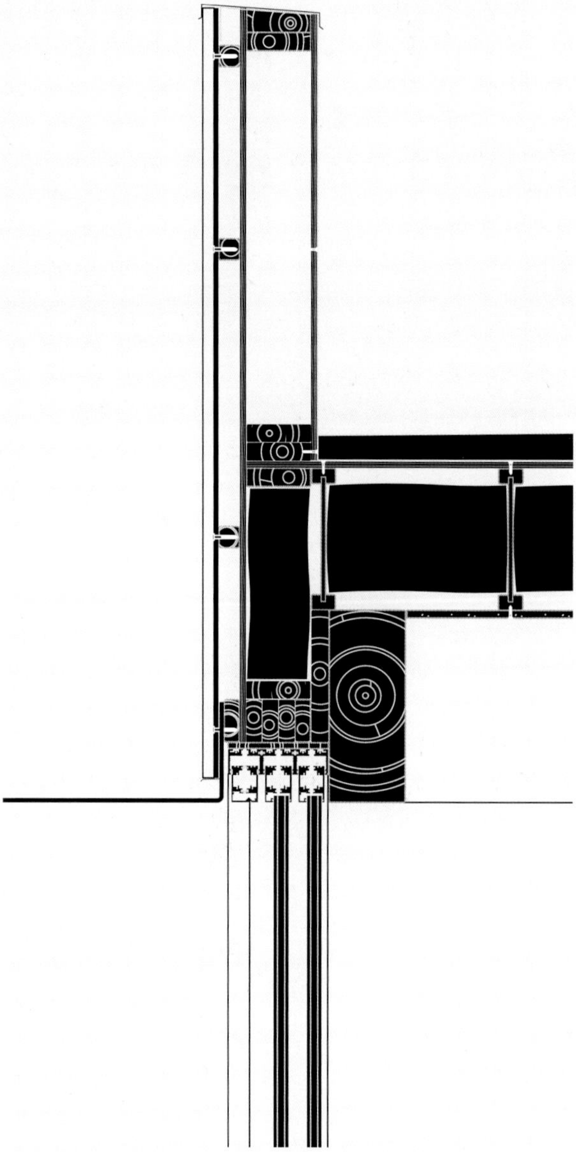

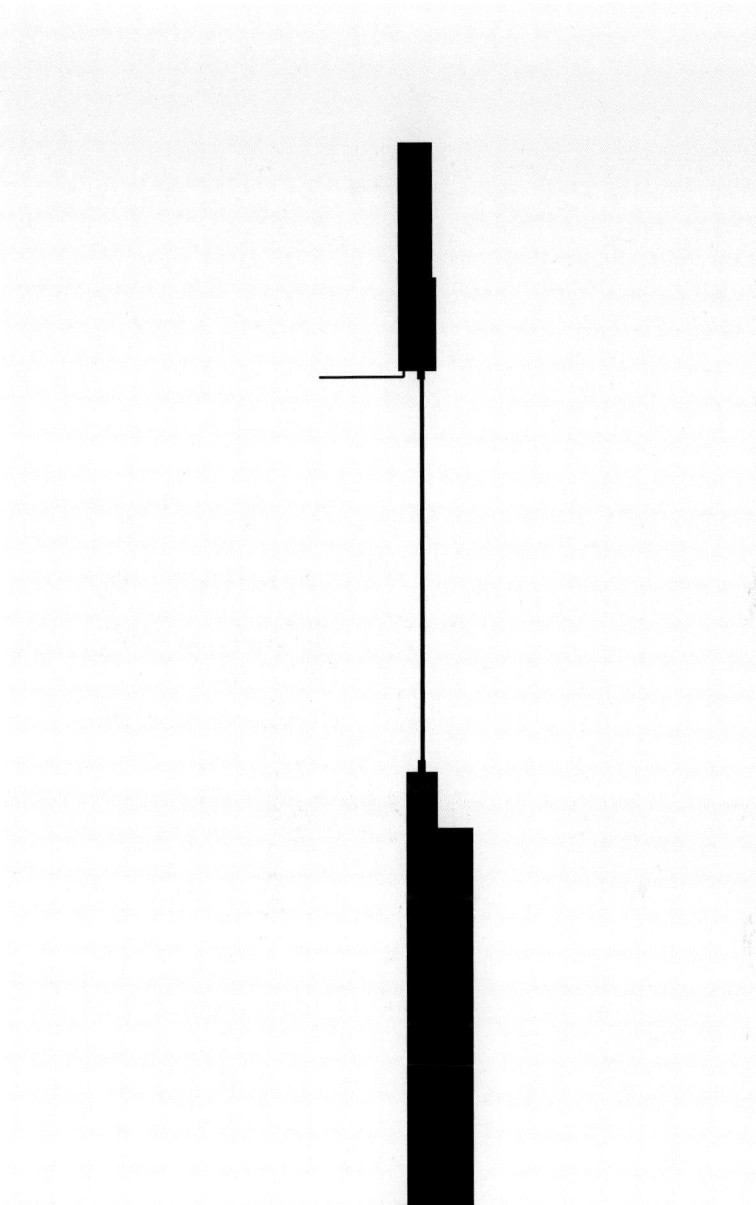

THIRTEEN WAYS
by Thomas de Monchaux

A House of One Shape

Stella and David are at home in their work. They live with it. Their small home, down a country-road-feeling driveway of respectable length in a lightly wooded stretch of the Hudson Valley, greets you with the most welcoming blank wall you have every seen. Pull up at night and your headlights illuminate it like a drive-in's movie screen, just as the beneficent film projector casts the lovers' kiss, silvery and numinous, across the dark piazza in Giuseppe Tornatore's 1988 *Cinema Paradiso*. The blank wall is friendly because it angles back: in the drawing of the floor plan, it looks like the business end of a scalpel. And indeed the whole of the house has the narrowness, the fine edges, the shine of a knife. But without the menace. Or maybe with just enough of the menace. The angle is welcoming because it tilts away, just a little, like your friend presenting a cheekbone for a peck of greeting; or like a half-bow from someone proper. It is an angle not of incidence but of deference. It sets up a procession within: with a signature LEVENBETTS right-trapezoidal shape to its floor plan, each room, depending on whether you enter it from its narrow or broad end, encloses you or opens out around as you move through it. You are embraced and released. No room is neutral. No room is impassive as you pass through it. The angled walls are, but for doors at one end or another, opaque; the parallel walls are, for the most part, walls of glass.

The interiors are as trim and snug and cedar-feeling as the sleeping quarters of a canal boat fresh from the drydock. But the place that feels most like home is, strangely, mostly right beside, right outside, the house: the covered porch, the first trapezoid in that procession of rooms, just behind that cinematic end wall, but without the enclosing glass; and even more, somehow, the patches of gravel, of swept and beaten earth, of low grass, just near, all around. Like the triangle—really the extreme trapezoid—of the headlight beam, or of the projector beam, each of these rooms beams some figurative light through the lens of its glass walls, out into the semi-domesticated landscape. To linger outside it is to be within it.

A Square House

Every home is a castle, of course. But what makes a home a castle, or a castle a home, is not always clear. This particular house is not what you think. It seems at first, brooding in cast concrete at the edge of its clearing in a wooded vale, like a redoubt. The most well-defended place can become, of course, a prison cell. "One of the essential characteristics of a bunker is that it is one of the rare modern monolithic architectures. While most buildings are embanked in their terrain by their foundations, the casemate is devoid of any, aside from its center of gravity, which [...] is the reason for our frequent discovery of certain upturned or tilted works, without serious damage [...] as a shipwrecked submarine on a beach." That is from the famous 1975 essay by Paul Virilio, based on photographs that he took, between 1958 and 1965, of fortifications and artillery emplacements along the coasts of the English Channel and the North Sea, left over from the Second World War. That word casemate—it might have been the contribution of a copyeditor to a 1994 English edition—is deeply speculative in its etymology. It might mean, from French from Italian from Latin, a house of woven mats, a house of reeds—casa-matta—in the sense of a hunting blind: and so from the carbines and fragile shelter of the hunter, we get the deep and tomb-like embrasures of the artilleryman. The house of straw becomes the house of stone. Canopy becomes cave. Matta also connotes the pliancy of reediness, and so of feebleness, and so, in an older English vernacular, of weakness or illness, and thus: Madhouse. Or—you can hear murder in mate—it might mean the house of death. Or, by the most charming and most apocryphal attestation, casemate might have something to do with the apotheosis that is checkmate—something of a nonsense word in English that resembles the phonemes of the words in Persian that signify, in the endgame, the king is amazed. The king, of course, not in his castle. But in his square house.

The lines that matter in chess are not the edges of the 64 squares of the square board, but the lines of movement between them: trajectories of vision and motion that build the story of the game. So it is with the Square House. Try to look at it and you find you can only look through it: aligned openings in tall glass send your gaze from the vale through the house to the woods beyond. The kitchen counter—slender and suspended, one sink indoors and one outdoors, in a state of permanent departure and arrival—reminds your eye to see through this building. This is in part because this house is less monolithic than sedimentary: not pushing into its hill like Virilio's submarine but cast into its contours in—seemingly, craftily, artfully—dozens, hundreds of fine layers, the layers suggested by the horizontal board forms that leave their grain on the outer walls. Inside, the floor steps up and down, like compressed earth on either side of tree roots. Inside, it is a glass house. Inside, walls are plastery and white. As your eyes adjust, they are drawn to every instance of varying texture and relative reflectivity; to every white-on-white profile; to every disc and every dot, on those pale walls. They are vents, panels for the projector, speakers, gadgets, face-plates, grilles, sliders, buttons, carefully-chosen old-fashioned plunger switches—everything that measures, calibrates, conditions, adjusts, accommodates. All the pawns in the game. See them and they are all you see. The Square House is also the House of Switches, manifesting out of all that white, a flock of small attending angels.

A House without Walls

The Primitive Hut is a dwelling that, invariably, all architects visit. It's Architecture 101. Up goes the slide: a 1755 engraving by Charles Eisen that serves as the frontispiece for the second edition of a book by a French Jesuit abbot, Marc-Antoine Laugier, which has the irresistible title—in full—of: *An Essay on Architecture; in which Its True Principles are explained, and Invariable Rules proposed, for Directing the Judgment and Forming the Taste of the Gentleman and the Architect, With regard to the Different Kinds of Buildings, the Embellishment of Cities, And the Planning of Gardens*. The engraving shows a fairly refined primitive—four trees, like four big columns, have obligingly grown in foursquare position; their living boughs have been bent towards each other at a tidy pedimentary angle; and braced by further sticks and twigs, they produce a woodsy house-sized facsimile of a humble Doric-order temple of ancient Greece. Laugier was an early exponent of neoclassicism—a kind of reining in and ordering of what he saw as the grotesque excesses of the previous century of the late Renaissance Baroque, especially for houses of worship: all those curves and swerves in which, he thought, the simple truths of the old way had gone astray. The Primitive Hut has no walls. Rain would fall through its patchy roof.

A pine forest is an array of straight and parallel lines, crossing the horizon, aligned with the axis mundi: earth to sky. No roof here, either. The leaf canopy in such a forest is not a plane. There is no canopy, really, but a cloud of still smaller straight lines: pine needles, all in crosshatch. But here in this forest is a deep floating plane, like the hull of a low-flying UFO, hovering in advance of a close encounter.

It's the roof plane of the Hillsdale House. The house is all roof—a roof whose outer edge sweeps and curves like any Baroque line. From inside the house, the aligned canopy and foundation curves turn everything you see into a panorama, a cyclorama, a wraparound vision. But it's all columns, too—the slenderest of them like pins, needles, pine needles. Their foreground presence disappears into all those lines in the panoramic background. Imagine the engineering and point load and cantilevers. All is principles, rules, judgement, taste. As orderly as a Doric temple. As the poet said: noble accents, and lucid, inescapable rhythms. Yet imagine the mazy and meandering path of a wanderer between them: all curlicue and Rococo.

Surprising rectangular courtyards, in some kind of pinwheel pattern beyond obvious grids, most smaller than what we think of as rooms, pierce the canopy like blown-out pixels: prisms of outside, brought within. The outside comes inside. Pieces of wilderness, not bent into building like the living boughs and branches of the canopy of the primitive hut, but somehow still wild. If A House of One Shape half-domesticates the adjacent landscape, here the wilderness comes home, and brings its wildness—dirt, light—with it.

Charles Eisen's engraving is out of time. In the foreground is an apparent goddess. Is she a muse? A dryad? With calibrated calipers encompassed in her hand, perhaps she is Architecture herself? She directs the attention of a cherub-like observer, the first little enrollee in Architecture 101, to the Primitive Hut in the background, stage right. And yet she reclines not on mossy banks, but on the ancient ruins of a stone temple, fluted Corinthian Composite columns and all. It is as if all has been lost. As if we were not at the start but long past the end, and trying to begin again.

A House in a Grid

There is a difference between shelter and enclosure. Not all that shelters also encloses. Not all that encloses also shelters. A cell can offer a particular kind of liberation, or the opposite. Between only a patch of shade on the ground and whatever casts that shade from above—the moving shadow under a bird in flight, the green light under a forest canopy, the indecipherable scintillations under a bough of bougainvillea—there is projected a space, a place, a room, a house of a kind. Even if only for a moment. Conversely, the pool of light from a lantern at the end of a road—that too, is a kind of open shelter. Warmth and light; or an emanation of cool conditioned air on a midsummer's day, whether from an unsustainable mechanical marvel in freon, or from a misty column of evaporation from a pool or well—these too offer shelter without limits. Without ceiling or wall.

Here is a house where shelter and enclosure are distinct. It's a Cartesian grid, something like a chessboard, of twenty five squares, projected up into prismatic volumes. But it's a shifted grid that's gone a bit adrift, with a different meter along its x and y directions. It is like the Square House because it is square. It is like the House without Walls because there is a forest of surprisingly slender columns and a seemingly floating roof plane overhead. It is like the House for the Next Site because, from a more central volume peripheral volumes have been unfolded or pulled like drawers from a dresser—two of them bedrooms, the beds looking out and away from the core, addressing the night. In the center of the center volume, one of Stella and David's signature pop-ups has somehow popped back down to the ground floor, enclosing bathrooms, laundry, things mechanical and watery. This volume, like the pop-up from the Houses in Five Shapes, is pill-profiled in plan, two arcs capping a rectangle, and so is all the more like the conning tower of a Paul Virilio shipwrecked submarine on a beach.

There must be, even all the way up here in New York State's Hudson Valley, some California dreaming. Craig Ellwood, Rafael Soriano, Pierre Koenig—especially that last master of the Case Study Houses, author of their epitome, Case Study House 22 at 1635 Woods Dr, West Hollywood, California 90069—would recognize the projected grid of slender steel; the finessed intersections, the knife-sharp lines, the paper-thin planes.

Between the regular square perimeter of the shelter and the irregular profile of the enclosure is an arrangement of patios and decks; grilles and grids and loggias and porches—liminal, littoral, blurring, blending. The edge also unmarked. Below, between the slender columns, the slender tree trunks in the surrounding glade, the prospect is no sea of lights over downtown Los Angeles, no Laurel Canyon, but a gentle slope. From which the house, along its broadest porch, cantilevers and arises—dissolving, just slightly, from ground to sky, from solid into air. Here is a house unbounded, without beginning or ending. Here is an open house.

A House of Lines

Most true beauty is accidental. Or at least incidental. Traditional agricultural and light industrial buildings, in farmhouses and outbuildings from Eastern Pennsylvania, up along the Hudson Valley, across the mountains to coastal Maine, sprawl with add-ons—enclosed porches, attached single-pitch sheds—called els. Often you see in them this vernacular detail: the housewright has realized that if the stairs are outboard of the floor plates, you don't lose interior square footage at both levels, and if you don't box in the space above or below the stair, but clad the angled soffit below and sloping ceiling above, you can cantilever the stair without any additional foundation, and you don't have that much more air to heat or cool—thus the typology, paradoxical, of the enclosed interior stair. An inadvertently radical parallelogram angling up some four-square volume. Here it is at A House of Lines: a long black eel of a house in which that angled ascent triggers, somehow, the back half of the house to raise itself up to address the horizon.

The volume that contains this stair is the eelier el of the house, he skinny sidecar or the long tail that, in classical modernist arrangement, contains what Louis Kahn called the serving space, versus the served space of the living and dining rooms below, the bedrooms above: long hallway closet, half bath, laundry room, pantry, refrigerator, upstairs bathrooms north and south—all the machines and routines of backstage life. Onstage and backstage order and disorder each other. When you are inside one half of the house, along its very long axis, you are outside the other half—even as both halves are both sheltered by the same roof. To live here is always to cross an invisible barrier. Along the other and wider bay of the house: the great table, the hearth, the scholarly desk—the ceremonial altars of a certain kind of domestic life. As at a Square House, the ground inside steps up and down, bringing you that much further into the refuge of the earth, into the idea of the air. Below: two steps up across polished concrete, the living area at the end of the long approach. Above: two steps up, across a narrow slot atrium—a passage just long enough for a breath and three heartbeats—that upper bedroom. These steps are a different material, something translucent or pearlescent, to let you know that even under that sheltering roof you are still, just a little, stepping up into the night sky.

Maybe the first work we do to the earth is furrow it. We trace and worry parallel lines of planting and sowing. Lines that grade the land or align to its contours. The cladding of a House of Lines is furrowed, too—like the enclosed exterior stair, it's pragmatic: the corrugations that add stiffness to sheet material in metal or composite. But like the horizontal striations, the board forms for cast concrete that evoke the sedimentary imagination of the Square House, these lines on the House of Lines send you back out into the land, back out to a thousand horizons. Earth outside, water inside. In the bathroom, flat bars of aluminum, slender but deep like the figure of the whole house itself, constitute a carriage in support of a single porcelain sink. Like designers Alison and Peter Smithson at the Hunstanton School in England in 1954—ground zero of the postwar New Brutalism—Stella and David have left only the heavy sink without its decorous countertop, and open to view, the pipes and pipe trap and gaskets, the supply cables, the valves, the unconcealed backstage, in all its intentional accidental beauty.

A House and a House

The only way to change something is to make it more like itself. This was an early house by Stella and David. Maybe the earliest, as built. Maybe there was a lot of Marcel Breuer in it. Or early Marcel Breuer, anyway. Back when he worked in wood, he was the architect who brought the modern house to America, in the form of the House in the Garden. That's the name that stuck for his 1949 exhibition house in the sculpture court of the Museum of Modern Art. It was the smartest and the coziest notional abode, at least for a season, in all of midtown Manhattan, before some Rockefellers bought it and moved it upstate to—naturally—the Hudson Valley. It's there, something about Breuer, in the First House, there in the pale cladding in cedar, and white-trimmed windows above the masonry base (It was rubble stone for Breuer— like all that white wooden trim in his own early American work, an influence of New England on the old Hungarian modernist—but smooth cast concrete here at a House and a House).

It's there in the twice-diagonally-corner-folded almost-butterfly roof on the House and a House; and in the actual butterfly roof, valley-folded along the cross axis of the long volume, of a House in the Garden. Breuer had a technical—or, rather, technical-sounding—name for this configuration, which was bi-nodal. One long line, two wings. The house raises up at its extremities: at one end, the master suite as a kind of mezzanine perched over the single-car garage below; far at the other end, nursery and guest or maid's room. This at least means you can have a double-pitched roof—good for the Northeast—but not look like an old-fashioned-looking housey-house. Other than the bedrooms and bathroom, in Breuer's house, interior partitions only went up part of the way: kitchen cabinets and other wooden volumes making sculptural boxes within the bent box of the larger house itself. Houses, almost, within houses. It's the same at the House and a House: so many folds and deflections, but a spine of sixteen wooden chests, tall as walls but not walls, broad as doors but not doors—somehow holding, from within, the line of all the house. Nothing else is quite parallel in this house. The walls angle about in plan, but only just. As the poet said: the beauty of inflections.

The idea behind Breuer's House in the Garden was that, since the butterfly roof was low at the center and high at the ends, you could build it in stages; you could build the low middle first and add that higher master suite and garage a little later. This was a very wartime home-front idea. A very 1949 idea. Austerity and abundance, all just around the corner from each other. But here at the House and a House, they really did it. The House became another House. They came back some years later and added to the high end. Two more bedrooms above and a garage below. But not seamlessly. A very clean scar in the form of a glass bridge to the new volume at one end. Below, a breezeway-driveway-carport like the one at the House with Three Yards at the new longer structure's new center of gravity. Another house you can drive through. Above this carport, a soffit pale and plastery like a second white sky, midwinter. And all the cedar stained black. As the poet said: The blackbird sat, in the cedar-limbs.

A House with Three Yards

The East End of Long Island, like the same island's northeast coast before that, like the southern coasts of Rhode Island and Maine before that, is where a certain old idea of a great American house once resided. And sometimes lives still. A house so big you call it a cottage. A summer house built, all stone and oak, to withstand the harshest Nor'Easters of winter. A country house to think about in the city. A house you use for thirty five days a year and keep in the family for a century. Ceremonially opened for one season and closed for another. Carraway's house in chapter one: "the house, a weather-beaten cardboard bungalow at eighty a month." Gatsby's house next door, in chapter nine: "that huge incoherent failure of a house once more." A house where summer is always starting and always ending. A house of memory and a house of anticipation. A house where you are always past the end and must always start again.

Here is not there. Not quite. Not really. Sure, it's a big house. There's a bunkhouse in the basement, after all. But it's on a suburban lot, neighbors' nightlines and all. And it eludes its own bigness. Where you expect volume, you find surface. Where you expect enclosure, you find openness. All the grounds are purpose-driven, not purely decorative—so three back yards. Maybe this is a new kind of Shingle Style. Like those old houses in that style, this is a house of wings. Three radial wings that make, from above, a stellar figure. Look closely at the layout of the ground floor and you see that—by topology if not typology—it's the same as a Garden in a House: over here, the two-car garage; over there, across a breezeway-driveway that loops through the center of the star, is all the rest: a hint of the courtyard suggested in the way the second volume angles in plan to cup the swimming pool that completes the composition. The pool like the fountain in a courtyard, like the rill in the walled paradise garden in the pleasure palace where the king is amazed. Checkmate.

Really, this is three slender houses—each house, each wing, right at the median American bungalow size of 2500 square feet—in convergence. And at the center of their convergence the whole is not closed but open: below, that breezeway driveway, where you slide without undue ceremony into the house itself; above, an outdoor room almost the full width of the wing, stepped up like a little amphitheater, to a further deck on the roof. Like that amphitheater stepped up to the sky, another one below down to the earth, illuminating that basement bunkhouse—like the two steps up into the night in the House of Lines, the two steps down into the day. Exposed conduit against fine finishes: high and low, rough and smooth, on and off. At the knuckle of the bend on the ground floor, at the heart of the house, not a great hall but—somehow neither onstage nor offstage, but sensibly near the kitchen and just downstairs from the bedrooms—the laundry room. Cool clean cotton, the feel of summer all through the year.

As with the Shingle Style, what matters here is pattern, texture: gray on gray. Here in this flat landscape, the furrows and parallels and contours that Stella and David build into their houses are turned vertical: board forms for cast concrete in the basement and ground- floor plinth, the seams between vertical bond-patterned cementitious boards, the vertical grain a kind of memory of a grove of pines, faraway here in the old potato fields where they never were.

A Snail House

A brick is made to be lifted by one hand. A concrete block is made to be lifted by two. The breeze block is a structural masonry unit in concrete often admixed with cinder for lightness, perforated to further reduce its weight, allow the passage of air, or add decoration. It was a defining feature of mid-century modernist domesticity. But not the fancy mid-century modernism—those bespoke Case Study houses and labors of love from California to Connecticut. They were the signature, rather, of the Alexanders and the Eichlers—homes, mostly of the lawned-over deserts of the American coastal and inland West, known not by the names of their designers but of their developers. Breeze blocks added durable but semi-see-through and graphically-exciting partitions and porches—where once might have been carpentered cabinetry or work in wrought iron—

to modern-styled tract subdivisions of the 1950s, 1960s, and 1970s. Once, maybe, the breeze block signified a forward-looking break with not only the look but the received meaning of the suburban house: not a colonial or a ranch from Sears or Levitt, but something better, sharper, finer, newer—something with a hint of Aerospace or Hollywood. Now, of course, it has somehow flipped back to signify just what it once seemed to resist: oldness, primness, ponderousness, staidness, unhipness of twentieth-century suburbanity as it was critiqued from within and without, from its very beginning. Anything but breezy.

A Snail House isn't exactly made of breeze blocks. But it isn't exactly not, either. Some kind of running bond pattern runs around it—where we might expect mortar it is solid, where we might expect cement it is void. But this screen, these breezy blocks, do exactly what such blocks usually don't: curve. A kind of radius-cornered hexagon has been unfolded, its opening calibrated to address—as the dot addresses the line above it in an exclamation point (!)—the linear volume of the double lap pool on its threshold. The whole composition looks from above like the figure of a key, a clavicle, still another cloister. Half of what's enclosed by this wall is courtyard; less than half is further enclosed—conditioned space, architects call it—by glass walls, some of which happen to slide, happen to be doors. Half of that conditioned half— the rest is a tight little core of services with a big watery shower—is the bed. A house for swimming and dreaming of swimming. A house for austerity and luxury, training and recovery.

Drawings are semi-see-through. As of this writing, the Snail House exists as a drawing, which in contemporary design practice tend to a kind of x-ray jellyfish translucency. Stella and David's drawings mostly don't, though: the solid is solid, the open is open. The cartographic line is there, and then not there. Once built, though, a Snail House will be a kind of drawing of itself: it will be more than most buildings an assembly of lines: a kind of wireframe that renders open those hunkered volumes that we expect to be heavy and solid—that radius- cornered unfolded hexagonal volume is the closest shape you might find in these pages to the geometry of the bunkers and escapements that fascinated Paul Virilio in his Bunker Archeology fortification documentation project of the late 1950s through the early 1970s. And yet the form is not heavy and closed but open and light.

In the caustic horror story that is John Cheever's much-anthologized 1964 tall tale, *The Swimmer*, an apparent critique of midcentury suburbanity is enacted by the writer, or by his doomed protagonist, who fancies to swim home through all the backyard pools of his area: "He seemed to see, with a cartographer's eye, that string of swimming pools, that quasi-subterranean stream that curved across the county." He completes the swim but the rest of the summer afternoon surreally takes the rest of the year, and by oneiric logic the swim ends in midwinter; and the swimmer, maybe both Ahab and Whale, having lost all to the water. The gift of a lap pool, like that of true Home, is the gift of venture and return, venture and return, of toes then fingertips, toes then fingertips, against the watery wall: of a place solid enough to propel and push you, a place constant enough to recognize and receive you.

A House-Shaped House

It is possible to say—and you know what I mean when I say—a house-shaped house: the triangle-over-square shape that is the shape of baseball's home base. The pediment-over-entablature shape that is the end facade of Laugier's Primitive Hut, of a Greek temple. The shape of Snoopy's kennel. Of a doll's house. Of a Monopoly house. The sort of housey-house that house-enthusiast Marcel Breuer, self- appointed futurist, couldn't allow himself—hence his insistence on the butterfly roof. Here are two house-shaped houses, aligned and shifted. One house for public life, one house for private life. A house without undue halls and enfilades. A house without undue procession. In the pitched profiles of the roof and ceiling, a valley overhead—a hidden butterfly pinned between two other pitches. Maybe one house is the guest, and one the host. In the two spaces defined by the end wall of one house and the notionally shifted side wall of the other house: two courtyards, or half-courtyards of a sort, each with only those two walls to suggest them. The shift turns linear symmetry into rotational symmetry. Many of Stella and David's houses make many moves—some like the House in Five Shapes are French Baroque. The House-Shaped House, like a pawn on a chess board, has just two moves to make. And it makes them. A move forward. A move that shifts a little to the side. Maybe these are two pawns, suspended in their own companionate checkmate.

A House in Five Shapes

Toward the middle of the 17th Century, one laboratory for the thinking and making of houses—grand ones—was the hôtel particulier of Paris. Louis Le Vau the archetypical architect of the era; the hôtels de Beauvais—68 rue François-Miron, 75004 Paris, the home of a royal mistress, typical of the social circle of these houses—and de Sully, not far away at 62 rue Saint-Antoine, 75004, are canonical examples. These places were paradoxes even in their name: hôtel from the Latin for a particular kind of hospitality, connoting welcomed strangers; particulier connoting not parts-versus-wholes but, in its time, privacy—so, your private place where you accommodate the public. Where you make strangers at home. This kind of house was a townhouse paradoxically disguised as a country villa, jammed by complex late-feudal social hierarchies and cultural customs into the city. Instead of grounds, a paved outer courtyard, and an unpaved inner courtyard, like a cloister, but called a garden—the house suspended between these two, entre cour et jardin, up against property lines and party walls. "Houses less beautiful than palaces," went the definition in a 1688 French treatise," and more beautiful than simple lodgings."

Certain paradoxes of the hôtel particulier also apply to the House in Five Shapes and its studies. The various versions of the house in these studies, too, are less beautiful than palaces and more beautiful—by a particular definition of beauty—than simple lodgings. They're a third to a half of the size of Stella and David's House with Three Yards in Amagansett, but they're of that scale and order. There are variations—an oval, a round-cornered triangle, a trapezoid. The trapezoid—the designers' favorite shape, surely—is the most finely developed: its lower level features a perimeter wall, partly a retaining wall, partly a kind of plinth for the trapezoidal volume and platform above; something about the unfurling geometry of that line retains a memory of the perimeter breeze block wall of the Snail House: a tight figure that has opened up. An unfurling; an opening hand. All iterations of the House in Five Shapes studies are courtyard houses: a triangle within a triangle, a circle within an ellipse (like the yolk of an egg), and in the trapezoidal variation—just as at the Hôtel de Beauvais—an arc-topped rectangle of a kind, symmetrical unto itself, asymmetrical and displaced from the centerline of an irregular perimeter. There is a paradox in this local symmetry, this global irregularity.

At the Hôtel de Beauvais, the perimeter figure is wild, a consequence of ancient property plats and immutable party walls. Order is carved out from this disorder, void from this figure. At the Trapezoid study, the symmetrical court is criss-cross to the symmetrical trapezoidal perimeter. For all the strong figures of these plan drawings, in both houses the revelation is in the cross-section. At the Trapezoid study, the earth slopes up through that courtyard, solving a way of moving and a way of seeing—not unlike the domestic amphitheater at the heart of the House with Three Yards. At Beauvais, the impossibility of a garden is solved by putting it up on the roof of the ground floor, adjacent to a pill-shaped pavilion that overlooks both it and the court on its other side, far below—like one of Stella and David's signature pop-up penthouses surveying its green roof, like the conning tower of a submarine shipwrecked on a beach. All this ingenuity in patterns and curves—a French Baroque against which architectural theorists like Marc-Antoine Laugier would pitch a new austerity, founded on the neoclassical ret-con of the Primitive Hut. At the hôtels and the studies, a complex life is folded into a complex place: within one scale and order of figure and ground, courtyard and perimeter, is—another paradox—a smaller scale and order; within privacy, publicity; inside the enclosure of the poché, sneaky pockets and chambers of assignation; into what seem only to be thick walls, rooms. Within closings, openings.

A Garden In a House

Cloister: a courtyard surrounded by a perimeter colonnade or arcade for promenade. Maybe a mazy medicinal herb garden in the middle. Dead center, a tiny pool like a birdbath or baptismal font. Monks and nuns. Or scholars. A dwelling place for people who do not live in houses—not sociably or neighborly as we think of those virtues—but in monastic and scholastic compounds; in which all daily routine is always already also ritual; in dormitories or cubicles like Le Corbusier's Le Cabanon cabin in Roquebrune-Cap-Martin, France. That cabin itself a miniature memory of the six-foot-wide domiciles in Corbusier's famous Brutalist priory at La Tourette, France. His own cloister at La Tourette suspended above a hillside courtyard—barely a court, barely a yard—that sloped away below, and so inaccessible but by pilgrimage and peripheral vision.

When in the first decades of the 20th Century, Princeton University looked to expand, they dropped the homely High Victorian Gothic, and invented something cooler and more pedantic—Collegiate Gothic. They sent their architect Ralph Adams Cram to look at the academical quadrangles of Oxford and Cambridge in the United Kingdom— themselves built in the image of the Catholic cloisters, many of whose ruins, thanks to some earlier king, were opened up and legibly plain to see all over the English countryside. Cram's gothic was stripped down but not austere, piquant and even charming in its details, sometimes abstracted in a way that knew about Art Deco; somehow scaleless and no matter how small, monumental; but also attentive to the daily routines of those students. With room to sprawl among the meadows made of drained swamps, Princeton's Collegiate Gothic was an architecture of pavilions, of long views, and the willful conjuring of a village scale, making with small cloisters surprising outdoor rooms.

In this way, Stella and David's Garden in a House—in the borough of Princeton, ten minutes from the University—for all of its international style flat roof and white walls and boxy shapes, for the fact that it is a corrugated white metal shed, it is Collegiate Gothic. It is organized around a square cloister, overlooked by five windows (one happens to also be a door) from a hallway, a staircase, the back of a kitchen, and, as they call it in real estate, a Great Room. Openings that turn all of the house into a kind of perimeter arcade—evoking not only the monastic cloister but the inward-looking and courtyard-facing Roman villa that was its typological antecedent. All windows are squares; all windows are set not to exterior alignments but to interior activities and ergonomics: Laugierian Principles, Rules, Judgements, Tastes—here apply. On the mostly blank walls, just as in the work of Cram, smaller and intricate details catch the eye: lights, outdoor faucets, a slot-like roof drain that is the most abstracted gargoyle in all of North America. In place of a rook-like tower it has one of the designers' signature moves—a pop-up, a box-on-a-box penthouse, with its maritime metal skin and rails, it's a conning tower for a landlocked Virilio submarine—and so the house is also a garden in a machine.

Overlooking a green roof, in proportions it almost evokes a smaller version of Stella and David's own home, A House of One Shape, in upstate New York, and that house's own smaller pop-up. Up here, the two bedrooms at either end must be for the kids or guests. The parent's suite is down on the ground floor. There's a two-car garage down there too—albeit connected by an abstract arcade of a breezeway, not directly accessing the kitchen in the usual suburban way—and an outdoor room, a slab-paved patio, just behind. In this way, at 2,400 square feet almost exactly the average size, this couldn't be a more standard suburban American house. Except of course it is anything but that. But in this way, it is the essence of its place: a gothic dream dropped into a sprawling American suburban landscape, somewhere off of I-95.

Cloister doesn't necessarily mean spiritual any more than Courtyard. You can hear in it the word closer, and—through French—the word key. (Clavicle, the key-shaped collar bone.) Cloister meant, originally, the part of the priory or monastery that was locked away, shut to the outside. In a world of Open Houses, the Garden in a House is a Closed House. It does block the sightlines—so suburban—of the neighbors. And yet walk inside, toward that inner courtyard, toward the light: don't you feel yourself opening up?

A House for the Next Site

Is a dream of a house also a dream of the road? Maybe somewhere in our minds or hearts there is an intersection between restfulness and restlessness. It is of course a privilege to choose to romance the road—the road can look so much better when you know it leads you comfortingly back to your door. And yet there's something about accommodations that are somewhere between stable and mobile: the sleeper car; the trim sailboat snug belowdecks; the VW camper; the old tricked-out tuned-up econo-line van; the contemporary fantasy of some van-life cabin-porn endless-summer of a domicile that can't be tied down. The prairie schooner. The canal boat. The gypsy caravan in a fairy tale. But also the hardcore pickup with the fiberglass backpack; the Toyota Hi-Lux with the big cab; the aluminum airstream recreational vehicle and trailer; the specific airstream trailer that Marcel Breuer literally built into a modern wooden house in the Hudson Valley; the cushicle; the Apollo LEM.

Some of it is the American dream of machines: of dream homes that are somehow also dream cars; of gear and gadget; of bikes and boats; of pop-ups and fold-outs. That house-locked airstream in the Marcel Breuer house in the Hudson Valley was, of course the building's kitchen: machines in machines, metal in metal.

Here is a house that arrives. Not literally, but figuratively. And narratively. In all the ways that count. And once it arrives, it unpacks. The central figure of a central square—could it be it's about forty feet square, just like the Square House?—accommodates attachments, add-ons, gear. Those attachments, those accommodations, those adjustments, are all smaller squares and double-squares and demi-squares. They adhere to the central square, or somehow emerge from it like drawers on all sides from some impossible dresser. It is as if a tiny city square has been turned inside out: public life center-stage: ceremonies of eating and entrance. More private life is to be lived offstage in the superstructure pop-up and slide-out, big beds and kitchen islands addressing the landscape. This is the way that a certain type of vernacular house grew: the northeast or upper mid-west farmhouse with its els, its porches, its lean-tos. Plant the house somewhere different, and like a seed it would grow a different way.

Here is another black house. Stella and David once described the palette of the House of Lines as, "black, white, gray, and glow," the glow, in that case, the misty white sky mother-of-pearl of daylight through translucent polycarbonate panels. Before broad spectrums of interior paint color became technically possible and fashionable in America in the later 19th century, early interior palettes were based on the hues of doves and oysters. The oyster encapsulated within its own walls. The dove, the original homing pigeon from the deck of the ark—that boat with its own little house-shaped pop-up superstructure. The dove, the symbol of being released to travel and then choosing to return—sometimes with an olive branch. In some versions of the story they send a raven, too, up from the ark. That black bird doesn't always come back. A black house looks very old—the oldest garrison houses of New England, all pitch and resin; the now-fashionable but centuries-old Japanese charred-cedar finish of shou sugi ban. But they also look very new: sharp, engineered, technical, vehicular, powder-coated—stealth. Out in the country, blackness recedes a house deferentially into the land-scape, the landscape the bride to the house's groom, the dove to its raven. Every house is a shadow. Every house is a lantern at the end of the road.

A House with a Swerve

And you may find yourself, living in a shotgun shack. And you may find yourself, in a beautiful house. Already, maybe, you may find yourself finishing the line in your head: And you may tell yourself, this is not my beautiful house. It's those former Rhode Island School of Design students The Talking Heads, of course: *Once in a Lifetime*, 1980. Can a shotgun shack be a beautiful house? The folk etymology for that ballistic name for a long narrow pitched-roof house comes from the American South, maybe mostly from New Orleans: open the doors, the explanation goes, shoot a shotgun at one end and the projectiles pass through and back out into the open air, uninterrupted. What domestic betrayals or invasions have inspired this thought—that experiment goes unsaid. New Orleans, whose riverine property plats meant long and narrow houses, whose heavy air somehow moved more briskly through the funnel of such a house. Through the kind of house that, shaped just the same for much the same weather, is in dense Japanese cities called an eel's nest.

There's also a dogtrot house or dog-run house. That's another Southern folk etymology, maybe mostly from South Carolina: an uninterrupted pitched roof travels from one enclosed end, above and across an open breezeway at the middle, to the other enclosed end. The central hall of a still older hall-passageway-parlor house typology has its two doors opened so wide that the passage becomes an outdoor breezeway. The breezeway becomes its own little cloister. The dog, presumably, runs across it, tongue cool in the breeze, feet hot on the boards or bricks below. A routine as ritualized as that of any monastic order, or any family getting through the week. In retroactive continuity, we could call it an 1840s precedent for ex-Bauhaus architect Marcel Breuer's modernist bi-nodal butterfly-roof house of the 1940s. Shots and trots and dogs and guns: the words are homely and homey.

And here is something the same but different. Here California comes to Columbia County, with that Craig-Ellwood-edged flat roof, and a few slender tubular steel columns as at a House Without Walls. But here combined are the logics of the shotgun and the dog trot: long, thin, open in the middle. Here the opening is the swerve. Below it, a new kind of porch—both front porch and back porch at the same time, pushing past the main house wing (or principal bedroom wing), and tucked behind the guest room wing (or secondary bedroom wing). The tight railroad-apartment layout within, one room leading to another, entrance hall doing double-duty as the kitchen, will be familiar to any dweller of a certain kind of Manhattan apartment—as may even be that tangent angle of the swerve, as in the lozenge-shaped light well of a tenement-block of a century or more ago. (At the same time it remembers that other landmark typology of rural America—the double-wide trailer, with its sixteen-foot beam, but extended and shifted to improbable length.)

Such an apartment is a strange association, admittedly, for a house that so lightly touches down, as if following a line of topography on some subtle ridge, in a country clearing. Some seventy percent of Americans live in freestanding single-family homes, and some twenty percent in apartments—a strange ratio given that some eighty percent of Americans live in cities. But all these percentages overlap—and don't—in complicated ways that remind us over and over that a house is not necessarily a home, nor a home a house. One way of looking at a house is finding the elements that take you in and open you up and, if you're even just a little lucky, may help you find yourself.

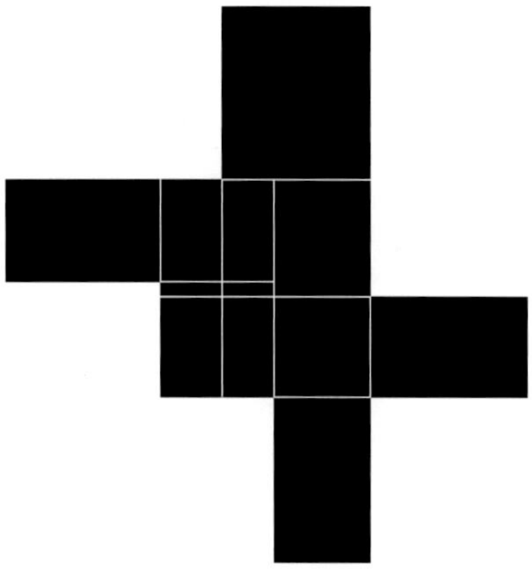

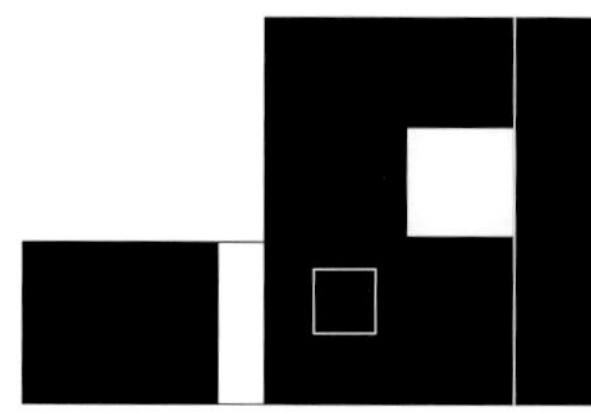

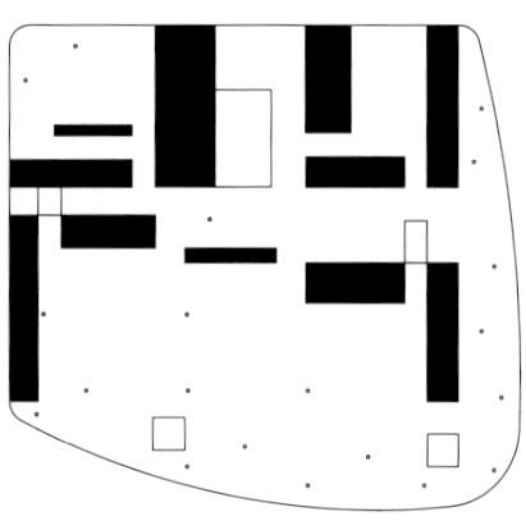

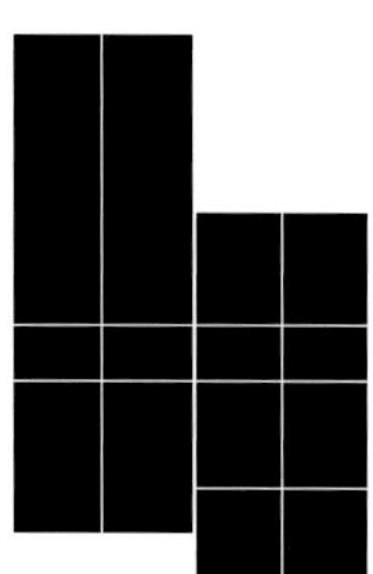

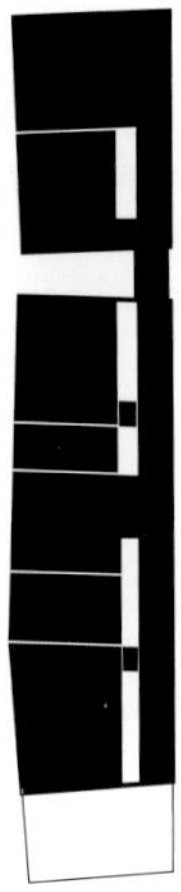
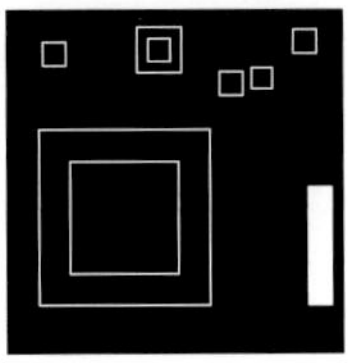
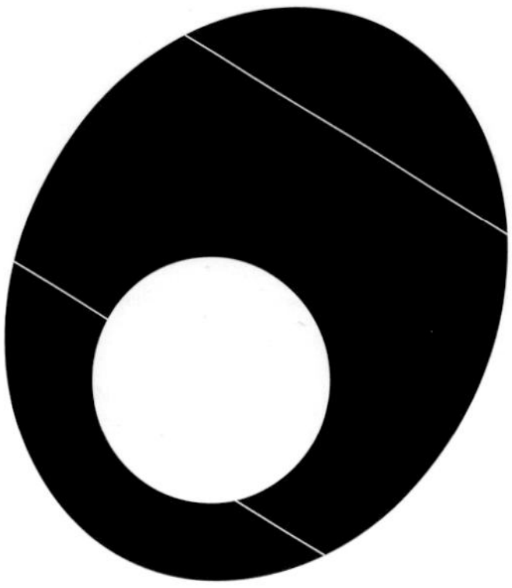
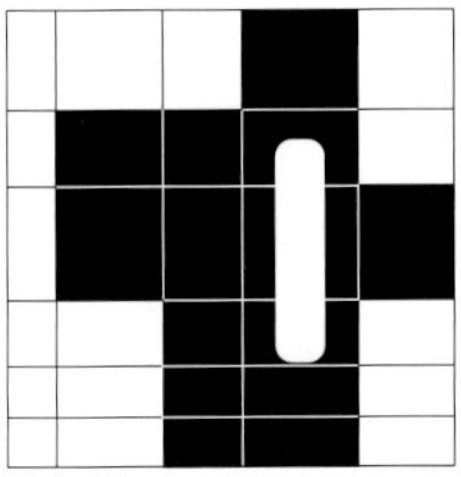
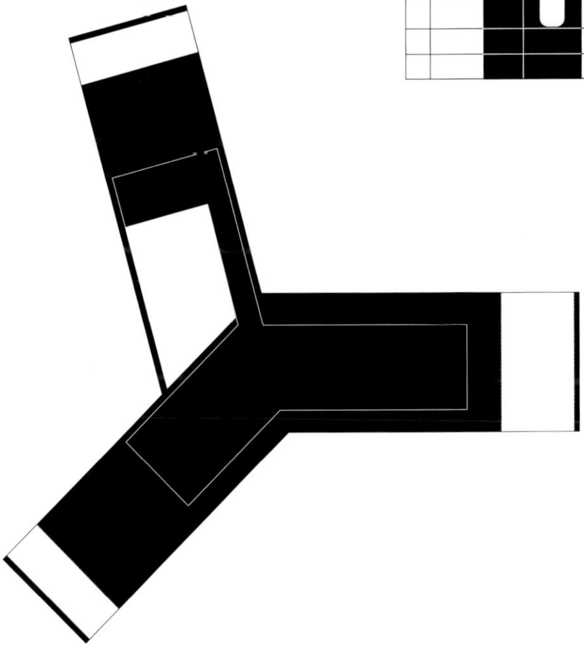
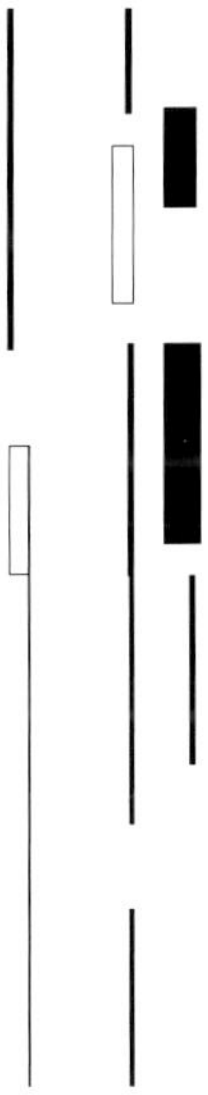

CREDITS

THIRTEEN HOUSES on pages 10–22.
Photography of 13 Site Models © LEVENBETTS.

OPEN HOUSE on pages 24–29.
page 26. Eco, Umberto. *The Open Work*. Cambridge: Harvard College, 1989.
page 26. Krauss, Rosalind. *The Originality of the Avant-Garde and Other Modernist Myths*. Cambridge: MIT Press, 1985.
page 28. Allan Wexler, *Bed / Sitting Room for an Artist in Residence*, 1988. © Allan Wexler Studio. Copyright the Artist.
page 28. Albert Frey, Frey House II, Palm Springs,1964. Photograph by Dan Chavkin. © The Colonial Williamsberg Foundation.Photograph of Interiors.
page 28. Albert Frey, Canvas Weekend House,1933–4, Fort Salonga, Northport, Long Island, New York. © Special Collections, John D. Rockefeller Jr. Library, The Colonial Williamsburg Foundation. Image courtesy of Trienal de Lisboa. Photograph of Building.
page 28. Paul Rudolph and Ralph Twichell, Walker House, 1952, Sanibel Island, Florida, USA. Photograph by Ezra Stoller/Esto. © Ezra Stoller/Esto. Photograph of Stairs.
page 29. Richard Neutra, Von Sternberg House, 1935-1972, San Fernando Valley CA, Getty Research Institute © J. Paul Getty Trust. Getty Research Institute, Los Angeles (2004.R.10). Black and White, Still Photograph.
page 29. Lina Bo Bardi, Casa do Vidrio (Glass House), 1950, Sao Paulo, Brazil. © Instituto Bardi / Casa de Vidro, Lina Bo Bardi / ARS, New York 2021. Photograph by Iñigo Bujedo Aguirre. Photograph of Building.
page 29. Lina Bo Bardi, Casa do Vidrio (Glass House), 1950, Sao Paulo, Brazil. © Instituto Bardi / Casa de Vidro, Lina Bo Bardi / ARS, New York 2021. Photograph by Iñigo Bujedo Aguirre. Photograph of Stairs.

CAMPSITE on pages 30–35.
page 33. Charles and Ray Eames, *Powers of Ten*, Documentary Short, 1977, Eames Office, California USA. © 1977 Eames Office LLC. Documentary Still.
page 34. Airstream, Inc., undated, Public Domain. Airstream promotional images.
page 34. Airstream, Inc., 1930, Public Domain. Airstream promotional images.
page 35. Andrea Zittel, *A–Z Wagon Stations*, 2004, Joshua Tree, California, USA. © Zittel Org, Photograph of Artwork.
page 35. Louis Kahn, Trenton Bath House, 1955, Ewing Township, USA. Photograph by John Ebstel © Keith De Lellis Gallery. Photograph of Building.

DOORS AND WINDOWS on pages 36–39.
page 36. William Faulkner. *As I Lay Dying*. New York: Vintage Books, 1930.
page 38. Marcel Duchamp, *Door 11: Rue Larrey*,1927, Paris, France, © Association Marcel Duchamp / ADAGP, Paris / Artists Rights Society (ARS), New York, 2021. Photograph of Artwork.
page 38. LEVENBETTS, House of Lines, Ancram, New York, USA. © LEVENBETTS. Photograph of Interior.
page 38. LEVENBETTS, Square House, Stone Ridge, New York, Photograph © Naho Kubota. Photograph of Facade.
page 38. LEVENBETTS, House of One Shape, Hudson, New York, Photograph © Naho Kubota. Photograph of Facade.
page 39. Blake Edwards, *Breakfast at Tiffany's*, 1961, USA. © Paramount Pictures Corp. All Rights Reserved. Movie still.

STEPS AND STAIRS on pages 40–43.
page 42. Jean-Luc Godard, *Contempt*, 1963, France. Movie Still.
page 42. LEVENBETTS, Square House, Stone Ridge, New York, USA. Photograph © Naho Kubota © LEVENBETTS. Photograph of Building.
page 42. LEVENBETTS, House of One Shape, Hudson, New York, USA. Photographs © Naho Kubota. Photograph of Interior.
page 43. John Cassavetes. *Faces*, 1968, USA. Distributed by Continental Distributing. BW Movie stills.

CORRIDORS on pages 44–49.
page 44. Evans, Robin. *Translations from Drawing to Building and Other Essays*. Cambridge: MIT Press, 1997.
page 46. Bruce Nauman, *Changing Light Corridor with Rooms*, 1971, Los Angeles, California, USA. © Tate, © 2021 Bruce Nauman / Artists Rights Society (ARS), New York. Photograph of Artwork.
page 46. Bruce Nauman, *Green Light Corridor*, 1970, Solomon R. Guggenheim Museum, New York Panza Collection, Gift, 1992. New York, USA. Photograph by Jonathan Hordle © Shutterstock Editorial © 2021 Bruce Nauman / Artists Rights Society (ARS), New York. Photograph of Artwork.
page 47. Wong Kar Wai, *In the Mood for Love*, 2000, Cannes, France. © Block 2 Distribution LTD acting on behalf of Jet Tone Contents Inc. Movie Still.
page 48–49. LEVENBETTS, Downtown Loft, New York, USA. Photographs © Naho Kubota. Photograph of Interior.

COURTYARDS on pages 50–53.
page 52. Toyo Ito, White O House, 2009, Marbella, Chile. Photograph by Nicolas Saieh © Toyo Ito.
page 52. Toyo Ito, White U House, 1976, Nakano, Tokyo, Japan. Photograph by Koji Taki © Toyo Ito.
page 53. Alfonso Cuarón, *Roma*, 2018, Orange, California, USA. Photos courtesy of Participant. © 2018 Espectaculos Filmicos El Coyul, S. De R.L. De C.V.. Movie stills.

CURTAINS on pages 54–59.
Page 56. Shigeru Ban, Curtain Wall House, 1995, Tokyo, Japan. Photographs by Hiroyuki Hirai © Shigeru Ban Architects. Still Photographs.
page 57. Akira Kurosawa, *High and Low*, 1963, Japan. © Everett Collection, Inc. Movie Stills.
page 58–59. LEVENBETTS, Downtown Loft, New York, USA. Photographs © Naho Kubota. Photographs of Interiors. Curtain Fabrication: Erik Bruce, Brooklyn, NY.

PLUMBING on pages 60–65.
page 63. Wong Kar-Wai, *Happy Together*, 1997, USA. © Block 2 Distribution LTD acting on behalf of Jet Tone Contents Inc. Movie Still.
page 63. Rudolph Schindler, Kings Road House, 1922, West Hollywood, CA. Photograph © LEVENBETTS.
page 63. Robert Gober, *Ascending Sink*, 1985, USA. © Robert Gober, Courtesy Matthew Marks Gallery,

Digital Image © The Museum of Modern Art/Licensed by SCALA / Art Resource, NY. Color, Still Photograph of Artwork.

page 64–65. LEVENBETTS, House of One Shape, Hudson, New York, USA. Photographs © LEVENBETTS. Photograph of Plumbing.

HOUSE PLANTS on pages 66–69.

page 68. LEVENBETTS, House of One Shape, Hudson, New York, USA. Photograph © LEVENBETTS.

page 68. Alain Resnais, *L'Année dernière à Marienbad*, 1961, France. Movie Still.

page 68. LEVENBETTS, House of One Shape, Hudson, New York, USA. Photograph © LEVENBETTS. Photograph of Garden.

page 69. LEVENBETTS, Square House, Stone Ridge, NY, USA. Photograph © Andrew Zuckerman.

PLANS on pages 70–73.

page 70. Le Corbusier. *Towards a New Architecture*. New York: Dover Publications, Inc., 1986 (1931).

page 70. Leon Battista Alberti. *On the Art of Building in Ten Books*. Cambridge: MIT Press, 1988 (1452).

page 70. Stan Allen. *Four Projects*. San Francisco: Applied Research + Design Publishing, 2017.

page 70. Robin Evans. *Translations from Drawing to Building and Other Essays*. Cambridge: MIT Press, 1997.

page 72–73. LEVENBETTS, House Plans, 2021, New York, USA. Drawings © LEVENBETTS.

STRUCTURES on pages 74–77.

page 76–77. Construction photos © LEVENBETTS.

page 76. Top Row Left to Right: A House With Three Yards, A House of Lines

page 76. Middle Row Left to Right: A Garden in a House, A House of Lines

page 76. Bottom Row Left to Right: A House of One Shape, A House and a House

page 77. Top Row Left to Right: A Square House, A House With Three Yards

page 77. Middle Row Left to Right: A House Without Walls, A Square House

page 77. Bottom Row Left to Right: A House Without Walls, A Square House

THICK AND THIN on pages 78–81.

page 80-81. Original drawings © LEVENBETTS. Comparative Wall Sections.

HOME on pages 82–85.

page 83. Lewis Baltz, *Tract Houses, Element #6*, 1971 © 2021 Estate of Lewis Baltz. Used by permission.

page 83. Lewis Baltz, *Tract Houses, Element #17*, 1971 © 2021 Estate of Lewis Baltz. Used by permission.

page 84–85. LEVENBETTS, House of One Shape, Hudson, New York, USA. Photographs © LEVENBETTS.

A HOUSE OF ONE SHAPE on page 86–103.

Design Team: David Leven and Stella Betts, Andrew Feuerstein, Jeff Rauch, Felipe Colin, Eli Back, Cornelia Foley.

Structural Engineer: Brett Schneider, Guy Nordenson and Associates

Contractor: Javier Gomez

All photographs and drawings © LEVENBETTS unless otherwise noted.

page 88–89, 92–99. © Naho Kubota Photography.

page 102. LEVENBETTS, Not To Scale chaise, Chamber Gallery, New York, NY. Photo © Guang Xu.

page 103. LEVENBETTS, House of One Shape kitchen and porch. Photo Kitchen and Patio © Naho Kubota Photography.

A SQUARE HOUSE on page 104–125.

Design Team: David Leven and Stella Betts, Andrew Feuerstein, Seung Teak Lee, Sebastian Mardi, Hans Tursack.

Structural Engineer: Nat Oppenheimer, Silman

Landscape: Marc Peter Keane

Contractor: Eric Glasser

All images and drawings © LEVENBETTS unless otherwise noted.

page 106–7. © Andrew Zuckerman Photography. Aerial Photographs.

page 110–21. © Naho Kubota Photography.

page 124. Eero Saarinen, Miller House, 1953, Columbus, Indiana. Photography by Carol M. Highsmith. © US Library of Congress. Photographs in the Carol M. Highsmith Archive, Library of Congress, Prints and Photographs Division. Still Photograph of Interior Sunken Living Room.

page 125. LEVENBETTS Square House Bath Photos © Naho Kubota Photography.

page 125. LEVENBETTS Square House Living Room and Construction Photos © Andrew Zuckerman Photography.

A HOUSE WITHOUT WALLS on page 128–43.

Design Team: David Leven and Stella Betts, Andrew Luy, Felipe Colin, You Chia Lai, Sasha Urano, Sungwhan Jean, Andrea Chiney.

Structural Engineer: Brett Schneider, Guy Nordenson and Associates

Lighting: Tillotson Design Associates

Landscape: Jamie Purinton Landscape Architect

Contractor: Rick McCue

All images and drawings © LEVENBETTS unless otherwise noted.

page 129, 132–39. © Naho Kubota Photography.

page 142. Piet Mondrian, *Composition 10*, 1915, Netherlands.

page 143. LEVENBETTS A House Without Walls. Bath Photo © Naho Kubota Photography.

A HOUSE IN A GRID on page 144–55.

Design Team: David Leven and Stella Betts, Felipe Colin, Andrew Luy, Andrea Chiney.

All images and drawings © LEVENBETTS unless otherwise noted.

page 154. Craig Ellwood, Zack House, 1949-1952, Los Angeles, CA, USA. © J. Paul Getty Trust. Getty Research Institute, Los Angeles (2004.R.10). Black and White, Still Photograph.

A HOUSE OF LINES on page 156–71.

Design Team: David Leven and Stella Betts, Andrew Feuerstein, Tim Furzer, Jonathan Man.

Structural Engineer: Nat Oppenheimer, Silman

Contractor: Scott Dean

All images and drawings © LEVENBETTS unless otherwise noted.

page 158–59, 162–63, 164 (left). © Christian Schaulin Photography.

page 160–61,164 (right)–167. © Michael Moran Photography.

A HOUSE AND A HOUSE on page 172–83.

Design Team: David Leven and Stella Betts, Andrew Feuerstein, Seung Teak Lee, Sebastian Mardi.

Structural Engineer: Nat Oppenheimer, Silman
Contractor: Eric Glasser
All images and drawings © LEVENBETTS unless otherwise noted.
page 174–75, 176–77 (top), 178–79. © Naho Kubota Photography.
page 176–77 (bottom). © Michael Moran Photography.
page 182. LEVENBETTS A House and a House Entry Photo. © Michael Moran Photography.
page 182. LEVENBETTS A House and a House Model Photo. © Andrew Zuckerman Photography.

A HOUSE WITH THREE YARDS on page 184–199.
Design Team: David Leven and Stella Betts, Andrew Feuersteln, Deric Mizokami, Sebastian Mardi, Alexis Kraft, Angi Tsang, Edwin May, Bret Quagliara.
Structural Engineer: Brett Schneider, Guy Nordenson and Associates
Lighting Designer: Tillotson Design Associates
Contractor: Roboco Inc.
All images and drawings © LEVENBETTS unless otherwise noted.
page 186–93. © Michael Moran Photography.

A SNAIL HOUSE on page 200–9.
Design Team: David Leven and Stella Betts, You Chia Lai, Andrew Luy, Caleb Sillars, Sasha Urano, Alexis Kraft.
Structural Engineer: Nat Oppenheimer, Silman
All images and drawings © LEVENBETTS unless otherwise noted.
page 208. Filip Fuxa, Nautilus Pompilius © Shutterstock. Black and White, Still Photograph.

A HOUSE-SHAPED HOUSE on page 210–19.
Design Team: David Leven and Stella Betts, Felipe Colin, You Chia Lai, Andrea Chiney, Andrew Luy.
Structural Engineer: Nat Oppenheimer, Silman
Contractor: Rick McCue
All images and drawings © LEVENBETTS unless otherwise noted.

A HOUSE IN FIVE SHAPES on page 220–39.
Design Team: David Leven and Stella Betts, Andrew Feuerstein, Sasha Urano, Andrew Luy, Caleb Sillars, Felipe Colin, You Chia Lai, Okki Berendschot, Andrea Chiney.
All images and drawings © LEVENBETTS.

A GARDEN IN A HOUSE on page 240–53.
Design Team: David Leven and Stella Betts, Andrew Feuerstein, Rachel Johnston, Rachel Chaos.
Structural Engineer: Nat Oppenheimer, Silman
Contractor: Allan Klein
All images and drawings © LEVENBETTS unless otherwise noted.
page 242–49. © Naho Kubota Photography.
page 252. LEVENBETTS A Garden in a House. Model Photos. © Andrew Zuckerman Photography.

A HOUSE FOR THE NEXT SITE on page 254–63.
Design Team: David Leven and Stella Betts, You Chia Lai, Sasha Urano, Valentina Angelucci, Andrea Chiney.
All images and drawings © LEVENBETTS unless otherwise noted.
page 262. Yana Tomashova, Paper Doll Man © Shutterstock. Black and White, Illustration.

A HOUSE WITH A SWERVE on page 264–75.
Design Team: David Leven and Stella Betts, Andrew Luy, Valentina Angelucci, Andrea Chiney.
Structural Engineer: Brett Schneider, Guy Nordenson and Associates
Contractor: Javier Gomez
All images and drawings © LEVENBETTS unless otherwise noted.
page 274. Unknown, Bust of Lucretius, Creative Commons. Black and White, Illustration.

THICK AND THIN on page 276–301.
All drawings © LEVENBETTS.
page 276–77. A House of One Shape.
page 278–79. A Square House.
page 280–81. A House Without Walls.
page 282–83. A House in a Grid.
page 284–85. A House of Lines.
page 286–87. A House and a House.
page 288–89. A House With Three Yards.
page 290–91. A Snail House.
page 292–93. A House-Shaped House.
page 294–95. A House in Five Shapes.
page 296–97. A Garden in House (original scheme).
page 298–99. A House for the Next Site.
page 300–01. A House With a Swerve.

THANK YOU

There may be thirteen ways to look at a house, but there is only one way, within the pages of a book, to properly acknowledge those who have worked with us, collaborated with us, hired us to design their houses, allowed us to confide in them, supported us in many different ways—and that is to say THANK YOU here and now on these final pages. Buildings and books take time. They also take money, insight, leaps of faith, methodical rigor, intelligence by many, really hard work, questioning and re-questioning, confidence, keen eyes, commitment, research, and ingenuity. And they take people working together in various capacities with different and complementary skills. Making architecture and making books are not things that are done by two people alone. Below are the names of all of you to whom we are deeply grateful.

EMPLOYEES of LEVENBETTS

Valentina Angelucci, Sarkis Arakelyan, Eli Back, Tamar Behar, Octavie Berendschot, Conor Byrne, Adriane Carvajal, Tim Chan, Pete Chang, Andrea Chiney, Dan Choi, Mathias Christiansen, Felipe Colin, Matt Corsover, Marlon Cruz, Shao Deng, Wing Deng, Mingyu Dong, Lucas Echeveste, Andrew Feuerstein, Cornelia Foley, Jorge Fontan, Tim Furzer, Trudy Giordano, Zack Griffin, Kate Heath, Olivia Heung, Jason Hudspeth, Yuliya Illizarov, Bart Javier, Sungwhan Jean, Gordon Jiang, Rachel Johnston, Eamonn Kelly, Alexis Kraft, Maciej Kusmierski, You Chia Lai, Jonathan Lampson, Seung Teak Lee, Andrew Luy, Jon Man, Sebastian Mardi, Ed May, Deric Mizokami, Tara Mrowka, Nick Na, Sohith Perrera, Christopher Pfiffner, Dawn Polak, Kara Pugh, Bret Quagliara, Erica Quinones, Jeff Rauch, Eric Rothfeder, Sean Sekumar, Jen Shin, Caleb Sillars, Chris Soohoo, Alex Stewart, Georg Thiersch, Jean Luc Torchon, Angi Tsang, Hans Tursak, Sasha Urano, Ari Vena, Jose Vidalon, Magnus Westergren, Sam Weston.

FRIENDS, CLIENTS, COLLABORATORS, PHOTOGRAPHERS, SUPPORTERS of LEVENBETTS

Jorn Ake, Stan Allen, Sean Anderson, Sunil Bald, Russell Barnes, Raphael Ben Yehuda, Christina Ben Yehuda, Nicole Bergen, Deborah Berke, Andy Bernheimer, Anna Betts, Charles Betts, Lucie Betts, Paul Betts, Petra Betts, Greg Birbil, Janine Birbil, Justine Birbil, Paul Birbil, Marlon Blackwell, Merritt Bucholz, Rachel Chaos, Felipe Correa, Alexandra Cunningham, Albert Dombrowski, Natasha Dombrowski, Merrill Elam, Martin Finio, Amy Fox, Jeff Fox, Nicole Francis, Jim Gainfort, Juan Garcia Mosqueda, Rosalie Genevro, Eric Glasser, Jim Godfrey, Paul Goldberger, Javier Gomez, Nicole Hamilton, Warren James, Rachel Judlow, Marc Peter Keane, Byron Kim, Allan Klein, Kent Kleinman, Liz Kubany, Naho Kubota, Anna Lehmann, Leslie Leven, Ron Leven, Stephen Leven, David Lewis, Paul Lewis, Anne Lindberg, Astrid Lipka, Kevin Lippert, Jordana Longo, Jim Luigs, Brian Mangum, Rick McCue, Karen McEvoy, Cathleen McGuigan, Brian McMahon, Chris McVoy, William Menking, Scott Metzner, Beth Mickel, Greg Miller, Michael Moran, Imtiaz Mulla, Guy Nordenson, Jim O'Brien, Beth O'Neill, Nat Oppenheimer, Nilay Oza, Hillary Park, Derek Porter, Ben Prosky, Rich Reinhart, Anne Reiselbach, Lyn Rice, Mark Robbins, Zach Rockhill, Suzie Rodriguez, Hanneline Rogeberg, Mayer Rus, Jonsara Ruth, Jerry Salama, Claudia Salomon, Sloan Schaffer, Christian Schaulin, Brett Schneider, Glenn Schroeder, Sam Seder, Lisa Sigal, Gabe Smith, David Sokol, Micheal Sorkin, Trevor Stahelski, Nader Tehrani, Jennifer Thompson, Suzan Tillotson, Mira Trezza, Billie Tsien, Marc Tsurumaki, Dylan Turk, Frank Van Etten, Tara Van Etten, Anthony Vidler, Claire Weisz, Greg Wessner, Allan Wexler, Sherry Williams, Janet Wong, Andrew Wong Schroeder, Sylvie Zannier, Andrew Zuckerman

We are also grateful to ALL of our family members. Thanks everyone!

Thank you to Gordon Goff at ORO Editions and Jake Anderson for your patience and assistance with shepherding the production of this book.

We'd like to express our deep gratitude to Prem Krishnamurthy and Chris Wu from Wkshps and to Siiri Tännler for your contribution of the graphic portion to this book. Your attentiveness to our architectural desires and process, along with your approach to design complemented the work in ways that far exceeded our expectations.

And to the LEVENBETTS team that assisted in the production of the drawings and model photographs specific to this book, we must thank Andrew Luy, along with Caleb Sillars, Valentina Angelucci and Andrea Chiney, in turn.

To Thomas de Monchaux we owe a special thanks. Thank you for helping us see our work in more than thirteen ways, for your prompts, your challenges, for the back-and-forth *ad infinitum* and most of all for your word-crafting that so beautifully elucidates the meaning behind the architecture.

This book's look was designed by Wkshps. Its cover was designed by Siiri Tännler, who also designed additional graphics, including this page. This book is typeset in Theinhardt, a grotesque sans-serif typeface from the Swiss foundry Optimo, designed by François Rappo and named in turn for Ferdinand Theinhardt, who first adapted Egyptian hieroglyphics for printed reproduction, and who around 1880 developed the typeface now called Akzidenz Grotesk, a quintessential example of timelessly modern design.